# DISASTER

## AND

## SOCIOLEGAL STUDIES

# DISASTER

## AND

## SOCIOLEGAL STUDIES

*edited by*

SUSAN STERETT

OÑATI SOCIO-LEGAL SERIES
Oñati International Institute for the Sociology of Law

**qp**

QUID PRO BOOKS
New Orleans, Louisiana

Authorized and supported by the Oñati International Institute for the Sociology of Law (Instituto Internacional de Sociología Jurídica de Oñati), as Volume 3, Number 2 (2013) in the *Oñati Socio-legal Series* (ISSN 2079-5971).

Published in 2013 by Quid Pro Books. Part of the *Contemporary Society Series*.

ISBN 978-1-61027-205-6 (pbk.)
ISBN 978-1-61027-208-7 (hbk.)
ISBN 978-1-61027-206-3 (eBook)

QUID PRO, LLC
5860 Citrus Blvd., Suite D-101
New Orleans, Louisiana 70123
*www.quidprobooks.com*

**qp**

Publisher's Cataloging-in-Publication

Sterett, Susan (ed.).
    Disaster and sociolegal studies / edited by Susan Sterett.
    Oñati Socio-legal Series, Volume 3, Number 2 (2013)
        p. cm. — (Contemporary society)
    Includes bibliographical references.
    ISBN 978-1-61027-205-6 (pbk.)
1. Disasters. 2. Natural disasters. 3. Disasters—Social aspects. I. Sterett, Susan Marie. II. Title.
III. Series.
KF 3748 .S41 2013

328'.37–dc22
2013384894
CIP

# CONTENTS

# ABOUT THE AUTHORS

**Thomas A. Birkland** is the William T. Kretzer Professor of Public Policy at North Carolina State University. Dr. Birkland is an internationally known expert on agenda-setting theory, public policy, and policies related to natural disasters and industrial accidents. He is the author of *After Disaster* and *Lessons of Disaster*.

**Lloyd Burton** is a professor of law and public policy in the School of Public Affairs, University of Colorado Denver. His teaching and research focus on the intersection between environmental management and disaster management. He is the founder of the Collaborative Research Network on the Jurisprudence of Disasters within the Law and Society Association. He holds a Ph.D. in Jurisprudence and Social Policy from the University of California, Berkeley.

**Ann-Margaret Esnard is** a Professor of Public Management and Policy at Georgia State University. Her expertise encompasses urban planning, disaster planning, hazard and vulnerability assessment and GIS/spatial analysis. She has been involved in a number of research initiatives, including three NSF funded projects on topics of disaster-induced population displacement and long-term recovery.

**Victor B. Flatt** is the Tom & Elizabeth Taft Distinguished Professor of Environmental Law and the Director of the Center for Law, Environment, Adaptation, and Resources (CLEAR) at the University of North Carolina Chapel Hill School of Law. His research focuses on environmental enforce-ment with a particular emphasis on climate change adaptation, including the evolution of disaster management.

**Valerio Nitrato Izzo** is is a Research Fellow at the Department of Law, University of Naples Federico II. A former Post-doctoral Fellow at the Centre for Social Studies, University of Coimbra, he holds a Ph.D. in Philosophy of Law from the University of Naples Federico II. He works mainly in legal theory and socio-legal studies.

**Petra Hiller** is Professor of Organization and Governance at Nordhausen University of Applied Sciences, Germany, and also Guest Professor at the Institute for Sociology at Vienna University, Austria. She received her doctor-ate and *venia legendi* in sociology from Bielefeld University, Germany, and was Visiting Scholar at Oxford University, England, and at the International Institute for the Sociology of Law in Oñati, Spain. Hiller has published on systems theory, cognitive theory of organizations, sociology of corruption and public governance. Most recently she was member of the expert commission for administrative reform in Thuringia.

i

**Arthur F. McEvoy** is Associate Dean for Research and Paul E. Treusch Professor of Law at Southwestern Law School, Los Angeles, and Professor Emeritus of Law, University of Wisconsin—Madison. He is the author of *The Fisherman's Problem: Ecology and Law in the California Fisheries, 1850–1980* (Cambridge University Press, 1986).

**Michelle A. Meyer** is a sociologist and an Assistant Research Scientist at the Hazard Reduction and Recovery Center in the College of Architecture at Texas A&M University. She has worked on projects including measuring disaster mitigation activities along the U.S. Gulf and Atlantic Coasts, and understanding environmental attitudes and behaviors.

**Pat O'Malley** is Professorial Research Fellow in Law at the University of Sydney, and a Fellow of the Academy of Social Sciences in Australia. Recent books focusing on risk include *Crime and Risk* (Sage 2010) and *The Currency of Justice* (2009). Current research focuses on the development of risk and resilience models in urban fire prevention.

**Juli Ponce** is a Law Professor and former Assistant Dean at the University of Barcelona School of Law, a former Director of the Public Administration School of Catalonia, and a frequent speaker on administrative law, zoning and urban planning and housing law. Dr. Ponce has published in professional journals throughout Spain, Europe, the United States, and Latin America. Dr. Ponce's consulting, research projects, and lectures have included projects for different universities and public administrations.

**Alka Sapat** is an Associate Professor of Public Administration. Her expertise includes disaster and crisis management, environmental policy and regulation, and research methodology. She has been involved in four NSF-funded projects on topics related to disaster-induced displacement, long-term disaster recovery and the role of NGOs, and state environmental policy.

**Susan M. Sterett** is a Professor of Political Science at the University of Denver. She has published on administrative states, constitutionalism, and accountability. Her books include *Public Pensions: Gender and Civic Service in the States, 1850–1937* (Cornell University Press, 2003) and *Creating Constitutionalism? Accountability and the Administrative State in England and Wales* (University of Michigan Press, 1997). She has published in *Law and Social Inquiry, Comparative Political Studies, Studies in American Political Development, Law and Society Review, Studies in Law Politics and Society,* and *Social and Legal Studies.*

**Jeffrey J. Stys** is President of Strategic Decision Associates, a Houston-based consulting practice. He focuses on strategic planning, development of high-performing collaboratives and community planning. He also works in preparedness planning and long-term recovery after disasters. Jeff has worked in Galveston in the aftermath of Hurricane Ike and oversaw the social services coordination for Hurricane Katrina evacuees in Houston.

**Lisa Grow Sun** graduated *summa cum laude* from Harvard Law School. After law school, she clerked for Judge J. Michael Luttig and then for Justice Anthony M. Kennedy. Sun is now a professor at Brigham Young University Law School and a disaster law scholar. She is a coauthor of the definitive U.S. disaster law textbook, *Disaster Law and Policy.*

# ACKNOWLEDGMENTS

We are grateful to the Oñati International Institute for the Sociology of Law for hosting the workshop on Disasters and Sociolegal Studies. We are also grateful to the United States National Science Foundation for its support, including support of the workshop (SES-1051408). The University of Denver also provided support as this collection reached publication. Alan Childress of Quid Pro Books first suggested we publish it with this press, and kept us on track.

Around the world many people find daily life charged with disorganization and devastation; the pictures of fires and floods can come after the people have fled, as we see on the cover of this collection. In bringing the law in, we also hope to bring the people in. We thank them as well.

# DISASTER

## AND

## SOCIOLEGAL STUDIES

# INTRODUCTION

## Susan M. Sterett

**ABSTRACT**

Disasters are treated as independent events external to law. However, social processes define the beginning, end, and extent of those events for mitigation, adaptation and response and recovery; those processes include the mobilization of law by people and organizations. Within the sociology of disaster, it is tempting to treat law as a problem-solving tool. Sociolegal analysis approaches law more skeptically: legal actors face problems and defer to the decisions others have made, or discount future problems as much as other institutions do and thereby contribute to problems, or offer compensation that does not ameliorate the inequality within and among countries that disaster can exacerbate. Law can signal that it is doing something about problems via national or supranational rights; for it actually to help requires legal actors to mobilize. Finally, the site of law has been displaced: from law being within public authority enacted through institutions to law as a matter of individual, self-governance set in expectation of disaster, and humanitarian assistance done through non-governmental organizations. This collection contributes analyses of individuals and organizations' action in disaster through legal processes.

Los desastres se tratan como hechos independientes externos al derecho. Sin embargo, los procesos sociales definen el principio, el final y el alcance de esos acontecimientos en lo que respecta a su mitigación, adaptación, respuesta y recuperación; esos procesos incluyen la movilización del derecho por personas y organizaciones. En el ámbito de la sociología de los desastres, es tentador tratar el derecho como una herramienta para la resolución de problemas. Sin embargo, los análisis sociojurídicos se aproximan al derecho de forma más escéptica: los actores legales se enfrentan a problemas y se adhieren a decisiones que otros han tomado, o descartan problemas futuros de la misma forma que otras instituciones, aumentando así los problemas, u ofrecen una compensación que no mejora la desigualdad dentro de y entre los países, que en parte se ve agravada por los desastres. El derecho puede defender que está tratando los problemas a través del derecho nacional o supranacional; pero lo que realmente hace falta para ayudar requiere que los actores legales se movilicen. Por último, ha cambiado el lugar que ocupa el derecho: ha pasado de ser una autoridad pública, que actúa a través de instituciones, a tener carácter individual, con la prevención de desastres basada en el autogobierno, y siendo organizaciones no gubernamentales las que ofrecen la ayuda humanitaria. Este número ofrece un análisis de las acciones de individuos y organizaciones en caso de desastres, a través de los procesos legales.

## INTRODUCTION: LEGAL PROCESSES AND DEFINING DISASTERS

The hazards of the late twentieth century that have created sudden, visible havoc include the tsunami in Japan, storms and oil spills in the United States, and earthquakes in Haiti and southwestern China. Including factory fires, wars, and the global financial crisis brings the destruction higher. The variety in the harm across groups in poor and rich countries and among poor and wealthy people within countries demonstrates the inequality in distribution of harm and the failure of regulation disaster usually marks. Although disasters such as earthquakes seem unavoidable or uncontrollable and they do indeed inflict harm across groups, it is a commonplace of the social science of disaster that while hazards may just happen, the disasters for localities that they bring have humans' choices embedded in them, and often the same people need to manage and respond to the aftermath, which means that analyzing disaster needs to include both earthquakes and factory fires.

A catastrophe is 'known by its works'; effects of an event are what we call a disaster (Quarentelli 1998). An earthquake without collapsing buildings is not a disaster. One way of answering what disasters are is tracking how people and organizations come together to delimit disaster, and the Red Cross and others who respond define disasters as time and place bound disruptions of daily life (Dombrowsky 1998). The conceptual lack of clarity concerning how to understand disaster invites mapping the mobilization of law that channels money for relief and compensation to individuals or to rebuild a place after an event. The earthquakes, tsunamis, and burning oil rigs that have occasioned human rights claims when people are displaced, or urgent calls for safer nuclear power plant construction, require mapping how powerful organizations and people mobilize help. Ulrich Beck has argued that the hallmark of modern risks is that they cannot be seen; they are the toxins that require specialists with esoteric knowledge to confirm the dangers. They are different from the widespread public health hazards or the industrial accidents that occasioned the modern welfare state, with social insurance to compensate people for workplace injuries or payments for the elderly when they were no longer useful in the industrial workforce (Beck 1992, pp. 13, 21, Sterett 2003). While toxins in our lives are widespread and sensing them requires the esoteric knowledge that Beck describes, storms, fires, and droughts have created immediate, visible, widespread suffering. Demands for response treat the risks as self-evident. These visible risks and the disasters they have occasioned are the center of concern for the studies in this collection.

The Oñati International Institute for the Sociology of Law hosted the workshop on disasters and sociolegal studies to extend the analysis of disaster within sociolegal studies, bringing in new scholars and shifting sociolegal attention from regulation and prevention to the effects of events that we delimit as disaster. Scholars of regulation map response to disaster that governs the mining, manufacturing and building that present the risk of disaster. People and organizations also mobilize the law to clean up after disaster: to shift the costs, to compensate, to hold people responsible (Haines 2009). The liability rules after mining waste ponds have failed and the allocation of property rights and responsibilities through the courts rather than through administrative agencies have been central to the governance of disaster, more than the prevention and governance of business activities that regulation sets as its task.

This collection complements the volume from a workshop at the Oñati Institute on climate change and sociolegal studies. Sudden weather-related disasters in Australia, or on the coast of the Gulf of Mexico, have been made more likely by climate change. Climate change has been a way of explaining the need to do something; the disasters come when we don't respond, and some of the disasters they bring are slow-moving, or 'crescive' (to use the helpful term applied by Beamish 2002), including the sea rise that has required relocating villages and that has occasioned beautiful designs to bring back storm surge protection to coasts that have lost marshland and oyster beds. Climate change can bring disasters, and disasters can have many precipitating events associated with them, from proximate sudden storms to choices about how to build and regulate nuclear power plants to the much broader framework of climate change.

Each disaster, crescive or sudden, has law and legal actors and organizations shot throughout: zoning decisions, decisions not to have or to differentially enforce building codes, decisions concerning whom to hold responsible and how, and decisions concerning compensation and assistance both through the state and through humanitarian associations. Disaster is variably juridified, or governed by reference to legal rules with accountability to legal institutions (Bilchner and Molinder 2008). How and why does juridification vary? Over time and cross-nationally? What does law *do* with disasters: solve them, enact through a public drama that states care for their subjects, soothe after disaster, or cause them?

## LAW AS SOLVING PROBLEMS

Making disaster in law the object of study can invite the belief that the purpose of law is an instrumental one: law fixes problems and helps the people who draw our sympathy. Our sympathy now is grounded in a belief that states owe care to all their people, and the duty to care is not differentiated by status, or work history, or citizenship or race (Calhoun 2010, Ophir 2007, Roberts 2007, Sarat and Lezaun 2009); the sympathy can extend to the case level workers responsible for administering the law on the ground; people experience law after disaster in case level work, and it is there that sympathy or exclusion will play out. However, the people and organizations bringing on disaster and reproducing inequality in responding to it are some of the same people responsible for remedying disaster. Businesses that drill for oil meet a demand for oil with the blessing of local and national governments; when British Petroleum must pay compensation for the oil spill that follows, they will be negotiating the payments, though they will face new pressures for compensation. The same demand to drill for oil that brought deepwater drilling to the Gulf of Mexico will shape remedies after the oil blowout (Freudenburg and Gramling 2012). If law is to impose justice from outside the event, we would need to know who could help bring that justice to pass. As the 1984 disaster in Bhopal demonstrated, if state officials see it as their responsibility to keep businesses producing in their state before disaster, they will also do so when negotiating response to disaster. The activity governments promote—manufacturing batteries, drilling for oil—could be inextricable from the problem (Haines 2009). Why, then, the belief that law will solve problems?

The commitment in liberal states to individual autonomy and to the obligation of states to protect their citizens from harm puts faith in the capacity and willingness of elites to mitigate or respond to harm. The belief that legal institutions can compensate puts faith in their ability to act independently of the organizations they govern. If law's value is instrumental, those who change laws or regulations or distribute post-disaster assistance must mean to solve problems and law and government policy must be a toolkit to allow them to do soothe problems cannot be so entrenched that they are insoluble. A belief in law's instrumentality states a pragmatic perspective, bringing the aspiration to responsive law that scholars of regulation have shared (Ansell 2011, Nonet and Selznick 1978, Parker and Nielsen 2011). Liberal states claim responsiveness. However much they do not achieve it, that aspiration allows those mobilizing for justice to fault the state when it fails, sometimes bringing partial compensation or regulatory improvement. However, claims are difficult to make and legal responses can signal that states are doing something, rather than adequately and equitably compensating for harm or mitigating the harm of the next disaster.

If it's the job of the law to do something, then officials will mobilize the law to show they are doing something. Nothing invites the public drama of rescue more than a disaster, and public policy can be public drama as much as public problem solving (Burke 1966, Edelman 1977, Gusfield 1981, Haines 2009). We might still find a close tie between the activities we want and the disaster to which it is inextricably tied, and remedying harm can accompany continuing a dangerous enterprise. Elites can articulate principles, and reassure publics; without pressure, they may make little progress toward mitigating catastrophe. A right to compensation or safety sounds much more satisfying than it is; without relentless pursuit to put the rights into action, the promise of rights is only the 'myth of rights' (Scheingold 1974). Reassuring publics can take different routes. Political elites claim expertise, control, and concern for citizens that stories of particular disasters often belie. Yet experts choose large scale works projects or development of business that put people at risk (Freudenberg et al. 2009). Companies build oil rigs and assure people of their safety when there is little experience with them, so estimates of the risks they pose are little more than guesswork (Clarke 1999). As Lee

Clarke argues, assuring publics that risks are manageable when risk is both unmanageable and unknown falsely implies that elites are keeping people safe.

Alternatively, Pat O'Malley (2013) argues in this collection that official responses to catastrophe have taken a *defensive* rather than falsely reassuring stance, where prevention of any imaginable harm is the aspiration of governance. Unprecedented catastrophes and the risks of new activities can make for completely unknowable harms, as Clarke argues; O'Malley argues that officials will claim prevention and precaution through imagining the worst that could happen, not that elites falsely reassure us that all is well. O'Malley traces this response to September 11 and the United States report following it. He also draws on the precautionary principle embedded in European law, which Juli Ponce (2013) discusses in his overview of land use planning and disaster in this collection. That principle invites decision-makers to imagine the worst possible disasters from any decision, and to make decisions that will avoid them. O'Malley argues that the precautionary principle and its accompanying requirement of preparedness are so cautious that they counter any freedom to act in the world, guaranteeing only a freedom from harm. He also argues that the turn toward governing the self has brought the concept of resilience from the management literature; if bureaucracies are to treat any imaginable catastrophe as possible, and it is impossible to be fully prepared, individuals and communities must be ready to learn from them and take advantage of the opportunities they offer. Alongside the defensiveness O'Malley finds is what he calls hyper-entrepreneurialism embedded in resilience, where everyone should be ready to re-invent their lives in response to any imaginable disaster.

States are both hyper-vigilant and cavalier about the harms to which people are exposed. A way to explore that tension could be through differences in vulnerability, as well as differences in the groups mobilized around the terrorism and financial crises central to O'Malley's discussion, as well as the groups mobilized around floods and hurricanes. Within any country, poorer people are often at greater risk of harm from hazards. In this collection Valerio Nitrato Izzo (2013) takes that point, long made within the sociology of disaster, and develops it through a post-colonial interpretation of what law does. Within families and neighborhoods, men and women often bear different responsibilities at work, for family and for community, and those differences expand in disaster (Enarson 2012; Peek and Fothergill 2008, Tierney 2006). Who is to prevent harm, and harm against whom? Who is to be hyper-entrepreneurial?

O'Malley argues that parallel governance frameworks operate across Western industrial states: states are to defend against all risks anyone could imagine, and at the same time encourage their citizens to respond rapidly to disaster, embracing disaster as an opportunity for new endeavours. Defensive and hyper-entrepreneurial responses match the tension that Fiona Haines finds in governments responding to disaster while finding response impossible because the disaster is unavoidably tied to businesses they invite. Governments eager to bring in capital investment induce companies to build manufacturing plants that can fail, with catastrophic results (Cassels 1993, Fortun 2004). The cleaning up that elites do afterwards, including investigating and imposing fines for wrongdoing, allocating responsibility, and paying to get people emergency supplies and housing do not ensure the next disaster does not happen. What, then, does law do if it only partially, sometimes addresses problems, and then only with persistent follow-through by people and organizations who are supposed to benefit?

Prevention and mitigation before an event happens is less expensive and causes less harm than responding to a disaster once it has happened. Therefore, the study of regulation has been tightly linked with the disasters to which new regulations can respond. Juli Ponce argues that the precautionary principle is essential to European law; the aspiration is to prevent harm when the costs of an activity are unknown and the results of a disaster could be costly. The principle signals states' commitments to protection, as Pat O'Malley argues; all the force of that principle can only be evident in the patterns of decisions states make. Many practices that are useful could have catastrophic results. In this collection, Lloyd Burton (2013) argues normatively that when states build in wildfire zones, they are making choices that will increase the chances that people will die, and that states too readily accommodate the desire to live in wildfire zones. Burton argues that the choice that is central to the liberal legal order—people are to choose their lives, and act on those choices—also dictates responsibility for preventing disaster. He argues that those who have not chosen to live with extreme hazards are those who should be most protected.

What political mobilization would bring states to implement that principle in the world that created the problems of risk and unequal vulnerability in the first place? Environmental justice movements have mobilized around unequal exposure to risk; understanding how protection has been accomplished, wherever it has, requires tracing how groups have organized to make claims, and how individuals have taken advantage of opportunities. Women and men are often positioned differently in the harm disaster brings because of responsibility for family and neighbors, or because gender segregation at work brings different risks. The claim to humanitarian care and sympathy in disaster bring opportunity where people can mobilize the law for themselves, or have access to representatives, even though the least well off are often the most harmed in disaster. Alka Sapat and Ann Margaret Esnard (2013) note that the earthquake in Haiti allowed people to claim temporary protected status, an immigration category that would allow them more legally stable legal residence in the United States than they previously had. That is a federal status, and federal law permits it. Federal policy alongside the hurricane brought many more people to local services in Miami. Local governments' need for federal money to meet a federal policy brought the new category of 'displacee' to Dade County as much as mobilization by those who wanted to claim temporary protected status. Local governments had learned that they needed to track people who had come to Miami after disaster; bringing people into view of the state served those displaced and the local governments more than the one unified state often envisioned in analyses of the state in disaster.

Care of a population has to provide that care efficiently and effectively, borrowing from a model of coordinated military response. Humanitarian crises are militarized, with the rapid distribution of goods and maintenance of order as goals (McFalls 2010). War provided the early models of the disasters to which states had to respond after having created them (Quarentelli 1998). In the United States, outside the individual compensation schemes for industrial accidents, federal disaster response first organized for civil defense (Rozario 2007). Militarized responses include mistrust of people helping themselves and each other outside of the hierarchy of organizations providing goods, even though non-governmental organizations are integral to humanitarian care, United States federal disaster response encourages responsibility, and both individuals and communities help themselves and each other (Cooper and Block 2007, Sterett 2012). Public portrayals hold that good citizens care for themselves and others responsibly, yet people who governing officials suspected before the disaster fit stereotypes of disorderly, dangerous, needy miserable people who must be controlled through the military and police during and in the immediate aftermath of disaster, as Lisa Sun (2013) demonstrates in her synthesis of post-Katrina media coverage.

Such perceptions allow officials both to require that people help themselves and each other and to rely upon a militarized response. A requirement that people should be responsible, and a suspicion that they are not, allows the inflammatory representation of people as disorderly and dangerous after a disaster, needing to be contained and policed. Lisa Sun argues in this collection that the repeated depictions of African American citizens as dangerous and disorderly after Hurricane Katrina invited violations of civil liberties and confirmations of the rightness of inequality in the United States, all in the name of protection. Sun argues that even noticing and discussing the misrepresentation of what people do, and countering it with stories of voluntarism, keeps the justification for militarized response before the public. Sun's critique of the misrepresentation of how people act after disaster fits neatly with the possibility that what we see is elite panic inflicted on the people for whom that elite is charged to care (Clarke and Chess 2008).

The belief that states are to protect their people is a normative commitment common to several of the studies here; if states are to protect, finding that they do not is implicitly a call to action. To criticize states for allowing people to remain in dangerous places or subject to dangerous industrial accidents requires that we believe that states will respond when reminded that they are neglecting people or putting them at risk for fires, floods and oil spills. As we will see in the next section, while within liberal legalism law explains itself as protective, law contributes to disaster by allocating property rights to allow dangerous activities.

## JURIDIFICATION OF DISASTER: LEGAL JUDGMENTS AS
### CAUSE, TRANSFORMATION, AND GESTURE

Giorgio Agamben's generative analysis of disasters and emergencies posits the disappearance of the rule of law, with states using the situation to suspend legal aspirations toward similar treatment across cases, predictability, rule-following, and that independent institutions be held accountable while making decisions (Agamben 2005). If the emergency happens in a system dense with rules and support structures that support legal accountability of institutions, we might expect that the lawyers, insurance companies, local governments facing new responsibilities without new money to pay for them, and institutionalized charities, will want to bring their preferred rules to emergency (Haines 2009).

The global proliferation of accountability to courts, international and supranational legal instruments, and an aspiration to legality, color the claims of advocacy groups cross-nationally and shape the governance of disaster as of other policy fields. However, disaster has been an opportunity for states to operate in exception, or outside the increasingly dense juridical practices that govern late modern states. How and when are the disruptions of disaster assimilated to the legal structures of late modern states? Juridification varies cross-nationally and over time; the global appeal of supranational instruments and courts can draw in lawyers and transnational advocacy groups, making disaster cross national boundaries even when the people who are hurt are within one country (Cassels 1993, Fortun 2004).

The forward-looking regulation of business can fail even after disaster when we know little about risks, and when there is a strong mandate to continue the risky activity. The allocation of property rights that the common law has historically done can allocate responsibility long after those responsible are gone, and it does not allocate responsibility well when disastrous outcomes are the result of many individual actions: when massive mudslides result from many small mines. Arthur McEvoy (2013) uses three case studies in which common use of resources and the litigation that assigns property rights and liability then creates problems. If mining does not result in liability rules that require the miners to pay attention to the downstream effects of what they do, there is little reason for miners to take future costs into account. Floods with damage that results from mining have been common enough in the United States from nineteenth century California to the twentieth century coal mines of West Virginia to lead to the suspicion that they are normal accidents (Perrow 1984). The mining created the problem. So did the laws that made the property rights in mining. Liability rules allocate responsibility retroactively; in California those who had mined the hillsides in the foothills of the Sierras were long gone by the time the hillsides washed away and filled the Sacramento Valley with cement-like sludge. Furthermore, responsibility was not concentrated in one miner or mining company. The retroactive compensation that liability rules and judgments provide, the possibility that people can be long gone, and the diffusion of responsibility when harm has cumulated across multiple actors all make accountability via lawsuits unlikely. Legal responsibility for harm can be individuated and isolated to the case at hand and to the most recent actor, although problems have long histories; the liability system truncates inquiry into the broader role property rules play, and how property rules contribute to normal accidents. In his discussion of irrigation and saturation of the ground in La Conchita, California, McEvoy also argues that liability rules are pointless when they focus on the current landowner and the initial landowner is in sight when the mudslides come.

Although property rules can make mud slide down a mountain, holding someone responsible only when the economic activity has disappeared, legal principles pay homage to prevention through planning as a liability rule, as Juli Ponce explains in this collection. He argues that national state law in Europe relies upon land use planning to prevent harms. States are held responsible when they allow an activity in a wrong place. States work to design out crime by keeping places publicly accessible and under surveillance. Studies of regulation draw attention to business activity; Arthur McEvoy's examples of landslides and fisheries that collapse as well as Juli Ponce's story of responsibility for a flood in a campsite remind us that disasters happen in places. The late modern governance of space alongside governance of activity constitutes the governance of disaster.

By definitions in statutes and the practices of humanitarian organizations, disaster disrupts the routines of daily life. It is limited in time and space (Redfield 2005). How? Not in the nature of an earthquake, or an industrial explosion, or a fire, where years later people may be grieving lost children, or artwork might remind us of the losses. The effects of disaster can be notoriously difficult to contain: the industrial explosion at Bhopal intensified the public relations in which chemical firms engaged, changing from 'better living through chemistry' to touting the environmental responsibility multinational corporations take (Fortun 2004). Turning to legal engagements highlights how often disasters cross boundaries, and the legal work it takes to contain or recognize disaster and its survivors. Few have studied the diaspora of disaster (Weber, Peek, and Social Science Research Council Research Network on Persons Displaced by Hurricane Katrina 2012), and how law constitutes diaspora: Alka Sapat and Ann Margaret Esnard argue in this collection that the delivery of services to the victims of the earthquake in Haiti happened in Miami, so tracking American delivery of services, and American regulation of immigration, is central to understanding governance of the earthquake in Haiti. Disasters change place through art: in his 2012 show in Washington, D.C., the Chinese international art superstar and dissident Ai Weiwei (2012) included rebar (construction material) recovered from the schools that disintegrated in the Szechuan earthquake in 2008. A long snake of backpacks ("Snake Ceiling"), one backpack representing each dead child, wound its way through the art gallery to remind viewers of how many children had died. Legal institutions define official ends and beginnings of responsibility when the effects still ripple through people's lives. Legal processes delimit disaster, not only in statutes but in the process of defining, preventing, and allocating responsibility for disaster in courts and administrative agencies.

Cleaning up toxic waste has been the kind of problem in which the costs are great and the benefits of the business that generated the waste long gone. With such an impossible problem, law may only be able to signal compliance with public priorities, rather than remedying the harms. As Petra Hiller (2013) explains in her analysis of administrative decision-making in Germany concerning toxic waste cleanup, even organizations charged with decontaminating land can find that the risk they manage is different from what the risk statutes charged them with managing. Cleaning up toxic waste after German reunification proved to cost more than the German state wanted to spend, when it also had the expenses of reunification. Hiller argues that the responsible organizations redefined the problem for themselves so they could solve it and avoid the political risks of failure. Organizations transform law, and in the case she discussed the responsible organizations made the toxic waste problem into one of risk of political risk for an organization. The risk of injury from contaminated land became the risk that the state agency would find itself under threat because it disrupted economic development that German authorities believed was particularly important after reunification, with the fear that the lack of economic development in East Germany would hinder all of Germany. Law within organizations changed the risk from one of harm to one of political failure.

How to reconcile the place of law in bringing on disaster or avoiding addressing it, and the belief that law is humanitarian and ameliorates the harm of disaster? First, disasters mobilize people, bringing people together within the law who may not have been working there before. Second, legal systems are loosely coupled organizations, with different courts and administrative agencies making decisions over time; the courts that would hold mining companies accountable for slides in Sacramento, California are not the same courts that earlier allocated water rights. Next, the instrumental vision of law misperceives the many times that law has been a site for constituting and enacting public dramas of care, and the responsibility of liberal legal states (Burke 1966, Edelman 1977, Gusfield 1981). Any actual change in behavior or mitigation of harm may be beside the point or at least not the only point for those with legal authority. When advocacy groups can follow through, insisting on implementation of the claims to care states make, sometimes the commitment to care can mitigate harms (Edelman 1977).

## LAW, SOCIAL WELFARE AND DISASTER

Legal actors' affirmation of legal rules that will bring about disaster would make us question when and how legal actors constituted by legal rules can *ever* act to mitigate harm. Nevertheless, the expectation that governments will care for their population allows advocates to make claims against the state. Compensating people for harm after disaster is grounded in sympathy and need rather than in insurance against the injuries of industrial urban life in which the modern welfare state was grounded (Beck 1992).

How would one get from the principle of protecting the most vulnerable, particularly those who have not chosen risk, to a practice of doing so? Large-scale spectacular disasters have led to compensation that values people based on losses, and those who lose more are often not the most vulnerable (Feinberg 2005). Even so, the story of helpless victims injured by forces well outside their control is compelling, and one that political regimes have used in mobilizing support for assistance. Michelle Landis Dauber has argued that the grounding of the United States welfare state was in disaster relief, and in assistance to those who seemed most helpless. She tells her story as one of the disaster of the Great Depression, and traces advocacy for the poor after the 1937 Mississippi River flood, noting slippage between explaining people's problems as grounded in a natural hazard they could not control and as grounded in long-term poverty made worse in the Great Depression, long term problems have less often drawn sympathy in the United States (Dauber 2005). That time was one of consolidation and creation of many federal spending programs, building from what states had been doing in the previous thirty years. Disaster is a provocative grounding for the welfare state, framing problems as indisputably outside one's control and therefore meriting state assistance. It is an invitation to expand the definition of disaster when other claims cannot gain a political footing. In other New Deal programs, money did not flow from the federal government to poor African Americans in the South.

Michelle Meyer (2013) shares the normative commitment to law as a force that will mitigate harm. She builds from studies of welfare states and definitions of people's needs to argue normatively for disaster relief administered through the institutions of the state. What she offers as prescription is what Giorgio Agamben and Ulrich Beck have argued is a fact of bureaucratic welfare states: they can provide disaster relief because they have rules and practices bringing people into the governance of the administrative state. States have required regularized biographies that fit into state-inscribed categories, including work, parenting and retirement, all of which are insured against the disruptions that risk brings. States are to be held responsible for the care of their citizens, and they can exercise that responsibility by choosing the appropriate means to the end of saving lives. She catalogues the range of vulnerabilities that people have, partially constituted by law. She argues that the risks people face in disaster complement or add to the traditional risks that welfare states have been addressing for one hundred years: the risks of industrial society, including injury, death, disability and retirement after working. She argues that when states ignore those risks, they create a misalignment between the risks people increasingly face and the responsibilities states actually take for their people. Her work points to the possibility of a different kind of analysis: how have risks shifted? More people are at risk for floods on the coasts because more people live on the coasts than did one hundred years ago; in Western postindustrial states, fewer people are at risk for death in fires than they were in the nineteenth century thanks to building codes and practices. Her analysis counters Michele Landis Dauber's argument that in the United States, disaster assistance has provided a ground for extending relief that is more sacrosanct than the industrial welfare state and indeed that disaster provided the grounding for long term relief in the United States. Both analyses are fresh in incorporating the risks of disaster into the framework of the welfare state, and both point the way toward deeper integration of the law of disaster response into legal frameworks of need and of what people deserve (see also Ophir 2007, Sterett 2009). For example, Meyer argues we need to care for people harmed by disaster as well as we do people who have grown old, and Dauber argues we need to attend to how disaster relief has trumped other claims to state assistance.

What happens to disaster relief when the social insurance model of the welfare state is being cut, as it has been after the global contraction after 2008? Throughout Western Europe countries have been subject to austerity measures. Conversely, integrating post-event temporary assistance with longer standing welfare state insurance would lead to considering how people put together the assistance and work they need to live. People tap more than one form of assistance—that is, people who collect old age pensions also collect housing assistance after disaster—so starting with how people live after disaster would capture how people experience disaster relief as part of making a living, including work, housing assistance, and public pensions. Starting with what people live on and how they understand it would also illuminate the inequality in relief that sociologists of disaster find. Legal systems divide work from social insurance and from disaster assistance or compensation. Analysis that begins from people's lives need not divide them.

Disasters and their potential for disruption of life have been gaining increasing attention, occasioned by the rise of global humanitarian assistance, debates concerning what global climate change will mean for national states, and the inability of international treaties to mitigate harms. As Sapat and Esnard argue in this collection, disasters often cross legal boundaries; the model that has communities helping themselves in their own disaster do not work when people flee, as when Haitians fled after the 2010 hurricane. After disaster, people engage legal rules that are new to them. Communities remain important in mobilizing the law, and displacement requires asking who is the community. That question can provide insight into the significance of race and ethnicity. People are not all the same in disaster, reduced to a common, bare element of humanity; communities are understood to share a culture, race or ethnicity (Sterett and Reich 2007). Sapat and Esnard argue that diasporas were central in assistance after the earthquake.

## VOLUNTARISM AND NGOS: LAW PLACING
### RESPONSIBILITY OUTSIDE ITSELF

Without bureaucratic regulation and compensation that came with the modern welfare state, whatever help people got after fires and floods came from neighbors, family and each other (Dynes and Tierney 1994, Krainz 2012). That doesn't mean it was enough; it's just what people had, and law might clean up the aftermath by providing relief for people who were disabled in accidents or fires. Now law intertwines with individual and community response; law designates voluntary organizations to respond to disaster, and emergency response teaches people that they must rely on each other, and on their ability to store goods for use after disaster. Disaster response coaches people to take responsibility for their lives, and that those who respond first to claims in disaster are neighbors, not firefighters or federal agency officials—the officials middle class people in western postindustrial states are most likely to believe are there to help. Once disasters strike, people often prove generous in helping each other and relying upon what they have to hand and what they could put aside. Those who have a harder time helping themselves during and after disaster often are isolated, or have disabled or very young or very old family members they can't leave behind in order to flee disaster. Yet in the public stories told, officials ask people to be responsible for themselves, while media accounts deplore irresponsibility, dependency, fraud and need. Social welfare payments for the elderly and disabled that have been instituted in late post-industrial states do not require that people work, making denunciations of dependency particularly troubling

The humanitarian impulse (Sarat and Lezaun 2009) to care for people after disaster is one that has spread throughout the world; non-governmental organizations have globalized the response to disaster. Global humanitarianism is what Médicins Sans Frontières and its sister NGOs do in the global South (Redfield 2005). Humanitarian response after disaster is something that happens to people in poor countries, with the sudden disruption a hurricane or tsunami brings, killing and displacing more people than they do in richer countries, and the short term rush of volunteers from abroad is targeted to places far from the global north. Humanitarian assistance in response to need is well-institutionalized in non-governmental organizations that operate within richer countries as well, including the Red Cross, the Salvation Army, and groups of volunteers that come together in localities after flood and fire. The aftermath of Hurricane Katrina in the United States brought globalization of humanitarian assistance back to the United States: global guidelines for internally displaced people framed the flow of international donations in the United States. Hurricane Katrina and the fall 2012 storm Sandy invited renewed attention to the place of humanitarian assistance organizations such as the Red Cross within the United States. After Katrina, as Victor Flatt and Jeff Stys (2013) describe in this collection, multiple nonprofit organizations were charged with delivering assistance. Accomplishing state purposes through NGOs and private charity mobilized for an event has long been the practice for aiding people who fled fires, suffered through drought, and experienced floods. The Red Cross is legally designated as a response agency for disaster in the United States. In the great Mississippi flood of 1927, the Red Cross allocated aid and helped to implement policies that starved out Black people who were stranded on levees (Barry 1998). The nongovernmental organizations frequently praised for their flexibility and generosity, their ability to respond without being bound by the bureaucratic intransigence of governments, are deeply intertwined with states and their purposes.

Valerio Nitrato Izzo (2013) theorizes disaster as postcolonial, with people in poor countries paying the price of disaster, whether through deaths in factory fires or greater vulnerability to flooding. Inequality in experiencing disaster is both internal to countries and happens across borders; Nitrato Izzo theorizes the vulnerability experienced within wealthier countries as a matter of internal postcolonial order, explaining the vulnerability of the Gulf Coast after Hurricane Katrina through Louisiana's status in the United States. Nitrato Izzo integrates disaster into broad themes concerning how law tracks international inequality, and his argument is an antidote to the appeal of the popular belief that disasters are equalizers, striking rich and poor alike. That perspective has frequently been found wanting within sociological analyses of disaster (Tierney 2006); the question for sociolegal studies is how law either systematically contributes to or mitigates inequality. Nitrato Izzo's postcolonial perspective is also a shift from Beck's argument that risk has become impossible to apprehend through the senses, widespread, with harms far from their origins. Although Beck describes risk as delocalized, Nitrato Izzo's innovation is in linking post-coloniality, law and disaster as analytical categories. Inequality across borders still allows for inequality within borders, and the large storms such as Sandy on the East Coast of the United States in fall 2012 are a reminder.

Disasters mobilize communities, and local communities often cannot meet the yawning need that loss of homes and family leaves. Coal mining disasters in West Virginia have continued to color the organization of disaster assistance in the United States, including the significance of voluntary assistance and the belief that it is tied to the local community that suffered the disaster, where neighbors help neighbors. The world of highly professionalized charities that work internationally, with contracts for volunteers and benefits for employees, contrasts sharply with the belief that communities care for their own after a disaster (Chandra and Acosta 2009, Hull 2006). After the industrial explosion in Bhopal in India, women whose husbands were too disabled to work came together in frustration, desperation and anger to claim compensation from the state (Fortun 2004). After the storm Sandy that hit the East Coast during the fall 2012 presidential election in the United States, the Republican candidate for president argued that localities and churches were best equipped to know what their communities needed, to which the American satirist Stephen Colbert (2012) responded that clearly the best people to respond to disaster were those whose homes had just been obliterated by it. The localism and voluntarism of help predated welfare state assistance, and captured what communities did after fires, drought, insect devastation and earthquakes (Krainz 2012). The bureaucratization of the welfare state and the accompanying bureaucratization of assistance would seem to displace the celebration of local emergent organizations, however much they might be necessary in the immediate aftermath of disaster. Administration by the states and by bureaucratized charities would also seem to mitigate the inequality that scholars have deplored in the distribution of assistance after disaster. Yet the celebration of voluntarism continues, and disaster response first coaches people to be ready, and to keep phone numbers to hand and a fresh supply of water nearby. Voluntary organizations are designated by law to provide relief and they operate responsively to need outside the law.

Advice for citizens raises questions about whether state practice will even act upon the principle that states are responsible for care of the citizenry after disaster. The resilient individual has been invented for governance in the uncertainties of late modern life. Regulation aspires to preventing disaster. In contrast, a resilience framework holds that disasters are inevitable, pointing to the onslaught of climate change and the increasing numbers of people who live on the coasts and in zones that are subject to drought and severe storms. If disasters are inevitable and states cannot care for everyone, then individuals must be resilient, Pat O'Malley argues that we are far from the welfare states with their risk assessment of predictable risks of the industrial state. Instead, people are now to be ready for anything, whether the devastating fires in the Australian outback, storms and droughts or the financial disasters of the early twenty-first century. The risks are unknown, of a hugely varying kind, and need to be embraced as opportunity rather than events for which people will need to be compensated. Properly designed regulation could still aspire to preventing the disasters of industrial fires, which sweep through buildings that have locked doors and, inevitably, kill people. Those accidents are still comprehensible in the twentieth century categories of the state. O'Malley argues that in the newer literature of internalized self-governance people are to be ready to become someone new when disaster strikes. O'Malley draws on management advice. According to O'Malley, the state is abandoning responsibility for managing known risks; instead, the world is one of uncertainty without predictable risks. Prevention is impossible and compensation for harm untenable. What is left is voluntarism and people who can move, rapidly develop new skills, and who keep everything they might need in their basement.

## CONCLUSION

The Buffalo Creek disaster of 1972 in West Virginia in the United States was the result of a failed dam that had been built to hold the waste from mining. The damage that it unleashed killed 125 people, and generated vast lawyering effort and attention, including Kai Erikson's beautiful and meticulous study of the loss of community that resulted from the flood (Erikson 1976). Even so, the legal settlement did not compensate people fully for their losses (Stern 1976). The settlement people in Bhopal received after the 1984 Union Carbide disaster often did not even compensate people for out of pocket expenses, and the Indian government did not want to cripple the international chemical industry in their country. Law consistently fails in compensating suffering after disaster *despite* the profound sympathy victims of disaster draw and the commitment in liberal states to caring for people. Sociolegal scholars can explain how that can happen and provide an explanation beyond the disappointment that meets every failure. Scholars of regulation within sociolegal studies take disaster as a failure and explain the mobilization for further regulation after disaster. If disaster is a failure, the mobilization of law and popular interpretation of rights and responsibilities during disaster is also a failure. Explaining how law works within disaster could disassemble the belief that law protects people, and that the problem with disaster is just that there needs to be more laws. From the point of view of regulation, disaster is already a failure of law. To then expect law would adequately compensate or fix the problem is to fail to take the analysis at the heart of studies of regulation far enough.

Rights embedded in administrative agencies and articulated through courts would seem to offer the hope of protection after disaster embedded in the law. International guidelines for displaced people list a right to judicial enforcement (Kromm and Sturgis, 2008). Expansions of rights are always based in analogies to something that already has a desired outcome, and advocates for care of populations suffering from environmental damage argue about whether people are thereby refugees (McAdam 2010, Piguet 2013). Refugees have well-established international protection, with rights institutionalized through both states and non-governmental organizations. Both sides in that debate assume that the law will indeed protect people. However, rights are easy to avoid without advocates to pursue implementation (Scheingold 1974, Scheingold and Sarat 2004). Remedies for harm after disaster are complex and negotiated, with the same political forces in the legal environment as the political environment that predated the harm. The lawyers for the victims of the disaster faced experienced lawyers who worked for a corporation that had few limits on the resources they could put into the case.

Law causes problems when it allows miners to strip earth bare; how it compensates then tells organizations whether causing disaster will cost them in a way that could reshape decision-making. Compensation for harm has a poor track record. Compensation can work like a lottery system, with some people doing very well and many getting only pennies on the dollar for the material harm done to them, let alone the less measurable losses of community. Early efforts in the United States included prosecutions for the Triangle Shirtwaist Factory fire in which hundreds of young women workers died, and myriad individual claims for compensation after industrial accidents. The tort system found doctrines that exempted employers from accountability for individual harms, and the Triangle Shirtwaist Factory Fire ended in exoneration for the factory owners (Von Drehle 2004). Advocates argue for laws, whether supranational or national liability. Tracing how lawyers, judges, case-level decision-makers and non-governmental organizations have mobilized law and have met or often disappointed the hopes embedded in a belief that law will fix problems is a crucial contribution that sociolegal scholars can make. As Tom Birkland (2013) shows in his overview of contributions to both disaster journals and sociolegal studies journals, too little has been made of the mobilization and understanding of law in disasters; disasters sometimes refocus scholarship as they refocus political agendas. We hope that this collection is only one part of expanding scholarship on legal mobilization, and a politics of rights, need and care in and after disaster.

In regulation, law has been widely critiqued: accountability to legal rules that pull in multiple directions can lead to a formalist rule compliance that does not advance the goal of reducing risks (Haines and Sutton 2003). Emergent understandings of law have turned to reaching goals that a regulator and regulated group reach together rather than commanding adherence to rules (Parker and Nielsen 2011). The gain in flexibility recognizes impossibility in the traditional model of law as accountability to publicly knowable rules. Even as students of regulation analyze the move toward 'regulating self-regulation' as a flexible, goal-oriented strategy that could accomplish goals and reduce risks, accountability for disasters that have already happened continues apace, in courts and in government compensation commissions. Since disasters draw media attention and the visible suffering of people who live through disaster draws sympathy, it demands short-term care in liberal states. Who is responsible for harm and/or care, and how legal institutions impose rules on a disorderly process, would reveal as much about legal systems as it would about managing inequality and responsibility.

## Bibliography

Agamben, G., 2005. *State of exception* [Stato die eccezione. English]. University of Chicago Press.

Ai Weiwei, 2012. *According to what?* [online]. Washington DC: Hirshhorn. Available from: http://www.hirshhorn.si.edu/collection/ai-weiwei-according-to-what/#collection=ai-weiwei-according-to-what [Accessed 4 April 2013].

Ansell, C.K., 2011. *Pragmatist democracy: Evolutionary learning as public philosophy.* New York: Oxford University Press.

Barry, J.M., 1998. *Rising Tide: the great Mississippi flood of 1927 and how it changed America.* New York: Simon & Schuster.

Beamish, T. D., 2002. *Silent spill: The organization of an industrial crisis.* Cambridge, Mass.: MIT Press.

Beck, U., 1992. *Risk society: towards a new modernity.* London; Newbury Park, Calif.: Sage.

Bilchner, L.C., and Molinder, A., 2008. Mapping juridification. *European Law Journal,* 14 (1), 36-54.

Birkland, T.A., 2013. Disasters, Focusing Events, and Sociolegal Studies. *Oñati Socio-legal Series* [online], 3 (2), 363-377 (Chapter 11 of this book). Also available from: http://ssrn.com/abstract=2221290 [Accessed 28 April 2013].

Burke, K., 1966. *Language as symbolic action: essays on life, literature, and method.* Berkeley: University of California Press.

Burton, L., 2013. The Comparative Jurisprudence of Wildfire Mitigation: Moral Community, Political Culture, and Policy Learning. *Oñati Socio-legal Series* [online], 3 (2), 234-253 (Chapter 4 of this book). Also available from: http://ssrn.com/abstract=2012287 [Accessed 28 April 2013].

Calhoun, C., 2010. The idea of emergency: Humanitarian action and global (dis)order. *In:* D. Fassin, and M. Pandolfi, eds. *Contemporary states of emergency: The politics of military and humanitarian interventions,* 29-58.

Cassels, J., 1993. *The uncertain promise of law: Lessons from Bhopal.* University of Toronto Press.

Chandra, A., and Acosta, J., 2009. *The role of nongovernmental organizations in long-term human recovery after disaster: Reflections from Louisiana four years after Hurricane Katrina* No. OP-277 [online]. Santa Monica, CA: RAND Corporation. Available from: http://www.rand.org/pubs/occasional_papers/OP277.html [Accessed 4 April 2013].

Clarke, L.B., 1999. *Mission improbable: Using fantasy documents to tame disaster.* University of Chicago Press.

Clarke, L.B., and Chess, C., 2008. Elites and Panic: more to fear than fear itself. *Social Forces,* 87 (2), 993-1014.

Colbert, S., 2012. Hurricane Sandy & Election Day. *Colbert Nation* [online], 31 Oct. Available from: http://www.colbertnation.com/the-colbert-report-videos/420666/october-31-2012/hurricane-sandy---election-day [Accessed 19 April 2013].

Cooper, C., and Block, R., 2007. *Disaster: Hurricane Katrina and the failure of homeland security.* New York: Times Books.

Dauber, M.L., 2005. The sympathetic state. *Law and History Review,* 23 (02), 387-442.

Dombrowsky, W.R., 1998. Again and again: Is a disaster what we call a 'disaster'? *In:* E.L. Quarentelli, ed. *What is a disaster?* London: Routldege, 13-25.

Dynes, R.R., and Tierney, K.J., 1994. *Disasters, collective behavior, and social organization.* Newark; Cranbury, NJ: University of Delaware Press; London: Associated University Presses.

Edelman, M.J., 1977. *Political language: Words that succeed and policies that fail*. New York: Academic Press.

Enarson, E.P., 2012. *Women confronting natural disaster: From vulnerability to resilience*. Boulder, Colo.: Lynne Rienner Publishers.

Erikson, K., 1976. *Everything in its path*. New York: Simon and Schuster.

Feinberg, K.R., 2005. *What is life worth? The unprecedented effort to compensate the victims of 9/11*. New York, NY: Public Affairs.

Flatt, V.B., and Stys, J.J., 2013. Long Term Recovery in Disaster Response and the Role of Non-Profits. *Oñati Socio-legal Series* [online], 3 (2), 346-362 (Chapter 10 of this book). Also available from: http://ssrn.com/abstract=2119879 [Accessed 28 April 2013].

Fortun, K., 2004. *Advocacy after Bhopal*. University of Chicago Press.

Freudenberg, W.R., *et al.*, 2009. *Catastrophe in the making: The engineering of Katrina and the disasters of tomorrow*. Washington: Shearwater Press.

Freudenburg, W.R., and Gramling, R., 2012. *Blowout in the Gulf: The BP oil spill disaster and the future of energy in America*. Cambridge, Mass.; London: MIT Press.

Gusfield, J.R., 1981. *The culture of public problems: Drinking-driving and the symbolic order*. University of Chicago Press.

Haines, F., 2009. Regulatory failures and regulatory solutions: A characteristic analysis of the aftermath of disaster. *Law and Social Inquiry*, 34 (1), 31-60.

Haines, F., and Sutton, A., 2003. The engineer's dilemma: A sociological perspective on juridification and regulation. *Crime, Law and Social Change*, 39(1), 1-22.

Hiller, P., 2013. Multi-level Governance in Environmental Risk Management. *Oñati Socio-legal Series* [online], 3 (2), 312-325 (Chapter 8 of this book). Also available from: http://ssrn.com/abstract=2221284 [Accessed 28 April 2013].

Hull, P., 2006. *Heralding unheard voices* [online]*: The role of faith-based organizations and nongovernmental organizations during disasters: Final report, December 18, 2006* No. RP006-44-01. Arlington, VA: Homeland Security Institute. Available from: http://permanent.access.gpo.gov/lps116727/Herald_Unheard_Voices.pdf [Accessed 19 April 2013].

Krainz, T.A., 2012. Fleeing the big burn: Refugees, informal assistance and welfare practices in the progressive era. *Journal of Policy History*, 24 (3), 405-431.

Kromm, C., and Sturgis, S., 2008. Hurricane Katrina and the guiding principles on internal displacement: A global human rights perspective on a national disaster. *Southern Exposure*, 35 (1 & 2).

McAdam, J., 2010. *Climate change and displacement: Multidisciplinary perspectives*. Oxford; Portland, Or.: Hart.

McEvoy, A.F., 2013. The role of law in engineering "natural" disasters. *Oñati Socio-legal Series* [online], 3 (2), 293-311 (Chapter 7 of this book). Also available from: http://ssrn.com/abstract=2221241 [Accessed 28 April 2013].

McFalls, L., 2010. Benevolent dictatorship: The formal logic of humanitarian government. *In*: D. Fassin, and M. Pandolfi, eds. *Contemporary states of emergency: The politics of military and humanitarian interventions*. New York: Zone Books, 317-334.

Meyer, M.A., 2013. Internal Environmental Displacement: A Growing Challenge to the United States Welfare State. *Oñati Socio-legal Series* [online], 3 (2), 326-345 (Chapter 9 of this book). Also available from: http://ssrn.com/abstract=2221286 [Accessed 28 April 2013].

Nitrato Izzo, V., 2013. Law, State and the Politics of Catastrophes: a Critical Perspective on Epiphanies of Injustice and the Need for Protection. *Oñati Socio-legal Series* [online], 3 (2), 221-233 (Chapter 3 of this book). Also available from: http://ssrn.com/abstract=2221287 [Accessed 28 April 2013].

Nonet, P., and Selznick, P., 1978. *Law and society in transition: Toward responsive law*. New York: Harper & Row.

O'Malley, P., 2013. Uncertain Governance and Resilient Subjects in the Risk Society. *Oñati Socio-legal Series* [online], 3 (2), 180-195 (Chapter 1 of this book). Also available from: http://ssrn.com/abstract=2221288 [Accessed 28 April 2013].

Ophir, A., 2007. The two state solution: Providence and catastrophe. *Journal of Homeland Security and Emergency Management,* 4 (1), 1-44.

Parker, C., and Nielsen, V.L., 2011. *Explaining compliance*. Cheltenham: Edward Elgar.

Peek, L., and Fothergill, A., 2008. Displacement, gender, and the challenges of parenting after Hurricane Katrina. *NWSA Journal,* 20 (3), 69-105.

Perrow, C., 1984. *Normal accidents: Living with high-risk technologies*. New York: Basic Books.

Piguet, E., 2013. From "Primitive migration" to "Climate refugees": The curious fate of the natural environment in migration studies. *Annals of the Association of American Geographers,* 103 (1), 148-162.

Ponce, J., 2013. Land Use Planning and Disaster: A European Perspective from Spain. *Oñati Socio-legal Series* [online], 3 (2), 196-220 (Chapter 2 of this book). Also available from: http://ssrn.com/abstract=2221235 [Accessed 28 April 2013].

Quarentelli, E.L., ed., 1998. *What is a disaster?* London: Routledge.

Redfield, P., 2005. Doctors, borders and life in crisis. *Cultural Anthropology,* 20 (3), 328-361.

Roberts, P., 2007. What the catastrophist heresy can teach public officials. *Administrative Theory & Praxis,* 29 (4), 546-566.

Rozario, K., 2007. *The culture of calamity: Disaster and the making of modern America*. University of Chicago Press.

Sapat A., and Esnard, A-M., 2012. Transboundary Impacts of the 2010 Haiti Earthquake Disaster: Focus on Legal Dilemmas in South Florida. *Oñati Socio-*

*legal Series* [online], 3 (2), 254-276 (Chapter 5 of this book). Also available from: http://ssrn.com/abstract=2221282 [Accessed 28 April 2013].

Sarat, A., and Lezaun, J., 2009. *Catastrophe: Law, politics, and the humanitarian impulse*. Amherst: University of Massachusetts Press.

Scheingold, S.A., 1974. *The politics of rights: Lawyers, public policy, and political change*. New Haven: Yale University Press.

Scheingold, S.A., and Sarat, A., 2004. *Something to believe in: Politics, professionalism, and cause lawyering*. Stanford Law and Politics.

Sterett, S., 2003. *Public pensions: Gender and civic service in the states, 1850-1937*. Ithaca, N.Y.: Cornell University Press.

Sterett, S., 2009. New Orleans Everywhere: bureaucratic accountability and housing policy after Katrina. *In*: A. Sarat, and J. Lezaun, eds. *Catastrophe: law, politics and the humanitarian impulse*. Amherst, MA: University of Massachusetts Press, 83-115.

Sterett, S., 2012. State policy and disaster assistance: Listening to women. *In*: E. David, and E. Enarson, eds. *The women of Katrina: How gender, race, and class matter in an American disaster*. Nashville: Vanderbilt University Press, 118-129.

Sterett, S., and Reich, J., 2007. Prayer and Social Welfare: race and service after Hurricane Katrina. In: H. Potter, ed. *Racing the Storm*. Lanham: Lexington Books, 135-156.

Stern, G.M., 1976. *The Buffalo Creek disaster: The story of the survivors' unprecedented lawsuit*. New York: Random House.

Sun, L.G., 2013. Disaster Mythology and Availability Cascades. *Oñati Socio-legal Series* [online], 3 (2), 277-292 (Chapter 6 of this book). Also available from: http://ssrn.com/abstract=2221283 [Accessed 28 April 2013].

Tierney, K., 2006. Social inequality, hazards and disaster. *In*: R. Daniels, D.F. Kettl and H. Kunreuther, eds. *On risk and disaster: Lessons from Hurricane Katrina*. Philadelphia: University of Pennsylvania Press, 109-128.

Von Drehle, D., 2004. *Triangle: the fire that changed America*. New York: Grove Press.

Weber, L., Peek, L.A., and Social Science Research Council Research Network on Persons Displaced by Hurricane Katrina, 2012. *Displaced: Life in the Katrina diaspora*. Austin: University of Texas Press.

# 1

# UNCERTAIN GOVERNANCE AND RESILIENT SUBJECTS IN THE RISK SOCIETY

## Pat O'Malley

**ABSTRACT**

Over the past decade or so, a series of new or revitalised strategies have been promoted to govern the highly uncertain threats that risk appears no longer able to prevent. Most owe their ascendancy to the lessons of 9/11, and the 'bureaucratising of imagination' that US sources have proposed as a response, by centring the possible, or even merely imaginable, rather than the statistically probable. Precaution, preparedness and speculative pre-emption have been particularly prominent, although new hybrid statistical and speculative techniques have broadened risk techniques to cope with labile conditions of high uncertainty. But while diverse, each establishes a negative and defensive framework of 'freedom from' that has been associated with creating a 'neurotic subject'. In the past decade, programs of resilience, and particularly resiliency training, have been developed with the aim of creating subjects able to thrive and prosper under conditions of extreme uncertainty. They constitute a form of governance promoting a positive 'freedom to'. Reflecting many of the assumptions and goals of neo-liberal politics, resiliency has already emerged as a principal technology for military and business, and may be the answer to the neo-liberal dream of a society of extreme entrepreneurs.

Durante la última década, se han promovido varias estrategias nuevas o renovadas destinadas a gestionar amenazas que el riesgo ya no parece capaz de prevenir. La mayoría deben su predominancia a las lecciones aprendidas tras el 11-S, y la "burocratización de la imaginación" que las fuentes estadounidenses han propuesto como respuesta, predominando lo posible, o incluso simplemente lo imaginable, por encima de lo estadísticamente probable. Han predominado la precaución, preparación y especulación preventivas, aunque las nuevas técnicas estadísticas y especulativas híbridas han ampliado las técnicas de riesgo para hacer frente a las condiciones inestables de alta incertidumbre. A pesar de que sean diferentes, cada una de ellas establece un marco negativo y defensivo de "libertad de" que se ha asociado con la creación de un "sujeto neurótico" En la última década se han desarrollado programas de resiliencia, y en especial de formación en resiliencia, con el objetivo de crear sujetos capaces de crecer y prosperar en condiciones de incertidumbre extrema. Constituyen una forma de gobierno que promueve una "libertad para" positiva. Como reflejo de muchas de las hipótesis y los objetivos de la política neoliberal, la resiliencia ya se ha constituido como una importante tecnología militar y empresarial, y puede ser la respuesta al sueño neo-liberal de una sociedad de emprendedores extremos.

## INTRODUCTION

In Ulrich Beck's (1992) overly familiar and alarmist language, the emergent 'age of catastrophes' forces us to move from the calculable to the incalculable future, or more precisely from governing through risk to governing by reliance on 'uncertainty'. Statistical risk techniques, he asserts, can no longer predict the global 'modernization risks' that are the most significant threats to our existence. Climate change, global terrorism, holes in the ozone layer, nuclear disasters and so on are all examples of human-generated catastrophes not recognised until their effects become manifest. To deal with these, it is argued that governmental prediction must abandon the precise probability techniques of risk, and enter the realms of 'uncertainty'—meaning that only estimation and imagination can prepare us for the future. Of course, this is a crude binary, suggesting that either we have statistical calculation of the future or virtually no useful capacity at all to calculate. Elsewhere I have argued that such a response itself falls into a trap that elevates the importance of risk, insofar as we are seen as plunging into chaos without it (O'Malley 2003). Yet, of course, governments relied solely on anticipatory governance before there was risk, and most modern institutions and arrangements, including Beck's Bell-Wether of Insurance, have long and profitably relied extensively on non-statistical estimation of hazards (O'Malley 2003, Bougen 2003, Ericson and Doyle 2004).[1]

Central to all such 'uncertain' techniques is what Jeremy Bentham (1962) termed the 'disposition to look forward'—the liberal duty of foresight. Formalised into doctrines of 'reasonable foreseeability' and 'negligence' in areas such as contract and tort law, they were equally the essence of a disciplinary regime for the poor essential to creating them as diligent and prudent subjects (O'Malley 2000). In this sense, uncertainty combines the act of imagination by which to project actions into the future,

---

[1] Like most social scientists unfamiliar with the actual workings of insurance, Beck assumes that it relies totally on actuarial method—the application of the laws of large numbers to extensive volumes of archival data in order to generate precise probabilistic predictions. While this is a preferred approach in many areas, such as life insurance and fire insurance, as Ericson and Doyle (2004) have shown, it is frequently not the case that insurance proceeds in this fashion, for example where small or localised markets for insurance are created. Such, often highly profitable, markets may exist even with respect to contemporary life insurance. Moreover, as O'Malley and his colleagues have shown (O'Malley and Hutchinson 2007, P. O'Malley and A. Roberts, personal communication, Eyeballing fire risks: How did fire prevention become actuarial? *Surveillance and Everyday Life Conference*, The University of Sydney 20-22 Feb 2012), even such major fields as fire insurance operated profitably and with considerable stability well into the 20th century without actuarial tables. Even where actuarial models do exist, it is clear that actuaries frequently rely on them only as a guide to business decisions rather than as a rigid determinant of insurance practice (Porter 1995, Ericson and Doyle 2004).

and the application of an everyday calculus—based on experience—in order to estimate their likely consequences. This 'reasonable foresight' became a skill and responsibility for all liberal subjects in the 19th century.

This foundational liberal technique for governing uncertainty has been updated and elaborated, and out of it new forms have recently innovated—especially since 9/11 so graphically illustrated the vulnerabilities of risk-predictive techniques. Most of these innovations, I will argue, are only slightly more sophisticated versions of what Bentham (1962) in the 18th century understood perfectly as the 'yoke of foresight'. These are discussed below as 'precaution', 'speculative pre-emption', and 'enactment' or 'preparedness'. They are marked by a shared defensive stance in which the future is littered with *imaginable* disasters. All share a belief that traditional statistical risk techniques alone are an inadequate defence. They also share a subject who is the subject of prudence. As noted, the prudent risk avoider was one of Bentham's subjects of foresight—for example the thrifty, self-denying and diligent worker who prepared for the rainy day. But while prominent, this was only one of Bentham's principal subjects. The other, tellingly, was the entrepreneur, and of late this has been influencing other innovative responses to the problem of governing situations of high consequence and high uncertainty. In the past quarter century, it has become commonplace to observe that we are witnessing a remodelling of liberal subjects in line with a neo-liberal vision of everyman as entrepreneur of himself (Foucault 2008, p. 256).[2] Extensively shaped by the fusion of a radical vision of business as uncertainty with the emergence of scientifically optimised training, a strategy or technology of individual resilience is being developed that is intended to create subjects who are not merely prudently defensive. The new subjects of resilience are being designed in ways of being human that allow them to live in *positive* freedom under conditions of radical uncertainty.

IMAGINING SECURITY

In its *Full Report of the National Commission on Terrorist Attacks Upon the United States* (National Commission 2004), the Commission asked how it was that that the US Government failed to anticipate and prevent the terrorist attack. Its conclusion was that the disaster was the consequence of a lack of imagination. Trawling through an enormous mass of information relating to intelligence and analysis leading up to the

---

[2] Of course such subjectifications existed and were prominent even in the 19th century. But overwhelmingly these were understood to be the preserve of wealthy white men: the explorer, the enterprising capitalist, mountaineers and big-game hunters. Important as they were, there was never an expectation that the masses would adopt such subjectifications, for to do so would be to risk becoming a burden on the community in the event of failure or injury (O'Malley 2004).

event, perhaps it was inevitable that among the hundreds of imagined scenarios, some resembled the Twin Towers catastrophe. The National Commission (2004, pp. 339-346) noted numerous 'telltale indicators' that had attracted little attention. Thus 'the North American Aerospace Defense Command had imagined the possible use of aircraft as a weapon' and 'one prescient pre-9/11 analysis of an aircraft plot was written by a Justice Department trial attorney' (National Commission 2004, p. 346). The National Counterterrorism Coordinator (Richard Clarke) informed the Commission that he had been concerned about the dangers posed by commercial aircraft, but he attributed this 'more to Tom Clancy novels than to warnings from the intelligence community' (National Commission 2004, p. 347).

Perhaps by ignoring the logistics of evaluating the stupendous array of other imaginable scenarios that had been toyed with by one or other of the thousands of experts in the field, the Commission concluded that the event could have been prevented if only these imaginings had been taken seriously—and of course, it meant in particular consideration of the one unlikely scenario that actually eventuated. The Commission convinced itself that 'the most important failure was one of imagination' (National Commission 2004, p. 9). As I have explored elsewhere with Phillip Bougen (Bougen and O'Malley 2009, O'Malley and Bougen 2009), the theme of imagination recurs throughout the report, leading to a general conclusion that 'the possibility was imaginable and imagined' (National Commission 2004, p. 344). While acknowledging that imagination is not a gift usually associated with bureaucracies, the Commission argued that 'it is therefore crucial to find a way of routinizing, even bureaucratizing imagination' (National Commission 2004, p. 344). The response is fascinating given that bureaucratization is something that had been ideologically on the nose of neoliberals and neoconservatives for decades. Bureaucracies have come to be regarded in this political environment as anti-entrepreneurial, inflexible and overly hierarchical. Much ink has been spilled on how government can be improved through replacing bureaucracy with 'government through foresight' which favours competition, market mechanisms, decentralization and entrepreneurialism. In short, what had been promoted widely before the Commission was a government that embraces uncertainty precisely by abandoning its bureaucratic character (Osborne and Gaebler 1993, du Gay 2000).

Thus it could be argued, at least if one accepts the nostrums of new managerialism and the entrepreneurial state, that any proposal to routinize imagination in bureaucracies is destined to fail. What is more interesting from a theoretical position is the fact that a specific tension is set up, for the claimed advantage of bureaucracies is precisely that they are rule-bound and thus calculable and predictable (Weber 1964). Yet bureaucracy is being set to foster imagining and governing through the incalculable.

Three principal strategies and associated technologies have emerged under this rubric: precaution, preparedness and enactment, and speculative pre-emption. A fourth approach—resilience (or at least one variant of it)—may be understood to have grown up rather to one side of this bureaucratization. To this development the last part of the chapter will turn, and suggest it as a response to uncertainty that better than 'bureaucratising imagination'—reflects the neo-liberal vision of entrepreneurial governance.

## REVOLUTIONIZING RISK? DATA DERIVATIVES

Yet before we move to consider these 'post risk' techniques, it must be pointed out that risk itself has not remained unchanged in the age of catastrophes. The image of risk relied upon by Beck and others is of a body of knowledge based on the long term accumulation of data, and resulting probability models that are formed around causal thinking. Mere correlation by itself is not sufficient. Thus Callon, Lascoumes and Barthe (2011, p. 206) argue that 'the probabilistic approach requires prior knowledge of the emergent event. It cannot be carried out if the latter has causes and modes of development that are still unknown ... or if it appears to rest on causal chains and interactions which are still poorly delimited'. Statistics on individual morbidity and mortality, on marine accidents to shipping and cargoes, on the determinants of building fires and so on, all advanced in this fashion (Lobo-Guerrero 2011). It is with this more or less causal-statistical model in mind that risk-based predictions are understood to fail in the labile environment of the 'age of catastrophes'. Thus with some hazards, statistical-causal modelling fails because is likely to be taken into account by human agents. In this vision terrorism, for example, is so hard to predict because terrorists can figure out likely 'causal' patterns of risk-profiling that would identify them and thus select agents who defy profiles. With other hazards, risk fails precisely because 'causal chains and interactions are still poorly delimited'. In climate science, for example, it is argued that correlations will only be attended to if they make causal sense—so that predictions of climate change can only take root once a theory can be produced to render the phenomena intelligible.

As Louise Amoore (2011) has shown, however, new forms of non-causal risk calculus are now widely in operation that resemble speculative trading on financial derivatives. Of course, others (Bougen 2003, Ericson and Doyle 2004) have pointed to the use of speculative 'catastrophe bonds' as a means of insuring 'uninsurable' catastrophic risks. There is an implication that such bonds are based merely on wild speculation—which some may indeed be. But Amoore identifies something more of a hybrid. 'Data derivatives' are a correlation or 'a score drawn from an amalgam of disaggregated fragments of data, inferred from across the gaps between data and projected onto an array of uncertain futures' (Amoore 2011, p. 24). Mobile, algorithm-based association rules are produced of the form 'if *** and ***, in association with ***, then ***'. For example, if ticket is paid in cash, and meal choice is X in association with flight route Y, then investigate further. The question becomes not who are you, but what are you doing here? The algorithm does not lead to a prediction but to another uncertainty, a potentiality: another question.

In this way, Amoore argues, it is not collected data that become actionable. Nor are the algorithms themselves stable, nor need they lead to scientifically established causal patterns. They may be ephemeral, only useful for brief periods or until some other question is answered and they are dismissed. It is a form of abstraction 'that is based precisely on an absence, on what is not known, on the very basis of uncertainty' (Amoore 2011, p. 25). This drives pre-emption not by predicting the future but by projecting fragments of data onto possible futures, producing a form of encoded intuition. Significantly, in light of what is to be said about resilience, Amoore is clear that this emerges from the practices of speculative business: from the realms of derivatives trading.

## PRECAUTION

As many have noted (Ewald 2002, Fisher 2007) one response to the emergence of the risk society and radical uncertainty has been the elevated resort to the precautionary principal, already widely deployed in Europe for example with respect to issues concerning climate change and genetically modified foods. In its most conservative form, this intensifies the negativity and paranoia of risk, for at its heart is a decision to cease and desist activities that generate high consequence hazards which are not precisely calculable. As Ewald (2002, p. 287) sees it:

> [T]he precautionary principle invites one to consider the worst hypothesis (defined as the serious and irreversible consequence'). I must, out of precaution, imagine the worst possible, the consequence that an infinitely deceptive malicious demon could have slipped into an apparently innocent exercise.

This is a specific formulation in which *imagining* the worst is pivotal. It is, as he (Ewald 2002, p. 288) suggests not just inviting one 'to take into account doubtful hypotheses and simple suspicions' but even 'to take the most far-fetched forecasts seriously, predictions by prophets, whether true or false'. There are, as will be seen, various ways of responding to such 'invitations'. However, because—in this interpretation—it takes the worst case scenario as its subject, precaution requires the curtailing or cessation of action. Significantly, Ewald (2002, p. 299) himself points out one consequence is that the 'spirit of enterprise, of creation, and of innovation' are no longer valued and promoted.

There are significant doubts about the extent to which this has been the case in practice. Ewald is adopting an extreme view of precaution, albeit one shared by other influential commentators (e.g. Sunstein 2005). In practice, precaution may stimulate research into the problematic effects of questionable developments, and in addition has opened up dialogues between democratic politics, science and business rather than closing down development by political fiat (Fisher 2007).[3] Thus the European Commission has defined precaution as a 'reasoned and structured framework of action enabling scientific uncertainty to be remedied' (European Commission 2000). Whether we accept the extreme interpretation or not, in precaution it could be said that two core elements are precisely as mapped by Ewald: the deployment of imagination and its coupling with possibility of harms that cannot be tolerated.

The resultant is something not clearly articulated in much of the precaution literature—for it shares with risk a fundamentally preventive logic. It assumes that prevention is possible. Where it differs from the data derivatives discussed by Amoore is therefore not in that it requires certainty or causal models to be established. It requires action 'even before a causal link has been established by absolutely clear scientific evidence' (1987 Declaration of the International Conference on the Protection of the North Sea, quoted in Callon, Lascoumes and Barthe 2011, p. 207). Rather it is that it does not work statistically: it does not require a correlation to be identified—only to be imagined. Thus even if we move beyond the extreme version of precaution discussed by Beck and Ewald, it remains the response par excellence of the risk society. It is a program of 'freedom from': there is no agenda of positive freedom per se, only one of removing some of 'freedom'—by closing down enterprise and discovery—in order to protect what is imagined as more important. It is, of course, the classic Hobbesian response of 'security' interventions translated into a world of only imaginable futures (Sunstein 2005).

## PREPAREDNESS AND ENACTMENT

The second major direction taken in the past decade—similarly negative—has been to assume that we cannot prevent catastrophes befalling us, even by retreatist strategies such as precaution, and had better get ready for the worst. Collier and Lakoff (2008, p. 11) have argued that this is a defining characteristic of 'preparedness' which has emerged as a federally institutionalised response post 9/11. By preparedness they mean 'a form of planning for unpredictable but catastrophic events ... the aim of such planning is not to prevent these events from happening, but rather to

---

3 Michel Callon and his colleagues (Callon, Lascoumes and Barthe 2011) have argued strongly against identifying precaution as being tied to the worst case scenario. In this light precaution would only lead to 'an impasse in decision making'. Rather they suggest that the worst case scenario forms limit case in precaution, which only requires that all hypotheses, even the most marginal, have to be considered. It is perhaps a moot point whether Ewald can be interpreted as promoting this view, or the 'extreme' view. Certainly it is the 'extreme' view that gets the most emphasis in his work. Callon, Lascoumes and Barthe (2011, p. 200) must think Ewald's position more moderate, since they suggest that the extreme view is a journalist's fiction that 'does not appear in any referenced text'.

manage their consequences'. Collier (2008) outlines enactment in detail, focusing on the role of expert reflection and the ways in which it is deployed to imagine catastrophic futures.

> Rather than drawing on an archive of past events, enactment uses as its basic data an *inventory* of past elements at risk, information about the *vulnerability* of these elements and a model of the threat itself—the *event* model. And rather than using statistical analysis, enactment 'acts out' uncertain future threats by juxtaposing these various forms of data.' (Collier 2008, p. 226).

This owes much to war-gaming as practiced in military circles for many years. In the simplest model, this may involve imagining scenarios and placing multiple transparent overlays on maps in order to simulate these, with the aim of giving emergency service planners a foundation on which to prepare. Recently, more sophisticated models have been developed, for example by Grossi and Kunreuther (2005) in which hazard, inventory, vulnerability and loss are deployed through the development of computer modelling based on analogous past events, rather than accumulated statistical data. With terrorism risk, for example, estimation of the timing and nature of the threat is 'elicited' from experts (cf. Ericson and Doyle 2004, pp. 150-151). While 'elicitation' is no more than expert-informed guesswork, as Collier points out, the use of analogous models of natural disasters, military damage assessments and nuclear reactor failures likely provide reasonable approximations to imaginable harms terrorism will produce (Collier 2008, p. 242). Similar modelling is used, for example, with respect to providing foundations for terrorism insurance—despite Beck's assertion that this is an 'uninsurable' risk (Bougen 2003).

No matter how sophisticated the modelling, the overriding characteristic of enactment-preparedness remains passive, defensive and negative, the attempt to create 'freedom from'. As with precaution, the spirit of innovation and enterprise is stifled, but this is not totally inescapable consequence of bureaucratising imagination, as may be seen in the case of speculative pre-emption.

## SPECULATIVE PRE-EMPTION

There is nothing new about pre-emptive strikes as such. However, it is an important development for several reasons. First, it is generated in an environment in which the precautionary principle had become well established but, as the National Security Strategy makes quite explicit, it offers a radical departure from the mind set mapped out by Ewald.

> The greater the threat, the greater is the risk of inaction—and the more compelling the case for taking anticipatory action to defend ourselves, *even if uncertainty remains as to the time and place of the enemy's attack*. To forestall or prevent such hostile acts by our

adversaries, the United States will, if necessary, act pre-emptively (National security Council 2002 quoted by Cooper 2006).

Speculative pre-emption relies precisely on high uncertainty for its rationale and this is argued to differentiate it from historical precursors. Previously, pre-emptive strikes would be founded on clear evidence that an attack was imminent. In 'the risk society', however, high uncertainty has become a justification in its own right Cooper (2006, pp 125-127) has gone further to argue that the logic of post-9/11 speculative pre-emption— to intervene in emergence precisely because of uncertainty linked to massive consequences—is being extended to such other fields as climate change and genetic engineering. In such areas its proponents advocate that 'we make an attempt to unleash transformative events on a biospheric scale before we get dragged away by nature's own acts of emergence' (Cooper 2006, p. 126).

Cooper's analysis is particularly significant because it also brings to the fore the nexus between speculative pre-emption and parallel radical shifts in the business domain. For Cooper, the genealogy of speculative pre-emption is founded in the shift toward the spectacular rethinking of capital during the neo-liberal years leading up to the turn of the 21st century. In the economic domain, 'it seemed that speculation itself had become the driving force behind unprecedented levels of innovation, allowing whole industries to be financed on the mere hope of future profits (Cooper 2006, p. 127). It was, as Cooper rightly observes, an era in which the imaginary of venture capitalism institutionalised a new model of economic activity.

I will return to this image of venture capital later in the piece, for it recurs in the development of another—and perhaps the most significant— 'post risk' strategy. But for Cooper, there is another genealogical step to take. The bursting of the dotcom bubble, reinforced later by the global financial crisis, shifted the entrepreneurial ideal on its axis. The neoliberal optimism in which the uncertain future was hailed and grasped as an opportunity for profit now was recast into a fear of uncertainty. The neoconservatives, she suggests, 'want to convince us that there is no end to danger'. After 9/11, this became the predominant vision that shaped warfare. Speculative pre-emption, she suggests, needs to be understood in the nexus between military security, the politics of life and new forms of speculative capitalization (Cooper 2006, pp. 128-129).

This is a telling argument. However, just as precaution was not the only 'logical' response to high uncertainty, so speculative pre-emption is not the only strategy that emerged from this triangle of the military, venture capitalism and 'the politics of life'—nor is it necessarily the most transformative one. The politics of the New Right, if we can still use this term in the 21st century, have long been unstable and contradictory, a legacy of the wedding of neo-conservatism and neo-liberalism in the Thatcher-Reagan years (O'Malley 1999). Consequently, there has not been only a trend toward defensive neo-conservatism but an ongoing contestation between allied and overlapping doctrines that have respectively valorised social and prudential authoritarianism and a more radically laissez faire 'social' entrepreneurialism. Thus while I accept Cooper's general argument, I want to suggest that there has been no succession of strategies, but rather a situation in which both strands continue to have an influence—in business and the military as in politics.

Speculative pre-emption shares with enactment a vision of an open and unformed future that nevertheless can be dealt with *as if* it were known. Intervention in Iraq went forward not simply on the imagined possibility of WMDs but on the assumption that 'we' could not take the chance of waiting to make sure. The resulting action, however, took the form of a vision of certainty—the invasion operated as if the WMDs existed; its form and operation would have been little different regardless of whether they proved to exist or, as turned out, to the contrary.

Enactment faces a problem that pre-emption evades, for if pre-emption operates as if there is certainty and obliterates the other uncertain futures by creating its own, the persistent doubt about which of the many imaginable futures is the most likely always haunts preparedness. If, as has been seen, the bureaucratisation of imagination demands that all imaginable futures be taken seriously, how do we proceed? Not all such imaginary threats can be rendered the subject of preparation. Of course, various techniques such as expert elicitation are used to select more likely imaginable futures. But that is precisely the trap that the bureaucratization of imagination sets. Imagination is the limit, then discounting *any* possibilities—such as the possibility of flying fully fuelled long-haul jets into buildings—negates the strategy. It must writhe in its own contradiction. Speculative pre-emption theoretically faces the same dilemma, of course, but by *remaking* the future appears to evade it. Even so, while 'enterprising' in form, it is still merely reactive, pursuing a negative goal of freedom from which is itself in tension with neo-liberalism's boundless faith in uncertainty and enterprise. This is where resilience comes into play.

RESILIENCE: ENTERPRISING IMAGINATION

As Walker and Cooper (2011, p. 27) suggest, 'with the post-911 revolution in homeland security, resilience has become a universal security perspective'. It integrates a wide array of disaster situations including terrorism, critical infrastructure protection, state failure, natural disasters and climate change within a single mode of analysis. Like other post-9/11 strategies, resilience is focused on critical events that we 'cannot predict or prevent but adapt to by "building resilience" '. As a consequence of the enormous scope of events to which it is envisaged applying, resilience—like risk—takes on a bewildering variety of forms. But it differs markedly from other strategies in that it does not imagine specific scenarios against which defences (or pre-emptive attacks) must be prepared. Rather, the focus is on building-in a capacity to adapt and survive in the face of *any* situation—a context of high uncertainty imaginable or otherwise (Lentzos and Rose 2008). More characteristically still, 'resilience is the capacity to adapt and thrive in the face of challenge' (World Economic Forum 2008, p. ix).

Note that there is no talk of disaster or catastrophe, nor specification of types of imaginable threat. There are 'challenges', and the aim is not simply recovery from disaster but the capacity to 'thrive'. It is a sea change from the other, ultimately negative and defensive strategies. This characterisation of resilience is diagnostic, for it identifies it precisely with the entrepreneurial, neo-liberal business models such as were developed in the 1970s for example in Tom Peters (1987) iconic *Thriving on Chaos*. Indeed, the parallel with the approaches to business that 'embrace high' uncertainty goes deeper than this. In order to explore this, we need to focus in on one specific field of security and uncertainty in the risk society: the transformation of military affairs.

Within a year of the announcement that imagination was to be bureaucratised, Defense Secretary Rumsfeld effectively summed up a rather different vision associated with a re-formation of the conception of the military and of its personnel along entrepreneurial lines. He urged:

> We must transform not only our armed forces but also the Department that serves them by encouraging a culture of creativity and intelligent risk-taking. We must promote a more entrepreneurial approach to developing military capabilities, one that encourages people, all people, to be proactive and not reactive, to behave somewhat less like bureaucrats and more like venture capitalists. (Donald Rumsfeld 2002).

Since just before the end of the 20th century, the military in the US and other 'western' powers have been radically changing the organisation and mentalities of the military in substantial ways—the 'revolution in military affairs' (RMA). Broadly speaking, the RMA reflects a view that the nature of warfare has changed. If once there were declared wars and set-piece battles, now warfare may occur at any time and in and through media that little resemble battlefields. 'Battlespaces' may involve contested landscapes, but they may be on the internet as hackers seek weaknesses in the enemy's defences, or in commerce and banking—anywhere the enemy is vulnerable. Even 'on the ground', armed warfare has shifted from set piece battles to highly mobile and fragmented conflicts. This is regarded as an era of 'asymmetric warfare' where each side plays according to its own rules and seeks weakness wherever it can be made to appear. The result is that 'our missions have become far more complex and our challenges and adversaries less predictable' (Alberts, Gratska and Stein 2000, p. 60). Warfare and military security have shifted dramatically in the direction of high uncertainty (Manigart 2003).

In response to this assessment, the RMA has drawn heavily on the radical models of business restructuring that are associated with the 'new managerial' revolution and neo-liberal visions of the entrepreneurial society. As business is perceived to have shifted toward innovative and highly competitive strategies in the globalized economy, so it has appeared to military leadership that 'in many ways the environment in which the military forces operate does not differ from that of the business environment' (DSTO 2004, p. 4),or as pointed out by the architects of the now pre-eminent 'network centric warfare' model, 'network centric warfare has its antecedent in the dynamics of growth and competition that have emerged in the modern economy' (Cebrowski and Gartska 1998).

In a nutshell, network centric warfare may be summed up by the idea that networked relationships become more critical to military flexibility, adaptability and multitasking than the traditional vision of 'silos' of military might and firepower. 'Co-evolving' with business, visible changes include simplification of hierarchies, use of smaller and more mobile formations, and increased autonomy and responsibility of personnel. The 'network centric warrior' is required to a far greater extent to be innovative, flexible and to act as an informed decision maker. (DSTO 2004) Here resilience emerges as a key to creating new subjects of high uncertainty.

In the wake of the destabilisation of the American economy post-9/11, the entrepreneurial ideal did not solely take the negative turn speculative pre-emption suggested above by Cooper. Among a raft of reformulations was the appearance in business and change management literature of a host of 'self improvement' manuals on how to become resilient. In Brooks and Goldstein's (2003) *The Power of Resilience: Achieving Balance, Confidence, and Personal Strength in Your Life*, the everyday idea of resilience as being able to 'withstand shocks' and 'bounce back' is joined by a more enterprising and positive vision 'that will lead to a more resilient, fulfilling life' (Brooks and Goldstein 2003, pp. 3-4). The same message is developed in Siebert's *The Resiliency Advantage: Master Change, Thrive Under Pressure* (Siebert 2005). For some advocates, in still more encompassing fashion, resilience 'is the basic ingredient to happiness and success' (Reivich and Shatte 2002, p. 1). In this sense, the constitution of new subjectivities not only is focused on risk and uncertainty as calculative ways of dealing with threats. At least equally it promotes what Baker and Simon (2002) refer to as 'embracing risk': the *positive* attitude that regards high uncertainty as opportunity and challenge.

A principal change ushered in by this new 'resiliency' literature was the argument that resiliency was a mindset or skill that could be learned, rather than a personality or character trait deeply inscribed in the individual. The elements of this mindset include such 'skills' as "displaying effective communication', 'possessing solid problem-solving and decision-making skills', 'establishing realistic goals and expectation', 'living a responsible life based on a thoughtful set of values' and 'learning from both success and failure' (Brooks and Goldstein 2003, p. 3). While such advice is easy to dismiss as the stuff of pop business shelves, it has been formalised by military and security establishments worldwide. The Australian Defence Force has had such a resiliency strategy in place since 2000, the British military and emergency services and the Canadian armed forces all have variations on this in place (O'Malley 2010). As part of the RMA, the US military now requires that all 1.1 million US troops undergo intensive training in emotional resiliency and that every sergeant effectively become a 'master resiliency trainer' (Reivich, Seligman and McBride 2011), and more recently the National Guard and Reserve have also begin resiliency training (Army News Service 2009, p. 2). In sum, the US military assumes that training in resiliency 'teaches self awareness, bringing mental fitness up to the same level as soldiers' physical fitness and creating 'supermen' and 'superwomen' (Army News Service 2009, p. 2).

The US Army's Fort Bragg program in psychosocial military resilience training focuses on a battery of 'factors' found to reduce stress reactions, and each has a training module:

> Positive emotions (optimism and humor); Emotional regulation (fear, anger etc.); Cognitive flexibility (positive explanatory style, positive reappraisal, and acceptance); Coping style (active approach vs. passive/avoidant); Spirituality (including religion); Moral code (including altruism); Social support (including unit support); Training (physical, psychological and spiritual); Purpose and meaning (mission) (Southwick, Vyhiligan and Charney 2005).

Each factor is broken down into components, each to be a focus of training. For example, 'coping style' involves focusing on an 'active approach' that involves gathering information, acquiring skills, confrontation rather than avoidance, problem solving, seeking social support and cognitive reappraisal (that is, 'redefining a crisis as a challenge') as opposed to blaming. Further, these resiliency training modules—like the business and change management literature—are based in research findings, most especially involving cognitive behavioural therapy. The 'coping style' module, for example, is based on research that shows this skill set was found to produce fewer post traumatic stress disorder symptoms in Gulf War veterans (O'Malley 2010).

The aim is to produce subjects—whether in business, the military or everyday life—who are capable of dealing with all situations of high uncertainty. In strong contrast to virtually all the other strategies, resiliency thus specifically rejects what Engin Isin (2004) refers to as the 'neurotic subject' he sees as integral to the subjectivity of the risk society. For Isin, the neurotic subject is 'someone who is anxious under stress and increasingly insecure and is asked to manage its neurosis ... neurotic because it governs itself through its anxieties, what it wants is impossible. It wants absolute safety' (Isin 2004, pp. 231-232). This, certainly is the subject of Beck's vision of the subjects of risk consciousness, but the new resiliency approach aligns far better with the neo-liberal imaginary of each subject being the 'entrepreneur of oneself' in an environment that is highly uncertain. This subject, in a sense scientifically designed, approaches uncertainty as a challenge and opportunity.

### CONCLUSION: UNCERTAINTY MAKES US FREE

The demand that governments 'bureaucratise imagination' has been met with a series of responses largely revising and developing strategies and techniques inherited from former years. The irony of encouraging the imagination of threats is that whereas risk could at least rein-in paranoia by the demand for statistical evidence, now as Ewald argued, evidence is hardly a requirement—if threats can be imagined then they could happen and we should be prepared, or strike first at any imagined source of threat. In all of these approaches, there is a specific kind of freedom being produced, what Isaiah Berlin referred to negatively as 'freedom from', associated with what Beck (1992) saw and 'paranoia, and Isin (2004) as 'neurosis'. Uncertainty appears as a problem for life itself and the command to bureaucratise imagination intensified this.

But from the 1970s, political and economic 'security' had begun to diverge as exposure to uncertainty and insecurity in the economic domain were defined by neoliberals as beneficial and essential to freedom and security. The less the security, the greater the freedom. Increased uncertainty now came to mean increased opportunity for the enterprising. Neoliberals such as Peter Bernstein (1998) argued that 'uncertainty makes us free'. If the future is predictable, the argument goes, then how can we be free? How could such a vision survive 9/11? How could uncertainty be sustained as a liberal condition of freedom when it had become the enemy of Western, liberal security? The answer was not to be found in bureaucratizing imagination. Nor as event are proving, was it to be found in speculative pre-emption, even though that preserved something of the enterprising mythology. Not through the search for solutions to every imaginable threat, but by creating new, resilient, subjects scientifically designed to 'thrive' on chaos and make every threat a challenge and opportunity. Thus, in the mythology of resilience, may the neo-liberal dream of freedom in uncertainty be imagined into existence in the 21st century.

From such a viewpoint, there is perhaps nothing particularly dark about this vision or its technologies for changing us. After all, it could be argued instilling people with techniques for optimism, resourcefulness, enterprise and social networking is no ad thing. Nor is it more objectionable than any of the other programs in the past that have tried to make better subjects of us. And at least this does not project a narrow band of repressive moral imperatives, as is true for many political, religious and aesthetic regimes of the past and present. Yet, as Dillon and Reid (2009, pp. 138-140) have argued, there is a very dark side to this. They note that resilience is part of a program to provide security to critical infrastructures since 9/11. Appearing as a reinvestment in 'human factors engineering' that can be traced back to the Second World War. Citing the 2004 US *National Plan for Research and Development in Support of Critical Infrastructures* (Office of Science and Technology Policy and Department of Homeland Security 2004), they point out that resilience is part of a program to harness the 'cognitive, emotional and social capabilities of the human' to defense ends.

> Human life, in this context of the War on Terror, is valued merely in terms of its utilities for the protection of the physical and technological infrastructures on which the liberal regimes depend for their se-

curity. The advance of such strategies and their application to population operates by reducing life to a logistical calculus of value on
account of its capacities to enhance infrastructure. (Dillon and Reid
2009, p. 139).

Even to the extent that this is true, the development of resilience programs in the business and 'lifestyle' sectors suggest that this is no more
than one tendency or application. As has been seen, there is no secret
about the military programs for researching and applying resiliency
techniques to troops, but equally it is clear that such techniques—even
accepting the unlikely hypothesis that they emerge solely from such
defensive ends—have escaped into everyday life, and put to work in
'enhancing' life itself. As such, they may represent a 'line of flight' whose
future trajectory is unknown, about which—we should be cautious rather
than negative; especially if indeed we live in an age of catastrophes.

## Bibliography

Alberts, D., Gartska, J., and Stein, F., 2000. *Network Centric Warfare: Developing and
Leveraging Information Security*. Washington DC: US Department of Defense.

Amoore, L., 2011. Data derivatives: On the emergence of a security risk calculus for
our times. *Theory, Culture and Society*, 28 (6), 24-43.

Army News Service, 2009. Resiliency training to be given army-wide [online]. *Army
News Service*, 8 October. Available from: http://www.defencetalk.com/
resiliency-training-to-be-given-army-wide-22468/ [Accessed 27 February
2013].

Baker, T., and Simon, J., 2002. Embracing risk. *In*: T. Baker and J. Simon, eds.
*Embracing Risk*. University of Chicago Press, 1-26.

Beck, U., 1992. *Risk Society*. New York: Sage.

Bentham, J., 1962. An Introduction to the Principles of Morals and Legislation. *In*: J.
Bowring, ed. *The Works of Jeremy Bentham Vol. I*. New York: Russell and
Russell, 1-155.

Bernstein, P., 1998. *Against the Gods: The Remarkable Story of Risk*. New York: Wiley.

Bougen, P., 2003. Catastrophe Risk. *Economy and Society*, 32, 253-274.

Bougen, P., and O'Malley, P., 2009. Bureaucracy, imagination and US domestic
security policy. *Security Journal*, 22 (2), 101-118.

Brooks, R., and Goldstein, S., 2003. *The Power of Resilience: Achieving balance,
confidence and Personal Strength in Your Life*. New York: McGraw Hill.

Callon, M., Lascoumes, P., and Barthe, Y., 2011. *Acting in an Uncertain World. An
Essay on Technical Democracy*. Boston: MIT Press.

Cebrowski, A., and Gartska, J., 1998. Network centric warfare: Its origins and future.
*Proceedings of the Naval Institute*, 34, 1-11.

Collier, S., 2008. Enacting catastrophe. Preparedness, insurance, budgetary rationalization. *Economy and Society,* 37 (2), 224-250.

Collier, S., and Lakoff, A., 2008. Distributed preparedness: Space, security and citizenship in the United States. *Environment and Planning D: Society and Space,* 26, 7-28.

Cooper, M., 2006. Pre-empting emergence. The biological turn in the war on terror. *Theory, Culture and Society,* 23 (4), 113-135.

De Goede, M., 2008. Beyond risk: Premediation and the post-9/11 security imagination. *Security Dialogue,* 39 (2-3), 155-176.

Dillon, M., and Reid, J., 2009. *The Liberal Way of War. Killing to Make Life Live.* London: Routledge.

DSTO (Defence Science and Technology Organisation), 2004. *The Network Centric Warrior. The Human Dimensions of Network-Centric Warfare.* Canberra: Australian Government Department of Defence.

Du Gay, P., 2000. *In Praise of Bureaucracy.* London: Sage.

Ericson, R., and Doyle, A., 2004. Catastrophe risk, insurance and terrorism. *Economy and Society,* 33 (2), 135-173.

European Commission, 2000. *Communication from the Commission of 2 February 2000 on the Precautionary Principle Brussels, 2.2.2000 COM(2000) 1 final* [online]. Brussels: European Commission. Available from: http://eur-lex.europa.eu/LexUriServ/LexUriServ.do?uri=COM:2000:0001:FIN:en:PDF [Accessed 27 February 2007].

Ewald, F., 2002. The Return of Descartes's Malicious Demon: An Outline of a Philosophy of Precaution. *In*: T. Baker and J. Simon, eds. *Embracing Risk: The Changing Culture of Insurance and Responsibility.* The University of Chicago Press, 273-301.

Fisher, E., 2007. *Risk Regulation and Administrative Constitutionalism.* Oxford: Hart.

Foucault, M., 2008. *The Birth of Biopolitics; Lectures at the College de France 1978-1979.* London: Palgrave MacMillan.

Grossi, P., and Kunreuther, H., 2005. *Catastrophe Modeling. A New Approach to Managing Risk.* New York: Springer.

Isin, E., 2004. The neurotic citizen. *Citizenship Studies,* 8 (3), 217-235.

Lentzos, F., and Rose, N., 2009. Governing insecurity: Contingency planning, protection, resistance. *Economy and Society,* 38 (2), 230-254.

Lobo-Guerrero, L., 2011. *Insuring Security. Biopolitics, Security and Risk.* London: Routledge.

Manigart, P., 2003. Restructuring of the Armed Forces. In: G. Caforio, ed. *Handbook of the Sociology of the Military.* New York: Kluwer Academic; Plenum, 133-159.

National Commission, 2004. *National Commission on Terrorist Attacks Upon the United States. Final Report* [online]. Available from: http://www.gpoaccess.gov/911/pdf/fullreport.pdf [Accessed 27 February 2013].

O'Malley, P., 1999. Volatile and Contradictory Punishment. *Theoretical Criminology*, 3 (2), 175-196.

O'Malley, P., 2000. Uncertain Subjects. Risk, Liberalism and Contract. *Economy and Society*, 29, 460-484.

O'Malley, P., 2003. Governable catastrophes. *Economy and Society*, 32 (2), 275-279.

O'Malley, P., 2004. *Risk, Uncertainty and Government*. London: Cavendish.

O'Malley, P., 2010. Resilient subjects. Uncertainty, warfare and resilience. *Economy and Society*, 39 (4), 488-509.

O'Malley, P., and Bougen, P., 2009. Imaginable insecurities: imagination, routinisation and the government of uncertainty post 9/11. *In*: P. Carlen, ed. *Imaginary Penalities*. Devon: Willan, 25-39.

O'Malley, P., and Hutchinson, S., 2007. Reinventing prevention. Why did "crime prevention" develop so late? *British Journal of Criminology*, 47 (3), 439-454.

Office of Science and Technology Policy and Department of Homeland Security, 2004. *National Plan for Research and Development in Support of Critical Infrastructure Protection*. Washington DC: Office of Science and Technology Policy and Department of Homeland Security. Available from: http://www.dhs.gov/xlibrary/assets/ST_2004_NCIP_RD_PlanFINALApr05.pdf [Accessed 9 April 2013].

Osborne, T., and Gaebler, T., 1993. *Reinventing Government. How the Entrepreneurial Spirit is Transforming the Public Sector*. New York: Plume Books.

Peters, T., 1987. *Thriving on Chaos: Handbook for a Management Revolution*. New York: Knopf.

Porter, T., 1995. *Trust in Numbers. The Pursuit of Objectivity in Science and Life*. Princeton University Press.

Reivich, K., and Shatte, A., 2002. *The Resilience Factor. 7 Keys to Finding Your Inner Strength and Overcoming Life's Hurdles*. Chicago: Broadway Books.

Reivich, K., Seligman M., and McBride, S., 2011. Master resiliency training in the U.S. Army. *American Psychologist*, 66 (1), 25-34.

Rumsfeld, D., 2002. Secretary Rumsfeld Speaks on "21st Century Transformation" of U.S. Armed Forces (transcript of remarks and question and answer period) Remarks as Delivered by Secretary of Defense Donald Rumsfeld, National Defense University, Fort McNair, Washington, D.C., Thursday, January 31, 2002 [online]. Available from: http://www.defenselink.mil/speeches/speech.aspx?speechid=183 [Accessed 27 February 2013].

Siebert, A., 2005. *The Resiliency Advantage: Master Change, Thrive Under Pressure, and Bounce Back from Setbacks*. Portland: Practical Psychology Press.

Southwick, S., Vyhiligan, M., and Charney, D., 2005. The psychobiology of depression and resilience to stress. Implications for prevention and treatment. *Annual Reviews of Clinical Psychology*, 1, 255-291.

Sunstein, C., 2005. *Laws of Fear. Beyond the Precautionary Principle.* Cambridge University Press.

Walker, J., and Cooper, M., 2011. Genealogies of Resilience: From Systems Ecology to the Political Economy of Crisis Adaptation. *Security Dialogue*, 42 (2), 143–160.

Weber, M., 1964. *From Max Weber.* Ed. by C. Wright Mills. London: Routledge and Keagan Paul.

World Economic Forum, 2008. *Building Resilience to natural Disasters. A framework for private Sector Engagement.* Geneva: World Economic Forum.

# 2

# LAND USE PLANNING AND DISASTER: A EUROPEAN PERSPECTIVE FROM SPAIN

## Juli Ponce

### ABSTRACT

The study deals with the role of EU and EU Member States in relation to disasters and land use planning. It considers how land use planning can evaluate and manage risks to avoid disasters, paying special attention to the European use of precautionary principle, sometimes explained with the sentence "Better safe than sorry". The analysis uses especially, but not only, the example of the Spanish legal system taking into account its inclusion in the more general EU legal system. The study also considers public responsibility in preventing disasters and possible consequences of maladministration when taking planning decisions, using real Spanish cases. Finally, the chapter explores the possibilities of planning as a tool to prevent disasters in relation to two specific areas: location of nuclear plants and new developments regarding the prevention of crime and terrorist attacks by means of urban planning (the so called *Crime Prevention Through Environmental Design*).

El estudio analiza el papel de la Unión Europea (UE) y los Estados miembros de la UE en relación con los desastres y la planificación del uso del suelo. Se describe cómo la planificación del uso del suelo puede evaluar y gestionar los riesgos para evitar desastres, prestando especial atención al uso europeo del principio de precaución, a veces resumido en la frase "Más vale prevenir que curar". El análisis utiliza especialmente, pero no sólo, el ejemplo del sistema jurídico español, teniendo en cuenta su inclusión en el sistema legal general de la UE. El estudio también tiene en cuenta la responsabilidad pública en la prevención de desastres y las posibles consecuencias de la mala administración cuando se toman decisiones de planificación, a través de casos reales españoles. Por último, el artículo explora las posibilidades de la planificación como una herramienta para prevenir desastres en relación a dos áreas específicas: la ubicación de centrales nucleares y los nuevos desarrollos en materia de prevención de la delincuencia y los atentados terroristas, por medio de la planificación urbana (el denominado *prevención del delito a través del diseño medioambiental*).

## INTRODUCTION

### *Disasters and land use regulations: a possible cause, but also a possible mechanism for disaster prevention*

Natural and man-made disasters are a major European worry, due to their increasing frequency and severity and their impact on human life, destruction of economic and social infrastructures and damage to the environment. For example, according to an official European Union (EU) document, the economic impact of disasters in Europe has been estimated at €15 billion annually (European Commission 2009a, p. 4).

Land use law (*Derecho urbanístico*, in Spanish, or *Droit de l'urbanisme*, in French) deals with the regulation of land use. There is a clear relationship between the use of land and disasters. On one hand, the regulation of land can allow urban expansion by means of several instruments (plans, zoning), and urban expansion can bring intensive use of land, industrial development and construction of infrastructures which can be a factor in future disasters. A good example of this is urban pressure on rivers and flood risks (Spanish Government 2010a, p. 44).

But, on the other hand, the proper regulation of land can be a preventive tool of disasters, by preventing disasters from happening and by minimizing their impacts when disasters are unavoidable. That point of view has not been traditionally explored in depth by European jurisprudence (but see recently Association internationale de droit de l'urbanisme 2011). That is the perspective I want to study in this work. Therefore, this is a study with a *legal* and *European* perspective whose limited goal is to expose the *state of the art* of the current legal framework in relation to disaster prevention and reaction through land use law.

### *Structure of this chapter*

My study will be organized in the following way. In the first place, I will consider the role of the EU and EU Member States in relation to disasters and land use planning. Secondly, I will consider how land use planning can evaluate and manage risks to avoid disasters, paying special attention to the European use of the precautionary principle, sometimes explained with the sentence "Better safe than sorry". In this analysis I will use especially, but not only, the example of the Spanish legal system taking into account its inclusion in the more general EU legal system.

Then, I will reflect on public responsibility in preventing disasters and possible consequences of maladministration when taking planning decisions, using a real Spanish case: the disaster at the *Biescas* campsite. In that case affected people brought a lawsuit against public authorities claiming for compensation for damages caused by inappropriate planning.

Finally, I will explore the possibilities of planning as a tool to prevent and mitigate disasters in relation to two specific areas which are of great relevance nowadays. Firstly, I will consider the location of nuclear plants (with some comments on the importance of administrative procedures to protect fundamental rights as the German Constitutional Court decision *Mülheim-Karlich* has underlined). Secondly, I will study new developments regarding the prevention of crime and terrorist attacks by means of urban planning (the so-called *Crime Prevention Through Environmental Design*).

Disasters caused by crime and specifically terrorism are considered in the European sphere as man-made disasters. As a document of the Danish EU presidency in 2012 underlines "Member States are responsible for protecting their civilian populations. However, the EU can support and complement the Member States in their coordination before, during and after major natural and man-made emergencies, *including terrorism*" (Danish Presidency of the Council of the European Union 2012). CPTED shows that urban planning is a flexible instrument used for a wide range of questions, including prevention of disasters caused by crime. It raises the question, again, of what happens in case of damages caused, at least partially, by a lack of enough planning design. The study will use the example of a real terrorist attack to show the Spanish legal response to that situation.

EUROPEAN UNION AND MEMBER STATES:<br>DISTRIBUTION OF POWERS AND ROLES

Although the EU has no powers in the field of land use planning, it can have an influence on national policy in several ways. On the other hand, although EU Member States are responsible for land use planning, they are bound by the EU legal framework and by the national constitutional distribution of legal powers. I will use the Spanish case to demonstrate this point.

### The European Union

The territory of the current EU occupies 4,324,782 sq km (less than half the size of the USA) (The World Factbook). The EU has a population of 492,387,344 (July 2010 est.) and a density of 112 inhabitants/Km2 (compared to a density of 31 in the US) (Population Division of the Department of Economic and Social Affairs of the United Nations Secretariat 2006). 75% of Europeans now live in urban areas and the figure is forecast to be 80% by 2020. Urbanization is spreading briskly, faster than urban population growth. It is estimated that the overall size of built up areas has grown by a fifth in the last twenty years, whereas the EU population increased by only 6%.

The European model is a concept invoked during discussions concerning European integration. But what does it mean? Obviously it is a concept in development with clear political roots in an ongoing debate (Faludi 2007). Some opinions conceive of the EU as a free-trade area, ascribing the poor performance of the economy to the "soft" European model being invoked. Those opinions would like to see the role of European institutions being restricted to policing the Single Market. On the other side, other opinions consider this perspective close to the *laissez-faire* approaches of Anglo-Saxon liberalism, seeing the European model as the foundations of a just and competitive society and wanting strong European institutions to fulfill functions otherwise reserved to those of nation states. This second stream conceives the European model as a human order based upon a mixed economy, civilized labor relations, the welfare state and a commitment to social justice (Faludi 2007).

Scholars and practitioners debating European spatial planning and territorial cohesion policy in the EU also take this discussion into account. In any case, the EU legal framework (as interpreted by an impressive amount of official documents following international developments) considers sustainability as a key concept composed of three complementary parts: economic, social and environmental (European Commission 2007). In other words, it cannot be stated that a society is sustainable unless the three elements exist.

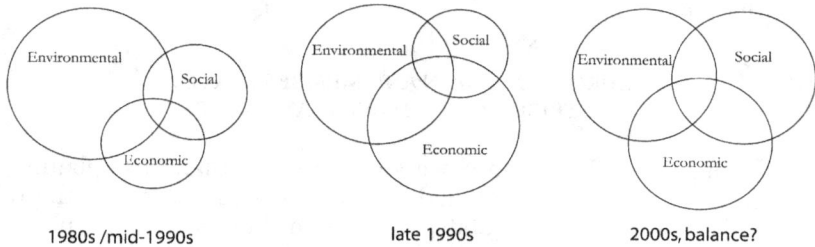

1980s /mid-1990s     late 1990s     2000s, balance?

European concept of sustainability (Colantonio 2007, p. 4).

The CIA's *World Factbook* states that "The evolution of the European Union (EU) from a regional economic agreement among six neighboring states in 1951 to today's supranational organization of 27 countries across the European continent stands as an unprecedented phenomenon in the annals of history." Well ... in any case, we should consider this unification as an ongoing (and difficult) process. The adventure started in 1957 and continues nowadays with a failed Constitution in 2004 and the late Treaty of Lisbon in 2007 which has changed the existing legal framework.

It is important to underline that, according to this "constitutional" framework, the EU does not possess powers in the field of land use. However, as Italian professor CHITI underlines, the goals of sustainable development, solidarity, the fight against exclusion and economic, territorial and social cohesion lead to increasing intervention in relation to European cities. The EU also has powers in the fields of the environment and other public policies with territorial impact (e.g. transportation), bearing in mind the *principle of subsidiarity* (that is, that matters ought to be handled by the lowest competent authority) (Chiti 2003).

Those related powers and the political will of taking into account territorial issues by means of the promotion of intellectual and public experiences networking (generating a huge amount of reports, studies and papers) and the use of substantial investments explain the relevant role of the EU in urban affairs. Moreover, EU environmental policy has a significant impact on land use law in European countries.

## The member states: the example of Spain

### Some data about Spain

Spain has a population of 45,200,737 (2007, according to official statistics) with an area of 506,030 km² and a density of 89 inhabitants/km² (according to United Nations World Populations Prospects Report 2004 revision), placing it halfway in the European ranking among the more densely populated central European countries and the less populated nations to the north (European Urban Knowledge Network).

Spain has seen rapid population growth, especially from 1960-1970 and 1970-1980, encouraged by the increase in industrialization of the metropolitan areas of large cities such as Madrid, Barcelona, Valencia, Bilbao and Saragossa. From 1960-1970 all of these urban areas had annual population growth rates of more than 3%, and in Madrid's case over 4%. 1970-1980 also saw rapid population growth but at a reduced rate, 2% (Madrid) or less. Population growth declined considerably in the decades which followed, bottoming out towards the end of 1990-2000. Since 2000 in particular continued migration has contributed to a steady increase in the natural rate of growth.

Rapid population growth from 1960–1980, concentrated in the metropolitan areas of large cities, produced a serious shortfall in infrastructure, housing and facilities, and a consequent deterioration in urban life quality. From the mid-1970s this combined with industrial decline in places such as Bilbao and the central area of Asturias, home to the iron and steel and shipping industry which went into crisis throughout Western Europe.

The housing development growth rate in recent years has been spectacular and remained buoyant until the crisis of 2008. But it has been coupled with sharp house price increases making it very difficult for a large percentage of the population to buy a home. A drop in average household size and a steady increase in immigration generate new housing demand.

Spain's urban population is concentrated in four major urban areas each with more than 1,000,000 inhabitants (Madrid, Barcelona, Valencia and Seville) and located, with the exception of Madrid, on the peninsula's periphery; 9 urban areas of between 500,000 and 1,000,000 inhabitants (Bilbao, Malaga, the central area of Asturias, Saragossa, Alicante/Elche, the Bay of Cadiz, Vigo/Pontevedra, Murcia and Las Palmas in Grand

Canary); 35 urban areas of between 100,000 and 500,000 people; and 30 urban areas of between 50,000 and 100,000 inhabitants. There are thus 78 urban areas throughout Spain with more than 50,000 inhabitants.

Physical characteristics, communications, the location of industrial enclaves and coastal tourist settlements all mean that the population is unevenly distributed and concentrated particularly in the peninsula's periphery and the Madrid metropolitan area, which is situated in the sparsely populated center of the country.

Apart from the Madrid metropolitan area which is witnessing high growth rates, the populations of smaller urban areas such as Malaga, Alicante/Elche and in particular Murcia and Vigo/Pontevedra are also expanding rapidly. The growth trend in the outlying regions of the peninsula (in the tourist areas along the Mediterranean coast) and the central area around Madrid thus remains constant.

Spain experienced a very slow natural growth rate from 1990 to 2000 as well as one of the world's lowest fertility rates, well below the European Union average. In 1996 Spain's average number of children per woman was 1.16 against 1.44 in the rest of the EU. The continued increase in immigration since 2000 has caused this indicator to climb, but it still remains below the European average. Population ageing raises many problems such as the provision of retirement pensions, health care and a greater demand for facilities for senior citizens.

An increase in migration produces diverse effects: on the one hand a rejuvenation of the population, more young workers in the job market and consequently more contributions to the social security system, while on the other hand it increases demand for facilities and housing and raises social integration issues.

### The framework of Spanish land use law

In this section I will focus on the general trends, (comparing the Spanish situation with American and other European land use laws) with reference to historical and current land use law. Case law is clearly very important, but the leading role has been played until now by the legislative branch which has created the modern land use law in Spain with the introduction of several very technical Acts.

On the other hand, urban planning has a major role in this scenario. Urban planning is compulsory, both on a regional basis (decisions made by the *Comunidades Autónomas*) and, more importantly, on a local basis. Urban planning in Spain implies a range of different legal elements: several kinds of maps, some documents and the rules for dividing the land into zones. A plan must exist to regulate land use, as it is a legal requirement in all the *Comunidades Autonomas* (there are currently 17 autonomous regions in Spain) (Ponce 2004).

## *The historical perspective*

### Situation before 1956

Regulation of land use has existed in Spain since the times of the *Ancièn Régim* (Brewer-Carías 1997). The modern context dates back to the liberal state of the 19th century, under the jurisdiction of the police (*policía*) on a local level. The regulation focused on the growth of cities (urban developments of *Ensanche*) and on problems of health and security. Public intervention was made possible by a wide range of laws, e.g. ordinances, alignments and compulsory purchases, which were first regulated in the Compulsory Purchase Act 1836 (Bassols 1973).

Land use law developed in a more technical way in the 20th century. From the 1920's more modern legal techniques were included in legal codes, such as the Municipal Charter of 1924, which introduced "zoning." In the 1930's, the idea of Regional Planning arrived in Spain. Catalonia was a pioneer with the "zoning distribution plan" in 1932, but the Spanish Civil War destroyed the possibility for concrete developments.

With regard to affordable housing, further with a bill in 1878 and the creation of several research committees, the Cheap Houses Act 1911 was the first law which addressed the issue of housing for the working classes. The Act relied on private investments and established some public grants for entrepreneurs. Unfortunately, this regulation was unsuccessful, mainly due to the lack of public resources to develop its provisions, and it was amended before the beginning of the Civil War in 1936 (Ponce 2008).

After the Civil War, public efforts were addressed to rebuilding the devastated country. Thus, the *Instituto Nacional de Vivienda*, a public specialized body, was created in 1939 to achieve this goal. Some years later, in 1957, a dedicated Department, the *Ministerio de la Vivienda*, assumed responsibility for housing policy in Spain until it was merged with the Department of Public Works at the end of the 1970's. In 2004, the Ministry of Housing was reestablished to deal with the serious problem of housing affordability. At the end of 2010, after a new political restructuration, this Ministry disappeared again.

### 1956 National Act: importance of planning in Spain

The modern land use law was introduced in 1956, in the middle of Franco's 40 year dictatorship. The 1956 National Act came into force when Spain was a centralized, non-democratic country. But in spite of this context, scholars agree that the act was of high technical quality and the foundation of modern Spanish land use law.

The departure point of the regulation was priority of agricultural land. Subsequent construction was granted by public powers through urban planning. As a general rule, the plans regulated the right of property, without expropriation. And the plan (at least formally) awarded decision-making powers to municipalities, with an element of discretionary interpretation. However, this discretion was not always used by democratic municipalities and there were regular abuses of power in favor of supporters of the fascist mayors.

Consequently, urban planning was the central *pièce de résistance* of the whole legal system. But twenty years after the 1956 Act, just 7,5% the Spanish territory had an urban plan implemented (Fernández 2008, p. 23). So, the failure of the plan was in reality the failure of law.

On the other hand, as regards the management of development, we do not know American type exactions or impact fees or French taxes about the use of law as a way of financing the new parts of the cities. The national Act 1956 established a legal system to develop public infrastructures and public facilities, still in work, based *grosso modo* on the owner's legal duties of giving freely a fixed percentage of land to the municipality (which is effective still today in general terms, with a national legal maximum of 10% and a possible minimum variable in each *Comunidad Autónoma*), of giving freely the necessary land to streets, green areas and local public facilities and of making all the necessary works to develop the area where the plot of land is included (López-Ramón 2009, p. 118).

But in the real world this rigid system is made flexible by means of development agreements between the city councils and the developer (a source, by the way, of corruption in some cases). Development agreements between municipalities and owners or developers are regulated in land use laws. The Spanish legal system accepts them but imposing certain procedural conditions in order to promote accountability.

**The reformation of 1975**

During the sixties and part of the seventies, Spain became and industrialized country, suffering great social and economic transformations. In the urban sphere, the important phenomenon was the migration of a large part of the population from agricultural areas to cities, with the inherent problems of adequate housing.

The growth of the cities was quite chaotic. Theoretically, the plans were in place to deal with this migration, but a large number of municipalities did not pass plans and in other cases, as I explained before, arbitrary decisions helped speculation and made it impossible to achieve orderly urban sprawl.

Due to this and other factors, it was decided to introduce a second act in 1975, to complete the 1956 National Act and to avoid all those problems. But the general structure of the legal system was untouched. In 1976 the regulations of 1956 and 1975 were merged in an act (the *Texto Refundido*).

**The Constitution of 1978**

The Constitution of 1978 highlighted the deep changes in Spain with the introduction of democracy and the autonomy of the regions (effectively we passed from a centralized model to an almost federal one).

Both elements had a legal impact in the field (see art. 148.1.3 of the Spanish Constitution) and on the local level (see art. 140 of the Spanish Constitution, establishing the autonomy of local government). An act in 1985 specifically mentions land use regulation among the local authorities

(Act 7/1985, Foundations of Local Regime).

According to the Constitution, Spain was declared a "Social State" (see art. 1), and several social rights were introduced including a right to environment, art. 45:

> 1. Everyone has the right to enjoy an environment suitable for personal development, as well as the duty to preserve it.
>
> 2. The authorities shall safeguard a rational use of all natural resources with a view to protecting and improving quality of life and preserving and restoring the environment, by relying on essential public cooperation.
>
> 3. Criminal or, where applicable, administrative sanctions, as well as the obligation to make good the damage, shall be imposed, under the terms to be laid down by the law, against those who break the provisions contained in the foregoing paragraph.

That legal system shows a high degree of complexity which has to be managed by means of different cooperative legal mechanisms (eg. sectorial conferences and public agreements, according to arts. 5 to 10 of the Common Administrative Procedure Act 1992, modified in 1999).

### The distribution of power among the public levels: regional legislation

Using the Constitutional Clause (148.1.3) the seventeen *Comunidades Autónomas* (and among them Catalonia, whose capital is the city of Barcelona, with a long history, its own language and a strong identity of nation status) have enacted laws, creating their own land use and housing law.

Although central government had delegated many of its powers, it continued making laws concerning land use using several constitutional clauses (especially art. 149.1.3, which allows it to enact supplementary legislation to complete the regional legal systems. According to this article, the Spanish Parliament can enact legislation establishing "basic rules and coordination of general economic planning", which are binding for the regional and local level). Using this argument, two National Acts came into force in 1990 and 1992, creating a common legal framework in spite of increasingly decentralized government.

Meanwhile, the price of land increased dramatically, especially in major cities, and the right to shelter became a myth for a lot of people who had to leave the inner cities (in Spain the better areas, where richer people usually live) for the suburbs (in Spain, areas with less facilities and therefore lower quality of life), in search of affordable housing.

### The Constitutional Court decisions of 1997 and 2001: fragmentation of land use law and the survival of a national hard core

The highly controversial decision of the Spanish Constitutional Court 61/1997 almost destroyed this common legal structure. It ruled that the 1990 and 1992 National Acts were partially (about 80%) unconstitutional and, consequently, void. It established that land use law was a regional business and that the national level could only exceptionally regulate this matter (e.g. basic rules about compulsory acquisition, art. 149.1.18, which are connected directly with property right).

Consequently, the National Act of 1998 tried to fill the gap and gave some general rules about classes of land and limits to local plans, as well as some rules about compulsory acquisitions. This act was modified in the current Land Use Act 8/2007 with similar contents but very influenced by EU approaches, as we will see later.

### The EU legal framework in disaster prevention and its impact on national legal systems

Beyond this previous general explanation, it is now necessary to analyze the current EU legal framework in the specific field of prevention of natural and man-made disasters. In that sense, the EU has developed both *soft law* and *hard law* in this area.

(a) As regards *the soft law*, the most relevant document is a European Commission (2009b) communication on the prevention of natural and man-made disasters. In this document, the European Commission confirms the lack of a common strategic approach for disaster prevention, and develops some ideas towards its creation. Among these ideas, the European Commission emphasizes three, in particular: the development of knowledge based disaster prevention policies at all levels of government; linking the relevant actors and policies throughout the disaster management cycle; improving the effectiveness of existing policy instruments with regard to disaster prevention. The European Commission develops different measures to be implemented in the future in relation to each one of these three ideas.

In relation to the development of knowledge, the European Commission expresses its intention to develop a comprehensive inventory of existing sources of information related to disasters and to launch a stakeholder group to review the existing information in order to take the measures necessary for filling any identified knowledge gaps. On the other hand, the European Commission states its intention of spreading best practices, developing guidelines on hazard/risk mapping and encouraging research activities.

Regarding links between relevant actors and policies, the European Commission will extend an already established program of "lessons learnt" from interventions conducted within the framework of the Community Mechanism for civil protection and will also develop specific courses on prevention. Moreover, the European Commission will increase the general public's awareness in relation to disasters. And it will create a network covering the departments in charge of land planning, risk and hazard mapping, protection of the environment, and emergency preparedness and response whilst reinforcing the link between early warning systems.

In connection with improving the effectiveness of existing policy instruments, the European Commission, in close cooperation with Member

States, will develop several public policies to strengthen the integration of disaster prevention in national operational programming of EU funding. Finally, the existing Community legislation will take account of disaster prevention during the planned review of a number of items of EU legislation and the European Commission will encourage Member States to fully integrate the common European design codes for buildings and civil works into their national planning regulation in order to mitigate the impacts of earthquakes.

(b) Regarding binding regulations, the EU has already developed a set of instruments to address different aspects of prevention of disaster, our main interest, and disaster preparedness, response and recovery. These legal tools are basically directives (e.g. European Parliament, European Council 2007, Council of the European Union 1996, Council of the European Union 2009) and also some regulations (e.g. Regulation 1726/2002 banning single-hull tankers from European ports and Regulation 2038/2006 on multi-annual funding for the action of the European Maritime Safety Agency in the field of response to pollution caused by ships), as we will see below when dealing with specific questions. From a legislative point of view, probably the most relevant tools are the EU Directives, which "shall be binding, as to the result to be achieved, upon each Member State to which" they are "addressed, but shall leave to the national authorities the choice of form and methods", according to art. 288 of the Consolidated version of the Treaty on the Functioning of the European Union (TFEU).

EVALUATION AND MANAGEMENT OF RISKS BY LAND USE LAW:
THE SPECIFIC PROBLEM OF SCIENTIFIC UNCERTAINTY

## Scientific uncertainty and precautionary principle

According to EU legislation and Member States legal frameworks (e.g. Spain), urban planning must evaluate risks to prevent natural or man-made disasters. But sometimes when identifying a phenomenon, product or process, scientific evaluation does not allow the risk to be determined with sufficient certainty. Scientific uncertainty can arise from controversy on existing data or lack of some relevant data. In these situations, EU legal framework calls for the use of the precautionary principle (art. 191 TFEU).

The Communication from the Commission on the Precautionary Principle (Brussels 02.02.2000 COM (2000) I) (European Commission 2000), is the most relevant EU soft law document in that field. I will provide an overview of this document in the following lines (in relation to abundant European jurisprudence on that topic, see for all Esteve Pardo 2009).

According to that Communication, the precautionary principle should be considered within a structured approach to the analysis of risk which comprises three elements: risk assessment, risk management and risk communication. Decision-makers need to be aware of the degree of uncertainty attached to the results of the evaluation of available scientific information. Judging what is an "acceptable" level of risk for society is a political responsibility. In some cases, the right answer may be not to act or at least not to introduce a binding legal measure. In the case of action, a wide range of initiatives are available: from a legally binding measure to a research project or recommendation.

In order to choose among these possible actions, measures based on the precautionary principle are guided by several principles:

(a) Proportionality: action chosen must achieve the appropriate level of protection. Principle of proportionality is a key legal principle in European law (e.g. art. 296 TFEU). Judicial review based on it relays on three "filters" or steps of control:

> (i) The means adopted must be suitable for the protection: they cannot be excessive, in the sense of restricting rights unnecessarily, nor insufficient, in the sense that they do not protect the public interest. In some cases a total ban may not be a proportional response to a potential risk. In other cases, it may be the only effective possible answer to a potential risk.

> (ii) The restriction of rights must be necessary. It means that public authorities must be satisfied with the mildest means if effective. Every excessive measure restricting freedom must be avoided and if used can be found illegal by judicial review.

> (iii) The third filter is proportionality in the strict sense. It means that benefits (of all types) associated with public intervention must be greater than inherent costs (of all types).

(b) Non-discrimination: another classic means of controlling public action in Europe (e.g. arts. 20 to 26 Charter of Fundamental Rights of the European Union). Comparable situations should not be treated differently and different situations should not be treated in the same way, unless there are objective grounds for doing so (which must be explained according to the legal duty of giving reasons). On the other hand, non-discrimination does not prohibit *positive* actions (the European term for affirmative actions or reverse discrimination) according to the circumstances.

(c) Consistency: measures should be consistent with the measures already adopted in similar circumstances or using similar approaches.

(d) Cost-benefit analysis: evaluation of the pros and cons cannot be reduced to an economic cost-benefit analysis. That evaluation must be wider in scope and includes non-economic considerations. But assessment should include an economic cost-benefit analysis where this is appropriate and possible.

(e) Examination of scientific developments: measures should be maintained as long as the scientific data are inadequate, imprecise or inconclusive and as long as the risk is considered too high to be imposed on society. Measures based on a precautionary principle shall be reexamined and if necessary modified depending on the results of the scientific research and the follow up of their impact.

(f) Burden of proof: measures based on the precautionary principle may assign responsibility for producing scientific evidence necessary for a complete risk evaluation. It is possible to ask for prior public approval of the activity and to move the burden of proof towards the private individual who should make clear that there is no unacceptable risk of causing disasters.

## *Evaluation*

Taking into account, if necessary, the precautionary principle, EU Member States have established regulations in relation to the public duty of evaluating risks when planning land uses. In that section I will use the Spanish example.

As a general framework, Article 10 of the Spanish land use act establishes that prevention of natural risks and serious accidents is one of the binding legal principles that must guide public regulation of land in all cases.

**Natural risks: the EU directives and their impact on a national level—the Spanish case**

As previously explained, the EU has approved several Directives that are binding as to the result to be achieved by each Member State to which they are addressed, but they shall leave the choice of form and methods to the national authorities. This classic EU legal technique explains why Spain, like other Member States, has been obliged to implement several Directives, by passing new legislation in relation to prevention and management of disasters.

**Natural risks: the legal requirements of evaluation by planning—the Environmental Impact Assessment and the Spanish land legislation**

*The Environmental Impact Assessment and the national Spanish land legislation*

Directives on Environmental Impact Assessment are good examples of the EU influence on Member States. Among these, I want to underline the Strategic Environmental Assessment Directive (European Parliament, European Council 2011). That Directive has been implemented in Spain by means of Act 9/2006, April 28, on environmental assessment of some plans and programs. This act demands an administrative procedure for the evaluation of environmental impact caused by urban planning. In connection with that, land use act of 2007 establishes compulsory risk maps to be included in the environmental sustainability report that the developer must prepare. This report must be included in a document called Environmental Memory which explains environmental impact (art. 15).

## ESQUEMA SIMPLIFICADO DEL PROCEDIMIENTO DE EVALUACIÓN AMBIENTAL ESTRATÉGICA

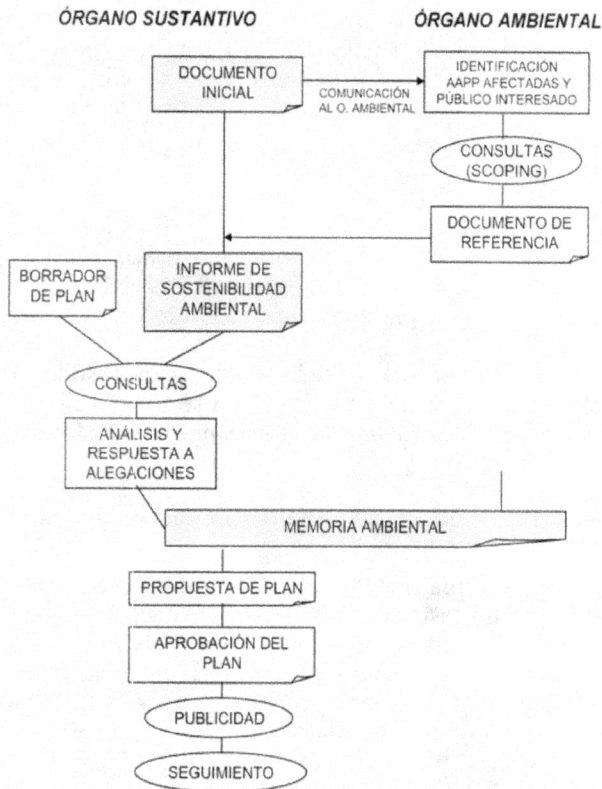

ÓRGANO SUSTANTIVO                                    ÓRGANO AMBIENTAL

```
  ┌──────────────┐                      ┌─────────────────────┐
  │  DOCUMENTO   │   COMUNICACIÓN       │   IDENTIFICACIÓN    │
  │   INICIAL    │   AL O. AMBIENTAL    │ AAPP AFECTADAS Y    │
  └──────────────┘                      │ PÚBLICO INTERESADO  │
                                        └─────────────────────┘
                                                 │
                                          ╭─────────────╮
                                          │  CONSULTAS  │
                                          │  (SCOPING)  │
                                          ╰─────────────╯
                                                 │
                                        ┌─────────────────────┐
                                        │   DOCUMENTO DE      │
                                        │    REFERENCIA       │
                                        └─────────────────────┘
  ┌──────────┐   ┌───────────────┐
  │ BORRADOR │   │  INFORME DE   │
  │ DE PLAN  │   │ SOSTENIBILIDAD│
  └──────────┘   │   AMBIENTAL   │
                 └───────────────┘
        ╭──────────────╮
        │  CONSULTAS   │
        ╰──────────────╯
  ┌──────────────┐
  │  ANÁLISIS Y  │
  │ RESPUESTA A  │
  │ ALEGACIONES  │
  └──────────────┘
                 ┌──────────────────────────────┐
                 │      MEMORIA AMBIENTAL        │
                 └──────────────────────────────┘
  ┌──────────────────┐
  │ PROPUESTA DE PLAN│
  └──────────────────┘
  ┌──────────────────┐
  │  APROBACIÓN DEL  │
  │      PLAN        │
  └──────────────────┘
       ╭──────────────╮
       │  PUBLICIDAD  │
       ╰──────────────╯
       ╭──────────────╮
       │ SEGUIMIENTO  │
       ╰──────────────╯
```

ÓRGANO SUSTANTIVO O PROMOTOR: Confederación Hidrográfica del Segura
ÓRGANO AMBIENTAL: Dirección General de Calidad y Evaluación Ambiental,
Secretaría General para la Prevención de la Contaminación y el Cambio Climático del
Ministerio de Medio Ambiente

A simple diagram of the Strategic Environmental Assessment.
Source:
http://www.chsegura.es/export/descargas/cuenca/sequias/pes/img/ESQUEMA_TR_AMB.gif

*Flood risks prevention and urban planning*

With regard to prevention of flood risks and urban planning, the Spanish regulation *Real Decreto* 903/2010[1] implements the EU Directive

---

[1] All the Spanish legislation is freely accesible at http://www.boe.es/legislacion/legislacion.php

2007/60/EC (European Parliament, European Council 2007) on the assessment and management of flood risks.

Cartagena (South East Spain). Town Hall square, 1919. 2 meters of water.
Source:
http://www.chsegura.es/chs/informaciongeneral/elorganismo/unpocodehistoria/riadas.html

According to this directive, the Spanish regulation creates different tools to assess flood risks (flood hazard maps, flood risk maps and flood management maps). The regulation makes clear that urban planning is bound by all three maps ("regional and local plans when regulating land uses can not include decisions against flood management") and establishes that construction will be prohibited on lands with identified flood risks (art. 15).

### Man-made risks: the example of the evaluation of crime and terrorism risks

The need for evaluation during the urban planning process extends to man-made risks. A good example is the compulsory evaluation of crime and terrorism risks during urban planning established by Catalan legislation and other European legislations (e.g. France). I will consider this kind of risk prevention in the last section of the study.

## Management

In some cases, legislation makes the evaluation and decides how to manage the identified risks. Measures can range from establishing guidelines for future local plans to introducing legal obligations for landowners to avoid factors that can lead to a future disaster. Again, I will use a Spanish example.

### Legal prohibitions binding land use planning

A good example of this technique is Article 12 of the Spanish land use act which stipulates that urban developments are prohibited in lands with natural or technological risks. This kind of land is declared rural (*suelo rural*). Therefore there is no right to build on them and urban planning must establish that condition (and there is no due compensation for it).

### Legal obligations binding land use planning and private owners: social function of property and prevention of disasters

*Regional planning and local zoning*

Local urban plans can be bound by guidelines which come from regional planning. Spatial planning in Spain (*ordenación del territorio*) is not in State hands, in principle. In accordance with the Spanish Constitution and the regional autonomous statutes, spatial planning is a regional power and the autonomous communities have specific acts regulating this policy. But it is true that the Spanish Constitutional Court has confirmed, in the decision 56/1986, the state's capabilities of influencing "*de facto*" regional planning by deciding the location of state infrastructures (e.g. the high speed train, *tren de alta velocidad*, AVE, which currently is instrumental in territorial cohesion through decisions about lines and stations all around Spain).

At the regional level, it is worth considering the Catalan example. The Catalan parliament passed an act on spatial planning in 1983 (Catalan Act 21/1983) using its jurisdiction in this field and has been developing a new generation of spatial regional plans binding local authorities in relation to land use and housing since 2004 (including plans protecting coastal lands). The last step in this recent process is the Right to Housing Act 2007, which has created the Housing Sector Plan for future approval (art. 11). This kind of regional planning can include provisions to prevent disasters. An example is the General Guidelines in Canarias. These Guidelines can establish criteria to prevent "catastrophic natural risks" which are compulsory to local urban plans (Canarias Act 19/2003).

*Limits to the right of property and disasters*

In Spain, land owners can not do whatever they want with their property. Although Spanish Constitution recognizes and protects a right to property, it must be developed in accordance with its "social function" (art. 33 Spanish Constitution). It means that legislation (and urban plans within its framework) can limit the right to property and guide it establishing positive duties. These limits are not takings and there is no compensation.

An example of this is Article 9 of the Spanish land use act which establishes that land and building owners in Spain have a duty of conservation of their properties. That legal duty includes the obligation of keeping rural land (*suelo rural*) in good condition to avoid risks of possible disasters (fires, floods...).

PLANNING AND CLAIMING DAMAGES IN THE CASE OF DISASTERS

## *(Lack of) Prevention: public and private liability*

Possible tort actions for disasters are established in accordance with each national legal system. Clearly, for example, the American legal regime differs from the European legal regimes (Pierce 2008, pp. 167 and ff.). Private liability and public liability can have different legal regimes, according to national administrative law systems (e.g. Spain). And even with this public-private distinction in mind, national legal characteristics can be quite different (e.g. England and Spain, where, as we will see, there is an "objective" public liability, that is without the necessity of administrative fault or negligence).

In the European case, we have a plurality of legal regulations of liability, rooted in each national legal system. But there is a (narrow) EU common framework created by the Directive 2004/35/EC of the European Parliament and of the Council of 21 April 2004 on environmental liability with regard to the prevention and remedying of environmental damage (European Parliament, European Council 2004). That common framework applies to private liability. Member States were obliged to implement the Directive by 30th April 2007. Spain fulfilled its legal obligation with regard to environmental liability by means of the Act 26/2007, on 23rd October of the same year.

That Directive establishes a common European framework for environmental liability (in the case of environmental damage, as defined in art. 1) based on the "polluter pays" principle. The Directive only covers occupational activities listed in Annex III to the Directive. Annex III includes mainly agricultural or industrial activities which require a license to be undertaken. These types of activities are deemed the responsibility of the operator even if he or she is not directly at fault. Out of Annex III there are other activities that can damage species or natural habitats protected by EU legislation (according to the definition of art. 1). In this second case, the operator will be held liable if, and only if, he or she is at fault or negligent. In both cases, this Directive shall not cover environmental damage caused by "a natural phenomenon of exceptional, inevitable and irresistible character" (art. 4, paragraph 1, letter b). It does not cover damages caused by nuclear risks (art. 4, paragraph 4). The competent authority (which is designated by Member States, art. 11), will establish which operator has caused the damage, assess the significance of the damage and determine the remedial measures which should be taken. The interested party will have access to a court or other independent and impartial public body with the competence to review the public decision (art. 13).

Regarding public responsibility for a lack of proper evaluation of risks, there is no common European legal framework. Therefore, each Member State will apply its own legal regime. In the Spanish case, art. 106.2 of the Spanish Constitution and arts. 139 and ff. Act 30/1992 establish a legal framework applicable to all public administrations in Spain in all activity sectors. According to this legal regime, a public administration will be liable if there is a real damage which citizens do not have the legal obligation of bearing, if administrative activity (or lack of administrative activity, when action was legally compulsory) is involved in the damage and if there is a relationship of causality between the public activity (or the lack of public activity) and the damage. In Spain, fault or negligence do not have to exist to recognize administrative liability. Payment is made through public budgets: as a general rule, administrative officials do not have to pay money from their pockets (the exception being when a public administration pays for damages caused by the serious negligence or fault of a public employee. In such cases, public administration must recover the sum paid from the public employee, art. 145.2 Act 30/1992).

A question that can arise in case of disasters and damages is whether the public activity of prevention was adequate. In other words, should public administration be liable for damages if urban planning does not assess properly natural or man-made risks and there are damages as a consequence of a disaster?

### A Spanish example about compensation claims in the case of disasters: the Biescas Campsite

This disaster in 1996 had a big impact on Spanish society. A sudden flood in the gorge of Arás (in Huesca, Northeastern Spain) destroyed the *Biescas* campsite resulting in 87 deaths. After lengthy discussions to define this disaster as an "act of God," a lawsuit was brought against the public authorities. A Spanish Court decision in 2005 faced directly the question of the possible existence of public responsibility due to a lack of proper assessment of risks when permitting the construction of the campsite in the ravine. The outcome was positive: state and regional administration were declared guilty and compensation for damages was recognized.

Biescas tragedy
Source: http://icogblogs.com/riesgos/category/noticias/catastrofes/page/2/

This noteworthy judicial decision stated that public administration did not evaluate the existent "natural and man-made risks of all kinds" for people and belongings. According to the Spanish *Audiencia Nacional*, public administrations are always obliged to prevent risks even if where there is a lack of specific legal provision establishing such a duty. Due to the fact that the disaster was neither unpredictable nor unavoidable, public authorities were obliged to compensate for damages (€12 million).

This disaster triggered several measures to develop policy for the prevention of disasters, e.g. the modification of the (above-mentioned) Spanish land use act and the creation of a Parliamentary Special Commission on Prevention and Assistance in Catastrophic Situations.

TWO EXAMPLES OF LAND USE PLANNING AND PREVENTION OF DISASTERS: LOCATION OF NUCLEAR PLANTS AND PREVENTION OF TERRORISM THROUGH ENVIRONMENTAL DESIGN
**(CPTED Strategies: Crime Prevention Through Environmental Design)**

In the last section, I will consider two relevant examples of the role of urban planning in avoiding and mitigating disasters, as the case of Fukushima in 2011 and terrorists' attacks in several cities around the world (among them, Madrid and London, in Europe) show. I chose both examples because although they are man-made disasters, the combination of the human action with natural conditions (fires, winds...) can create the conditions for huge devastations.

## Location of nuclear plants and prevention of risks through urban planning: administrative procedures and fundamental rights

Prevention of disasters caused by nuclear energy is a main concern, as demonstrated by the tragedies of Chernobyl (1986) and Fukushima (2011).

The International Atomic Energy Agency has developed safety requirements in relation to the location of Nuclear Plants (IAEA 2010).

In the European sphere, nuclear power stations currently produce around a third of the electricity and 15% of the energy consumed in the European Union, according to European Commission information (European Commission 2012). This explains the Council Directive 2009/71/EURATOM of 25 June 2009 establishing a Community Framework for the Nuclear Safety of Nuclear Installations (of compulsory translation by member states by 22 July 2011) (Council of the European Union 2009). But this Directive says nothing about the location of nuclear plants. It reminds us that "National responsibility of Member States for the nuclear safety of nuclear installations is the fundamental principle on which nuclear safety regulation has been developed at the international level", and it is still true at a European level.

So, it is necessary to go to national legal systems of EU member states to know about evaluation of risks and urban planning. In the Spanish case, according to the regulation 1836/1999, before gaining a public decision for the licensing of a nuclear plant, it is necessary to get a "previous license or site license" which is a recognition by national public authorities for the possibility of locating a nuclear plant in an specific site. After getting this previous license, and only then, the previous license holder can apply to get a building permit to construct the nuclear facility.

The interested party must apply for the previous license by submitting several documents, including an evaluation of any possible risks detected. After a due administrative procedure with public consultation, the Ministry of Industry will either deliver the previous license or will refuse the application. Therefore, we are dealing with the exercise of discretionary powers.

In this context, the role and importance of due process to guarantee citizens' rights and good administration, i.e. the exercise of discretionary powers which respect the obligation of due care, is essential.

That importance of administrative procedures in protecting fundamental rights was underlined by a famous German Constitutional Court decision concerning the Mülheim-Kärlich Nuclear Power Plant (BVerfG, 20.12.1979 – 1 BvR 385/77).

Mülheim-Kärlich Nuclear Power Plant.
Source: Wikipedia.

In that decision, the German Constitutional Court emphasized the huge relevance of administrative procedures (as the moment for risk assessment). Administrative procedure is a tool to protect the right to life and physical integrity, not just a defensive tool, but an active tool to promote the respect for fundamental rights by imposing the duty of protecting and promoting them on public authorities.

## Planning and prevention of terrorism risks: A Spanish example—the car bomb attack against a Guardia Civil barrack

Interest in *public policies for the prevention of delinquency and terrorism* is growing, particularly in relation to urban environmental design (Ziegler 2007).

Various European institutions are involved in efforts to prevent delinquency and improve urban living conditions. One report by the Regional Committee on "delinquency and security in cities" (18 November 1999), points out:

> It is important to take into account, right from the outset of any major new building works or the renovation of dilapidated areas of a city, measures to prevent urban violence. This can be achieved by close collaboration between the authorities responsible for urbanisation, building owners and the authorities responsible for the safety of the community.

In a meeting on 15 March 2001, the Council of Justice and the Interior of the European Union gave its political approval to the conclusions of the conference of European experts, *Towards a strategy based on understanding to prevent crime* (Sundsvall, Sweden, 21-23 February 2001), who highlighted:

CPTED or DCO ["CPTD" and "DCO" stand for *Crime Prevention Through Environmental Design* and *Designing Crime Out*] has proved to be an effective and practical strategy in the prevention of delinquency and the sense of insecurity, integrated by multidisciplinary collaboration. The best practices referred to CPTED/DCO should be gathered, evaluated and made accessible to all those concerned. This process should use a common framework and the transferable concepts, processes and principles should be identified.

Finally in the European Union, the connection between housing policy and security and, in particular, urban design for the prevention of delinquency, has recently been discussed in the Regions Committee Report on 13 February 2007 (point 1.8), "Regional and Housing Policy":

The projects should fit together adequately and in the space which surrounds them. When new housing is built or renovated, the regions and the local authorities should take into consideration such issues as design, in order to discourage delinquency and create zones of quality, sustainable development and patrimony, in addition to the needs and aspirations of the local communities and the widest possible impact on cohesion.

This European interest in the situational prevention of crime explains the development of a European standard for the prevention of delinquency by means of urban planning and architectural design (ENV 14383-2). As we know, the European standards are voluntary (complimentary not obligatory) between countries, institutions and individuals as to how a product or process should be. The key components of the European market unit, are the technical specifications approved for an organization recognized for standardization for its repeated or continuous application, which can be international (elaborated by the ISO, *International Standardization Organization*, e.g. ISO 9000), European (EN, arising from the European Committee of Normalization, e.g., EN 50130-501136 about alarm systems, EN 1522/1523 about bullet-proof doors and windows, ENV – pre-standard – 1627-1629 about anti-burglary properties of doors, windows and window bars...).

In the mid 1990s, a decision was reached to standardize procedures (as opposed to products) in order to help local and regional authorities, urban planners, architects and engineers in their efforts to reduce delinquency in collaboration with the police, security companies, insurers and residents associations.

The European Committee of Normalization set up a technical committee – 325 (tc 325) in 1996 in Denmark to work on the new standard. The project was divided into three work groups (wg 1, 2 and 3). Wg 1 is presided by France and concentrated in terms and definitions. Wg 2 is for urban planning and is presided by the Netherlands. Wg 3 is presided by the UK and is concerned with housing design, shops and offices.

Wg 2 has developed a European pre-standard (ENV) approved by the European Committee of Normalization in 2002, with provisional application for 3 years, and the possibility of becoming an EN. The ENV 14383-2 is important as it is the first effort to establish common terms and definitions regarding the situational prevention of crime. Finally, in 2006 the EN 14383-1:2006 standard was approved for terms and definitions. Moreover, during the period 2005 to 2007 two technical specifications have been approved (dwellings and offices: CEN/TS 14383-3:2005, CEN/TS 14383-4:2006) and a technical report (urban planning: CEN/TR 14383-2: 2007).

Among the member states of the European Union, the United Kingdom and, to a lesser extent, France and Spain are examples of countries who have applied this idea to the concrete development of public security policy, introducing new standards and/or changes to administrative practices.

In the case of Britain, various official reports and the legal system itself have incorporated this perspective. Among these reports, *Safer Places: The Planning System and Crime Prevention* (Office of the Deputy Prime Minister 2004), highlights the fact that crime and the fear of crime can compromise social cohesion and, as a consequence, the sustainable development of communities, insisting that it is more efficient from an economic point of view to consider the variables of crime prevention at the planning stage, since it is less costly than to correct or manage badly designed urban development. In the same way, the connection between security and social cohesion is emphasized, which has been a crucial element of the British political agenda since 2001, with the creation of the *Community Cohesion Unit*, within the *Home Office*.

With regard to the legal system, the *Crime and Disorder Act* of 1998 contains the public competence for the prevention of crime and disorder (Section 17), which in the urban environment has been defined in the *Planning Policy Statement I: Delivering Sustainable Development*, 2005.

The *Safer Places* report connects public security with urban planning and emphasizes the link between security and social cohesion, establishing the need, at the planning stage, for local authorities to take into consideration the best practices established in the official reports mentioned, which include an analysis of different experiences with regard to access and mobility in the urban space (well defined access, avoiding isolated stairways, tunnels etc., appropriate road design...), urban structure (for example, avoiding buildings which can be used for anti-social behavior), vigilance (for example, adequate nocturnal lighting and the installation of CCTV), *relevance* (referring to urban design which encourages a sense of community, with clearly defined divisions to avoid confusion between private and public spaces), physical protection of private property (a more traditional perspective which we can identify with), activity (avoiding monofunctionality and urban segregation and encouraging mixed use and different types of housing) and management and maintenance (to avoid urban environments which incite vandalism and increase the risk of crime).

These reports and legal documents also include some new practices in the area of administrative security policing, such as the creation of

*Architectural Liaison Officers,* specialized officers experienced in the risks of delinquency who advise on urban planning issues, and in the development of the *Secured by Design*[2] initiative, supporting the principles of "designing out crime" by use of effective crime prevention and security standards for a range of applications.

In the case of France, the well known urban problems this country faces have also led to think on urbanization as a tool for the prevention of delinquency and urban violence (Bauer and Raufer 2005), with similar official reports on the subject, as in Britain (e.g. Peyrat 2002). Moreover, since 1995, the French legal system incorporates what we could define as an evaluation of the crime impact of specific developments (see art. L111-3-1 of the *Code de l'Urbanisme,* modified by Law 2007-297, 5 March 2007, relating to the prevention of delinquency).

In Spain, an addition to the Catalan regulation was introduced in 2006, specifying the content of the already mentioned Social Memory (The Social Memory is a specific element of Catalan comprehensive plans which must take into account several elements and include explanations for alternatives decided. See art. 69 Catalan Decree 305/2006, 18 July). The new regulation states that "an evaluation of the impact of proposed urbanization" with regard to "gender, should also form part of the Social Memory, as well as social groups who need specific attention, including immigrants and senior citizens," so that "planning decisions, based on information about social realities, can contribute to the development of equal opportunities between men and women, as well as favoring other groups in need of protection." This evaluation must contain a diagnosis of the situation and an evaluation of the social and gender impact of the urbanization plan, and must justify, among other aspects, the coherence of the proposed plan with the needs of men and women and of other groups with regard to various parameters, including "security and the use of the urban fabric" (See art. 69 Catalan Decree 305/2006, 18 July).

What happens if there is a criminal attack which causes a disaster and public authorities do not have take all the possible planning measures to avoid it? A second interesting Spanish judicial decision concerning public responsibility in the prevention of disasters (for the first, see above, the disaster of the *Biescas* campsite) is the Spanish Supreme Court decision of November 2, 2004. In this case, the judges considered the car bomb attack against a barrack of the Spanish security forces (specifically, the Guardia Civil). The explosion caused one death.

---

[2] http://www.securedbydesign.com

Images of a car bomb attack at a Guardia Civil barrack in Vic in 2001.
Source: http://jquinyonesblog.blogspot.com.es/search?q=VIC

The plaintiff argued that personal and material damages were caused by the lack of a proper plan to introduce security measures (a previous attack had been attempted against the same police station a year earlier). The Spanish Supreme Court refused the claim for damages, arguing that although it was possible to plan for more security measures in the urban design, the damages were caused by the terrorists and not due to a lack of public action (in the Spanish legal regime this case is called the breach of causal nexus: there can be a maladministration but the cause of damages is not this maladministration but the activity of the victim or a third party, e.g. the terrorist attack) (Tribunal Supremo de España 2004).

### SOME FINAL CONCLUSIONS

That study has adopted a legal perspective to expose the state of the art of disaster prevention in Europe, using as an example the Spanish case. Although the EU does not possess powers in the field of land, the treaties regulating its functions give it several goals to achieve (sustainable development, solidarity, fight against the exclusion, economic, territorial and social cohesion) as well as powers in the field of the environment and other public policies with territorial impact. Those goals and powers, investments of money and promotion of intellectual networking give the EU a place in the area of disaster prevention and mitigation. EU role is developed by means of *soft law* and *hard law*.

European Commission Communication of 2009 on the prevention of natural and man-made disasters is important among the *soft law*. In relation to *hard law*, the EU has enacted several Directives and Regulations which bind member estates in different degrees. On the other hand, Article 191 TFEU calls for the use of the precautionary principle in case of scientific uncertainty, a principle that has been considered in the Communication from the Commission in 2000.

According to that EU framework, Member Estates must evaluate disaster risks when planning land uses. The paper analyzes the Spanish case as an example, studying how the Spanish legal system has implemented EU directives (environmental impact assessment, flood risk prevention) and how it manages the identified risks (using direct legal prohibitions or allowing regional planning to limit local land use planning when necessary). Moreover, the study has considered public and private liability in case of disasters. Focusing on the public responsibility for a lack of proper risk evaluation, the study underlines the lack of a common European legal framework and the need of applying each national legal regime in that area. After explaining the legal Spanish regime briefly, it has been considered if a public administration should face liability in case of damages caused by inadequate land use regulations. The case of the *Biescas* campsite has shown clearly that it is perfectly possible in Spain.

The study finishes with two examples of land use planning acting as a factor of prevention and mitigation of disasters. In both cases we are in front of possible man-made disasters. In the case of the CPTED, the study explores public responsibility for a lack of due prevention through land use planning, using a second Spanish judicial decision in that field.

Therefore, the study shows the limited but important role of the EU level; the relevant member states' responsibility in preventing and mitigating disasters and the legal mechanisms used to connect both levels (*soft law*, treaties, directives, regulations) and to ensure a proper evaluation of risks when planning the uses of land.

## Bibliography

Association internationale de droit de l'urbanisme, 2011. *Risque et droit de l'urbanisme en Europe*. Paris: GRIDAUH.

Bassols, M., 1973. *Génesis y evolución del Derecho urbanístico español (1812-1956)*. Madrid: Montecorvo.

Bauer, A. and Raufer, X., 2005. *Violences et insécurité urbaines*. 9th ed. Paris: Presses universitaires de France.

Brewer-Carías, A., 1997. *La ciudad ordenada*. Madrid: Instituto Pascual Madoz, Universidad Carlos III, BOE.

Chiti, M.P., 2003, Il ruolo della comunità europea nel governo del territorio. *In*: S. Civitarese, E. Ferrari and P. Urbani, eds. Il governo del territorio. Milán: Giuffrè editores.

Colantonio, A., 2007. Measuring Social Sustainability: Best Practice from Urban Renewal in the EU [online]. Oxford Institute for Sustainable Development. Available from: http://oisd.brookes.ac.uk/sustainable_communities/

resources/SocialSustainability_Metrics_and_Tools.pdf [Accessed 15 April 2013].

Council of the European Union, 1996. Council Directive 96/82/EC of December 1996 on the control of major-accident hazards involving dangerous substances [online]. Available from: http://eur-lex.europa.eu/LexUriServ/ LexUriServ.do?uri=CELEX:31996L0082:EN:pdf [Accessed 22 February 2013].

Council of the European Union, 2009. *Council Directive 2009/71/EURATOM of 25 June 2009 establishing a Community framework for the nuclear safety of nuclear installations* [online]. Available from: http://eur-lex.europa.eu/LexUriServ/ LexUriServ.do?uri=OJ:L:2009:172:0018:0022:EN:PDF [Accessed 22 February 2013].

*Danish Presidency of the Council of the European Union* 2012 [online]. Available from: http://eu2012.dk/en/EU-and-the-Presidency/About-EU/Politikomraader/ JHA/Civilbeskyttelse [Accessed 21 February 2013].

Esteve Pardo, J., 2009. *El desconcierto del Leviatán. Política y Derecho ante las Incertidumbres de la Ciencia.* Madrid: Marcial Pons.

European Comission, 2000. *The Communication from the Commission on the Precautionary Principle, Brussels 02.02.2000 COM (2000) I* [online]. Available from: http://ec.europa.eu/dgs/health_consumer/library/pub/pub07_en.pdf [Accessed 21 February 2013].

European Comission, 2007. *The Urban Dimension in Community Policies for the period 2007-2013* [online]. Available from: http://ec.europa.eu/regional_policy/sources/docgener/guides/urban/index_en.ht m [Accessed 21 February 2013].

European Comission, 2009a. *Communication from the Commission to the European Parliament, the Council, the European Economic and Social Committee and the Committee of the Regions, A Community approach on the prevention of natural and man-made disasters, [COM(2009) 82 final—Not published in the Official Journal]* [online]. Available from: http://europa.eu/legislation_summaries/ environment/civil_protection/pr0005_en.htm [Accessed 21 February 2013].

European Comission, 2009b. *Communication from the Commission to the European Parliament, the Council, the European Economic and Social Committee and the Committee of the Regions, A Community approach on the prevention of natural and man-made disasters* [online]. Available from: http://ec.europa.eu/echo/civil_ protection/civil/pdfdocs/com_2009_82en.pdf [Accessed 21 February 2013].

European Commission, 2012. *Nuclear energy* [online]. Available from: http://ec.europa.eu/energy/nuclear/safety/safety_en.htm [Accessed 22 February 2013].

European Parliament, European Council, 2004. *Directive 2004/35/CE of the European Parliament and of the Council of 21 April 2004 on environmental liability with regard to the prevention and remedying of environmental damage* [online]. Available from: http://eur-lex.europa.eu/LexUriServ/

LexUriServ.do?uri=CELEX:32004L0035:EN:PDF [Accessed 22 February 2013].

European Parliament, European Council, 2007. *Directive 2007/60/EC of the European Parliament and of the council of 23 October 2007 on the assessment and management of flood risks* [online]. Available from: http://eur-lex.europa.eu/LexUriServ/ LexUriServ.do?uri=OJ:L:2007:288:0027:0034:en:pdf [Accessed 22 February 2013].

European Parliament, European Council, 2011. *Directive 2001/42/EC of the European Parliament and of the Council on the assessment of the effects of certain plans and programmes on the environment* [online]. Available from: http://eur-lex.europa .eu/LexUriServ/LexUriServ.do?uri=CELEX:32001L0042:EN:pdf [Accessed 22 February 2013].

European Urban Knowledge Network, 2013. EUKN—Spanish National Focal Point [online]. Available from: http://www.eukn.org/spain/en [Accessed 21 February 2013].

Faludi, A., 2007. The European Model of Society. In: A. Faludi, ed. *Territorial Cohesion and the European Model of Society*. Cambridge: Lincoln Institute of Land Policy.

Fernández, T.R., 2008. *Manual de Derecho Urbanístico*. 20th ed. Madrid: La Ley.

IAEA (International Atomic Energy Agency), 2010. *Evaluación de emplazamiento de instalaciones nucleares. Requisitos de seguridad* [online]. Available from: http://www-pub.iaea.org/MTCD/publications/PDF/Pub1177s_web.pdf [Accessed 21 February 2013].

López-Ramón, F., 2009. *Introducción al Derecho urbanístico*. Madrid: Marcial Pons.

Office of the Deputy Prime Minister, 2004. *Safer Places: The Planning System and Crime Prevention* [online]. Tonbridge: Thomas Telford. Available from: http://www.communities.gov.uk/documents/planningandbuilding/pdf/147627. pdf [Accessed 21 February 2013].

Office of the Deputy Prime Minister, 2005. *Planning Policy Statement 1: Delivering Sustainable Development* [online]. Available from: http://www.ukcip.org.uk/ wordpress/wp-content/PDFs/LA_pdfs/ODPM_planningpolicystatement.pdf [Accessed 21 January 2013].

Peyrat, D., 2002. *Habiter Cohabiter. La securité dans le logement social* [online]. Paris: Secretariat d'État au Logement. Available from: http://lesrapports .ladocumentationfrancaise.fr/BRP/024000101/0000.pdf [Accessed 21 February 2013].

Pierce, R.J. Jr., 2008. *Administrative Law*. New York: Foundation Press.

Ponce, J., 2004. Land Use Law, Liberalization, and Social Cohesion Through Affordable Housing in Europe: The Spanish Case. *The Urban Lawyer*, 36 (2), 322-331.

Ponce, J., 2008. Breve reseña histórica de la regulación de la vivienda en España y Cataluña existente con anterioridad a la Ley 18/2007, de 28 de diciembre, del derecho a la vivienda. *In*: J. Ponce and D. Sibina, eds. *El Derecho de la Vivienda en el Siglo XXI: sus relaciones con la ordenación del territorio y el urbanismo. Con análisis específico de la Ley catalana 18/2007, de 28 de diciembre, en su contexto español, europeo e internacional.* Madrid: Marcial Pons.

Population Division of the Department of Economic and Social Affairs of the United Nations Secretariat, 2006. *World Urbanization Prospects: The 2005 Revision* [online]. New York: United Nations. Available from: http://www.un.org/esa/population/publications/WUP2005/2005WUPHighlights_Final_Report.pd f [Accessed 21 February 2013].

Spanish Constitution, 1978. *Constitución Española* [online]. Available from: http://www.lamoncloa.gob.es/NR/rdonlyres/79FF2885-8DFA-4348-8450-04610A9267F0/0/constitucion_ES.pdf [Accessed 22 February 2013].

Spanish Government, 2010a. *Restauración de ríos: bases de la Estrategia Nacional de Restauración de Ríos* [online]. Madrid: Spanish Government. Available from: http://www.magrama.gob.es/es/agua/publicaciones/Rios_B_Restauracion_tcm7 -27570.pdf [Accessed 21 February 2013].

Spanish Government, 2010b. *River restoration: basis of the Nacional Strategy for River Restoration* [online]. Madrid: Spanish Government. Available from: http://www.magrama.gob.es/es/agua/publicaciones/River_B_Restoration_tcm7 -27571.pdf [Accessed 21 February 2013].

*The World Factbook* [online]. Washington, DC: Central Intelligence Agency. Available from: https://www.cia.gov/library/publications/the-world-factbook/index.html [Accessed 21 February 2013].

Tribunal Supremo de España, 2004. *Sentencia 6998/2004, de 2 de noviembre de 2004* [online]. Available from: http://www.poderjudicial.es/search/doAction?action=contentpdf&databasematch=TS&reference=1813102&links=c uartel&optimize=20041204&publicinterface=true [Accessed 22 February 2013].

Ziegler, E.H., 2007. American Cities, Urban Planning, and Place-Based Crime Prevention. *The Urban Lawyer*, 39 (4), 859-875.

# 3

# LAW, STATE AND THE POLITICS OF CATASTROPHES: A CRITICAL PERSPECTIVE ON EPIPHANIES OF INJUSTICE AND THE NEED FOR PROTECTION

## Valerio Nitrato Izzo

**ABSTRACT**

While the phenomenon of catastrophes is emerging as a growing threat that humanity should face in the next years, legal studies have disregarded the issue for a long time. Recent extreme events have motivated a new attention towards the legal dimension as part of the context in which disasters take place. Catastrophes are a powerful breakdown of our normative world. Paradigms of regulation in this field have usually been identified in terms of prevention, anticipation and amelioration, theoretical schemes that can be applied to various branches of the law. Nevertheless, this is only a part of the challenge that the legal study of extreme events must face. They should in fact include into these abstract schemes the factors of inequality that contribute to producing higher rates of vulnerability. In this chapter I propose to conceive catastrophes as legal epiphanies, through which it is possible to evaluate the effectiveness, the efficiency and the sustainability of regulatory choices.

Mientras el fenómeno de las catástrofes se está convirtiendo en una amenaza cada vez mayor que la humanidad deberá afrontar en los próximos años, durante mucho tiempo los estudios jurídicos no lo han tenido en cuenta. Hechos extremos recientes han hecho que adquiera mayor relevancia la dimensión legal como parte del contexto en la que ocurren los desastres. Las catástrofes suponen una poderosa ruptura en la normativa de nuestro mundo. Los paradigmas de la regulación en este campo se han identificado generalmente en términos de prevención, anticipación y mejora, esquemas teóricos que se pueden aplicar a distintas ramas del derecho. Sin embargo, esto es sólo una parte del desafío que debe afrontar el estudio jurídico de los fenómenos extremos. En realidad, deberían tenerse en cuenta los factores de desigualdad que contribuyen a producir mayores ratios de vulnerabilidad. En este trabajo me propongo concebir las catástrofes como epifanías legales, a través de las cuales es posible evaluar la eficacia, la eficiencia y la sostenibilidad de las decisiones reguladoras.

## INTRODUCTION AND DEFINITIONAL ISSUES

Dealing with the vague concept of catastrophes, the search for a sound definition can be an issue on itself. In common sense, there is a tendency to put together different terms such as "emergencies," "disasters," "catastrophes," "cataclysms," etc.[1] As in many language matters, all these terms share a common intuitive essence of an event, negative in its outcomes, which evokes sinister scenarios of destruction, death, or other issues. Notwithstanding, in this chapter I will mainly use the term "catastrophe." I will do this for two reasons. The first one is that there is the possibility to grasp the meaning of the differences between the events that we name with these words, according to some indicators, such as the magnitude of the event, the pervasiveness, the impact on the social structure, the amount of destruction of physical goods, etc. From this point of view, disasters are quantitatively and qualitatively different from catastrophes (Quarantelli 2000). This can be summed up in the sentence "all catastrophes are disasters, but not all disasters are catastrophes" (Douglas, Sarat, Umphrey 2007, p. 2). The other reason to do this is that catastrophes are prodigious cultural objects that have a distinct place in the history of risk. It is not by chance that catastrophes are regarded as remarkable events in many religious texts, as well as in plots or literary texts. The link with culture can also be reflected in the choice of terms by international organizations such as the United Nations General Assembly that, in its International Strategy for Disaster Reduction terminology summary, defined disasters as "A serious disruption of the functioning of a community or a society involving widespread human, material, economic or environmental losses and impacts, which exceeds the ability of the affected community or society to cope using its own resources" (UNISDR 2009). The choice to avoid the term catastrophe probably reflects the attempt to obviate exactly such a cultural connotation, a surplus of meaning that could have inevitably made more vague the working definition as dependent of human understanding and interpretation of such events.

Law and catastrophe is, surprisingly, quite a recent topic. While there is a substantial amount of disaster studies, the link between legal studies and catastrophes has been under focus only recently. Recent events such as 9/11 and general terrorist threats, the number of tsunamis and Hurricane Katrina, had the effect of stirring a new interest on them, especially within the North American literature (Malloy 2009, Farber *et al.* 2010, Sarat, Douglas, Umphrey 2007, Miller 2009, Posner 2004).

In some ways, law contributes to the very definition of catastrophes

---

[1] Note that I will use the terms in the plural forms to underline not only the fact that each event of widespread harm is unique in its features but also to highlight the fact that such events are growing in numbers and in the spatial space of damage, that render them a feature of today's world.

and disasters. For example, we can find the typical self-reference of legal thinking in a definition of disaster that relies on "what the intervention of disaster relief units make necessary" (Dombrowsky 1998, p. 14). Regarding the issue of definition the legal field is also influenced by the dialectics between the naturalistic and the human/social/cultural elements. According to Ségur (1997), the relationship between law and catastrophe regarding its definition oscillates between a nominalistic approach and a causal one. The features of the nominalistic approach are based in the fact that law avoids defining the elements that identify a catastrophe, recognizing only its already known ways of manifestation, preferring a descriptive attempt to define catastrophes that can open space to more vagueness than to more legal clarification. The other side of the issue, and the dominant one, is the reduction of catastrophe to its human impact, stressing the causal element.

It is possible to ground some general points in the relationship between law and catastrophe. First, a catastrophe is an event producing a subversion of the very concept of order itself. From this point of view, a catastrophe is a breakdown of the normative world: confronting the law, catastrophe is Janus-faced, juris-generative and antithetic to law, all at the same time (Douglas, Sarat, Umphrey 2007, p. 4). Catastrophes are "moments when we confront the limits of our normative world" (Meyer 2007, p. 20). In fact, catastrophes can be seen as powerful *legal epiphanies* in which, by stressing the limits of our normative world, we can more profoundly comprehend the way law really works or what goods and values it protects. At the same time, we need to face one of the most challenging aspect of catastrophes, namely the fact that risk is now globally spread, indifferent to national boundaries that normally constitute the territorial space where a single legal system is sovereign. So these legal epiphanies reflect this ambiguous structure: they are global and local at the same time, as are its effects and origins.

## FROM CATASTROPHE SOCIETY TO RISK SOCIETY

It has been argued that with modernity we have moved from a society of catastrophes to a risk society (Walter 2008). This assumption can be questioned, but catastrophes still remain important and powerful events that challenge the conventional risks approaches. This is due to the extreme harm that such circumstances can produce. These events are, in the end, a peculiar mix of natural and human driven elements. The very happening of natural disasters is something totally (e.g. earthquakes) or partially (hurricanes, floods) unforeseeable and that is not directly dependent on human contribution for their coming into existence. This is, nevertheless, a very narrow way of looking at extreme events. What makes a natural event a catastrophe is the social context of the event. There are no catastrophes without an affected human community, directly or indirectly involved by the outcomes of the event. That is the reason for looking at the category of vulnerability as crucial for the understanding of the complex of social elements that contribute to such impacts which we can relate to catastrophes. A naturalistic outlook is incomplete as it cannot fully explain what causes the harm without taking into account the social, political, ecological elements concerned (Blaikie *et al.* 1994). The tool through which we can evaluate the role of these elements in the occurrence of a catastrophe is the concept of vulnerability, understood as "the characteristics of a person or group in terms of their capacity to anticipate, cope with, resist, and recover from the impact of a natural hazard" (Blaikie *et al.* 1994, p. 9).

Another distinction is also relevant for the purpose of this work: the distinction between natural and human-made catastrophes, which is a thin one from a social sciences perspective. There is still the need to introduce a more detailed account of human agency in the causal contribution to the creation of catastrophes. Posner (2004, p. 12) distinguishes between four types of catastrophes: among the first two types, natural and technological catastrophes, he lists natural pandemics and asteroid collisions, as well as laboratory and scientific accidents with the aim of stressing the role of technology in the production of disasters. The third category includes unintentional albeit man-made catastrophes such as exhaustion of natural resources, global warming, and loss of biodiversity. The fourth one takes into account deliberately perpetrated catastrophes as "nuclear winter," bioweaponry and other forms of technological terrorism. Among those listed, it is the third category I am more interested in and that can better be used to highlight the complexity of the interactions between different levels of legal and social policies, at a national and international level.

A good example of the tension at the interaction of these levels is the position claimed by Ulrich Beck. Since his famous contribution to sociology that resulted in the global success of the term "risk society," catastrophes found a place in his analysis. Risk society is in fact a "catastrophic society" (Beck 1992, pp. 24, 79-80). Beck is aware of the important political meaning of catastrophes as he states that the re-distribution of risk on a worldwide level will lead to a society in which politically potential catastrophes can include a "reorganization of power and authority" and exceptional conditions threaten to become the norm. So, in the risk society Beck gives to catastrophes an enabling power that seems capable of challenging the production of risk as a consequence of the reflexive modernity, in which the policy choices regarding the elimination of the causes of hazards in the modernization process become political (Beck 1992, p. 78). In Beck's analysis of the possible role played by catastrophes in risk society, he argues that such an enabling political power of catastrophes is the substitute for revolution in the risk society. Catastrophes enable a shift from a normal state to a state of emergency, in which the administration of risks can include a reorganization of power and authority. Here people fight a crucial battle, as with increasing risk production new types of challenges to democracy arise, namely a tendency to a legitimate authoritarianism of hazard prevention.

Beck's interest in the relationship between catastrophes and the risk society continues to be important also in his most recent works, where we find a more explicit link based on his concept of cosmopolitanism. Cosmopolitanism in his view is the method in social sciences to make sense of our contemporary world. Understanding and facing the challenges of a global risk society means leaving aside methodological nationalism in social sciences. Cosmopolitanism in this perspective differs radically from a sociological analysis centred on the state. Beck claims cosmopolitanism as a new form of analysis that envisages the state as one of the actors among others, providing a new perspective on the whole global power game. In *World at Risk*, Beck has sketched an explicit link between catastrophes as the main object of a risk analysis and a cosmopolitan perspective. In his view, risk is not the same as catastrophe. It is, however, intimately related because risk is the *anticipation of the catastrophe*. While a catastrophe is always limited in its spatial, temporal and social dimensions, the anticipation of the event is not limited. What counts in the end is its staging: to have an idea of the meaning of the global dimension of catastrophes we need to question the staging of the catastrophe, which fills in the gap between the anticipated catastrophe and the actual one (Beck 2009, pp. 10, 67). The lesser a risk is evaluable, the heavier is the weight of cultural assumptions about it: this in the end leads to an elimination of the gap between a risk and its cultural perception. This is a distinctive feature of the new world risk society. Global risks lead to an imposed cosmopolitanism in which nation-states and national methodology are not anymore useful tools to understand society.

I will now concentrate on some elements that are relevant for the implications of Beck's position on global risk distribution. The first one is that in the global risk society "dealing with catastrophic risks, the present of the future planetary state of exception, which can no longer be contained and managed at a national level, is being negotiated" (Beck 2009, p. 73). Such a state of exception would be not a "national" one but a "cosmopolitan" one. To understand this conceptual link, a distinction is introduced between intended and unintended catastrophes. The difference here lies in the fact that while side effect catastrophes, as unintended, are a mixture of bad and good (e.g. new technologies, global warming), intentional ones (such as terrorist attacks) have no benefits (Beck 2009, p. 79). Both contribute, in any case, to a planetary state of exception that goes beyond national borders, and that is no longer declared by state authorities: it is an imposed state of exception, where social, spatial, and temporal boundaries are so wide that a single nation cannot give any sound answer to these threats. Beck's "cosmopolitan" account of the state of exception differs explicitly from Carl Schmitt's view of the exception, which he linked with the sovereignty of a state. It also differs from the recent influential account by Giorgio Agamben, who argues that the state of exception has been replaced by "a generalisation of the paradigm of security as the normal technique of government in Western societies" (Agamben 2005, p. 14). Here is a classical treatment of catastrophes as productive of a state of exception, but Beck's argument goes further, extending it not only to local authorities but labelling it as a distinctive feature of cosmopolitanism in a world risk society. As the argument carries on it seems that any boundaries should be destined to be trespassed by global risks. Some questions arise here: is Beck not too quickly dismissive on the relevance of the state in the social determination of risks? And, more specifically, is such an analysis attractive in the context of legal and social studies?

Before trying to answer these questions it is important to stress another element of the cosmopolitan approach that has to do with the asymmetry between who decides, who takes the risk and who suffers from such a decision. Focusing on the case of social inequality, Beck first states that "the predetermined irrelevance of large inequalities enables powerful and wealthy nation-states to burden poor states with the risk entailed by their decisions" and that "the cosmopolitan perspective opens up negotiation spaces and strategies which the national strategies preclude" (Beck 2003, pp. 463, 466). While social inequalities remain invisible in an analysis centred in the national-states' context, in a cosmopolitan perspective these gain a chance to become visible thanks to a normative claim for equality and respect, through the staging of the catastrophe, in a global public sphere that goes beyond the national boundaries. Understanding risk as *conditio humana* will have the effect of a necessary recognition of the *other* on normative and cultural levels, which is no longer possible by looking at the nation-states framework of society. On a legal basis this should lead to the emergence of a risk cosmopolitan law that is transnational in its nature (Beck 2009, p. 191).

It is at this point that this theoretical proposal is at the same time more interesting and more doubtful. It is interesting because it takes into account the emergence of risks as global actors in the shaping of society on a global level. At the same time, Beck argues that catastrophes are worse for poor people and states. He also argues that cosmopolitanism is *imposed* from below on a global level. This crucial passage can be challenged by giving a different perspective that looks at the same time *inside* and *outside* the state when regarding cultural and social differences and the legal structure of risks. To do so I will sketch a brief alternative proposal, inspired by a critical approach with a "post-colonial" emphasis. By using the term post-colonial I mean an approach that takes into account differences between the global North and the global South in exposure to risk in relationship to decision making exclusion. Another consequence of this critical approach will be to ascribe a normative duty of protection of the communities on the government and the state.

## FIRST SKETCHES OF A CRITICAL APPROACH TO LAW AND CATASTROPHE

The main issue when discussing risks, and particularly global risks as catastrophes, is to take into account the profound asymmetry that divides those who decide from those who will be affected by such decision. Considering such an asymmetry between the risk-creator and the risk-bearer,

I would like to propose to understand it as a matter of different lines of risks that govern the world in the era of globalization. We should qualify such lines as "abyssal lines," a concept that I borrow from Santos (2007). According to Santos, "Modern Western thinking is an abyssal thinking. It consists of a system of visible and invisible distinctions, the invisible ones being the foundation of the visible ones. The invisible distinctions are established through radical lines that divide social reality into two realms, the realm of "this side of the line" and the realm of "the other side of the line (...) What most fundamentally characterizes abyssal thinking is thus the impossibility of the co-presence of the two sides of the line" (Santos 2007, p. 45). Knowledge and law are at the core of the production of abyssal lines. Regarding modern law, "this side of the line is determined by what counts as legal or illegal according to official state or international law. The legal and the illegal are the only two relevant forms of existence before the law and, for that reason, the distinction between the two is a universal distinction. This central dichotomy leaves out a whole social territory where the dichotomy would be unthinkable as an organizing principle, that is, the territory of the lawless, the a-legal, the non-legal, and even the legal or illegal according to non-officially recognized law" (Santos 2007, p. 48).

Abyssal thinking can be an alternative way for risk society to comprehend the placement and diffusion of risks in contemporary world (Santos personal communication at *Law and Justice in the Risk Society* conference, Plenary Session "Law, Democracy and Risk" of the Research Committee on Sociology of Law Annual Meeting, Milan, Italy, 11th July 2008). Risk in fact is not democratic. The profound asymmetry between who produces risks and who has to suffer its outcomes is a distinctive feature of different lines that divide our social and legal worlds. I argue that these lines do not only divide different areas of the world, as the North/South gap, but are also present within Western societies and states, reflecting differences in inequality and vulnerability levels inside the states and between different states. Moving between an internal and external view regarding the state is an important feature of a post-colonial approach to catastrophes. While the imposed cosmopolitanism focuses on the global fight for the definition of risks in the global arena, the effort to move away from a narrow national pattern can lead to an under-evaluation of the state as a crucial actor in the ascription of risks, in its definitions and for the accountability for vulnerability in societies.

It is possible to apply a post-colonial framework on the issue of climate change. Even if it is not possible to draw a strictly direct and causal link between some climate shocks as hurricanes, floods, and other hydrometereological disasters, data analysis regarding disasters in the last 20 years, showing a rising in the number of disasters,[2] demonstrates the

---

[2] See the reliable data from the International Disaster Database (CRED 2013) (used also by the UN International Strategy for Disaster Reduction).

consequences predicted by climate change scientists. As a recent work shows, the way a country is inserted into the world economy bears heavily upon its ability to cope with climate related disasters (Roberts and Parks 2007). Roberts and Parks have argued that there is a connection between a colonial legacy and the vulnerability of a community. Extraction based economies in former colonial areas generate more vulnerability in all crucial indicators, such as social, economic, environmental and institutional ones. It is not simply a matter of being a poor country in the sense of a smaller per capita GDP, but of designing a society in a way to better serve others' interests (e.g. extractive goods economy, tourism industry) that lead to see other indicators as more relevant: income inequality, urban and coastal populations, press freedom, and property rights (Roberts and Parks 2007, p. 131). Due to the incidence of these factors on the overall vulnerability level, a preventive approach that takes into consideration the colonial legacy will be more effective than one of "risk management" based on intervention after the event. It should also be added that a colonial legacy can also lurk within the wealthier countries. Katrina's hurricane is the perfect example. The state of Louisiana, in fact, presents all the characteristics of a state with a colonial history, sharing with those high levels of inequality, political exclusion, racism and a poor enforcement of environmental regulations. The failure in the resilience strategy relies almost on the same factors of a less developed country (Roberts and Parks 2007, pp. 98-101). Hurricane Katrina was, thus, an abyssal line of risk. As disasters hit areas such as New York, where a 'superstorm' at the end of October 2012 put out power for over a week throughout the metropolitan area, internal inequalities that sociologists of disaster have long discussed made coping with power and heat loss differently challenging. If a post-colonial framework is useful, it must allow thinking through how internal inequalities fit when disasters hit very populated and often very desirable coastlines.

Thus, it is possible to defend the utility of an analysis based on a critical approach as the one sketched before. Lines of risk can move outside and inside states, demonstrating that catastrophic risks can affect any area in which lines of risk are moving. It must be added that lines of risks move not only when linked to a colonial element. More generally, sometimes they just indicate how risks are distributed and grow in an unequal way, contrary to what is pretended by a cosmopolitan egalitarian approach. Heat waves in wealthier countries demonstrate the gaps of exposure to risk and vulnerability between different social groups (Klinenberg 2002, Acot 2006).

## REDUCING VULNERABILITY AND THE NEED
## FOR PROTECTION: A NORMATIVE CLAIM

The reconstruction offered here is just a very rudimentary demonstration of an alternative route to the cosmopolitan approach to global catastrophes. The reflection on the link between a colonial legacy and higher levels of vulnerability show that, to some extents, climate-related catastrophes are colonization through different means.

Legal instruments raise a normative claim that can ground a sociole-gal approach to risk. International instruments presume that the right to life as a fundamental human right, and preserving life is a legal duty for all states. In political theory, the Hobbesian argument for the necessity of the state was grounded on the need to protect the citizen from physical harm. Emphasis on life is not anymore sufficient to consider the complex rela-tions with risk that each individual experiences nowadays. So we face a transformation of what it means to be "protected," which is in the first instance a duty of the state. Even if in the Western world we live in the safest societies ever, rising uncertainty in society is linked to the progres-sive individualization in modern societies: vulnerability, as a consequence of the growing uncertainty and the need for protection are two faces of the same medal (Castel 2003). As a consequence of the affirmation of the paradigm of a risk society, as an unavoidable consequence of modernity, elites assume that risks are inevitable. Some authors argue that the inclu-sion of the worst-case scenarios in the normative horizon of the state, leads to a "biopolitics of catastrophes" (Neyrat 2008). This is a new form of governance that has catastrophes—in a wide sense—as its object. It regards catastrophes as a constant, widespread possibility of the worst happening, something that must be faced with defense tools such as pre-caution and prevention. Regulation in this way resembles a kind of im-munization from catastrophic events, claiming the control on the possibil-ity of existence (Neyrat 2008). It is worthy to note that a recent report by Oxfam International (2009) on the importance of defending vulnerable people from catastrophes was entitled "*The Right to Survive*." Such a linguistic shift is very revealing of a re-definition of the very sense of being protected these days: there is not a *right* to life, but a right to *survive*, of individuals who are abandoned acting in a world where threat to their lives is the rule.

A common ground for a critical approach to catastrophes in this sce-nario is needed. The point can only be sketched here but it is crucial. The re-framing of the need for protection in an age of catastrophes implies an attempt to answer a simple question: is there a right to do not risk? Who holds it? And whose duty is it? Some expressions of such a right could be seen, for example, in the principle of precaution as embedded in various national and international legislation. It is still more a matter of aspiration than of a justiciable right. An attempt to ground a right not to face risk could seem an idealistic exercise best conducted in the domain of morality and legal philosophy rather than justiciable rights (Oberdiek 2009); however, it is becoming not just a generic claim for safety from harm, but a *legal* claim. The obligation to protect puts again at the center the role of the state that the cosmopolitan approach is likely to discard. For example, in the aftermath of the 2006 earthquake in Indonesia, Coalisi KPHY, an association of cause lawyers, sued the Indonesian State for 'having not arranged any prevention measure' (Bultrini 2009). The same could be said of Katrina where the failure of civil protection systems has been considered one of the most striking features of the event, though the judiciary did not hold the state responsible. The inertia of the civil protection system produced a clear demonstration of serious gaps in the ability of the legal system to respond to natural disasters and other catastrophic events (Chen 2009), revealing that the right to survive Katrina was not granted to all people living in the affected area.

## THE POLITICS OF CATASTROPHES: THE SHAPING POWER OF LAW

The politics of catastrophe outlined at this point could also be read as revelatory of emerging trends in the legal and social shaping of vulnerable subjects. This feature can be an interesting tool to analyze the creation and the shaping of subjects by law. I will briefly explore this feature regarding two possible fields: one related to the relationship between crime and catastrophes and the emergence of patterns of criminalization of victims of catastrophes, and another more focused on the consequences of environmental crises.

In the wake of Katrina, the absence of law as supporting a right to survive was evident, as most vulnerable people lacked assistance. Nevertheless, in this situation law claimed its indispensability in assuring order. The projection of traditional crime attitudes and biases regarding crimes committed during the catastrophe was initiated by wrong reports of crime related to the event. The model of disaster management centered on fusing natural elements such as floods or earthquakes with violent criminality and terrorism, with the risk of a growing amount of coercive law enforced by the state and local authorities (Simon 2007). After its breaking impact on the legal system, the law tries to exploit and colonize the catastrophe (Meyer 2007, p. 21) by avoiding recognition of the particularity of the situation. As the analysis of concepts such as looting during catastrophes seems to confirm (Green 2007), criminal law aims first at reaffirming the coercive power of the state as if the catastrophe had not happened, so that the law continues to operate normally, through ordinary legal categories, even in the exceptional conditions that the law helped create. For example, 'shoot on sight' order against looters shows the attempts of the law to reaffirm its authority, even in a time in which the law seems to have been depleted by events apparently out of its control. This pretension of the law to control the aftermath of a catastrophe seems to be more a matter of a power-driven relationship that one based on a protection-needs pattern of governmental structures with a duty to mitigate damages. From this point of view the criminalization of a catastrophe can be seen as a conscious strategy that relies more on a myth than on empirical findings (Sun 2011). Such a mythology can have practical effects in the way the response to catastrophes is directed, moving the attention from emergency plans to anti-social behaviors.

The analysis of looting in the aftermath of catastrophes confirms that the law *legalizes* the catastrophe in a way that does not allow legal subjects to ask the state to take responsibility for protection or safety, in turn the justification for the state. That is because law sometimes can only serve the aim of protecting state irresponsibility and legitimating immunities and suffering (Veitch 2007). The role of law and the state is to *design* catastrophes as *natural* ones: abdicating its role of protection, endorsing a naturalistic attitude towards these events, such as the myth of "looting in a state of nature," can hide the criminalization done with very different aims from protection. The *(un)natural* catastrophe revealed its racial injustice imposing a different criminal construction for a whole group of persons mainly belonging to a specific racial group.

Environmental refugees can also be seen as another category of legal subject emerging directly from a politics of catastrophes. As a consequence of climate change, we are going to face not only sudden climate shocks but also a slow degradation of the environment: desertification, deforestation and the rising of the sea level are some of the most evident. Technological catastrophes related to pollution and industrial accidents are also relevant here. These events affect larger sections of population in the world and this can cause compulsory displacement. The legal status of these persons is still largely debatable from the point of view of international law (Segal 2001). Scholars in the field have recognized that the legal status of refugees, as the one enshrined in the Geneva Convention, is ambiguous with regard to refugee status as a consequence of environment-related catastrophes.[3] But again we see how catastrophes shape the sense of life on a global scene more as a matter of survival, with an ambiguous legal meaning, rather than as an enforceable right to life that entails a right to be *protected*. The dialectics between a national level and an international one show their intimate link and the difficulty of any analysis only focused on a "global" level that does not try to include the ambiguous role of the state. In both situations, the subsequent criminalization of Katrina and the difficult legal status of environmental refugees, we can find a normative claim to protection, a claim to a right to survive that goes beyond the rights discourse. The indifference of the moving lines of risk to state boundaries make the case for a different understanding of the position of the victims of catastrophes. If we think about them as the recipients of humanitarian response, we reduce the responsibility of the government and argue for a natural event, moved by the forces of nature, that cannot be really reduced in its impact. If we pose the question from a normative stance, intending to translate a claim into rights-discourse, there will be clear interest in de-naturalizing the event and highlighting the failure and the gaps in the system that did not reduce vulnerabilities

---

[3] See the Draft Convention elaborated by the CRIDEAU (Interdisciplinary Center of Research on Environmental, Planning and Urban Law) and the CRDP (Center of Research on persons rights), thematic teams of the OMIJ (Institutional and Judicial Mutations Observatory), from the Faculty of Law and Economic Science, University of Limoges, with the support of the CIDCE (International Center of Comparative Environmental Law) (Prieur *et al.* 2008).

or were not able to help in the aftermath of the extreme event. The normative dimension is all that is left to people that hold rights formally but are excluded from effective citizenship (Somers 2008, pp. 63-117, 114).

## CONCLUSIONS

In this chapter I have shown how law has a role to play in the shaping of the many dimensions of a catastrophe. The legal answer to extreme risk is essentially *undetermined* as globalization is able to spread risk far away from the context in which the hazard can occur. In this scenario, it is important to be aware that there is an unequal exposure to risk and that any extreme event is going to show dramatically how society has been shaped till that very moment. From the legal point of view, a state-based approach and a cosmopolitan one must be combined in a way that can assign a place to a general need to be protected, a normative claim that emerges as a struggle for justice—intended here as protection—from injustice—here the individual left alone in a world of uncontrollable risks. A critical political theory of disasters is urgently needed and this chapter is intended to be a small contribution to such an enterprise.

Catastrophes are just another expression of the Promethean gap between humanity and the world of its products, a gap enlightened by the work of the Austrian philosopher Gunther Anders (Anders 2005). Such a gap can only be filled in by facing catastrophes as a constant presence and threat in our world, minding that the worst-case scenario can only materialize as a dramatic reality: we just don't judge catastrophes possible before their coming into existence (Dupuy 2002).

The treatment of catastrophes by law and governmental institutions is a powerful indicator of how our societies are going to deal with risks of a great harm. We can use catastrophes as "legal epiphanies," since these events can help to understand a bit more about our laws, what values they protect and how they work or should work with the aim of protecting us from vulnerability in the global arena of risks. Law tries to claim control, in an eternal struggle between the break of order and its reaffirmation.

## Bibliography

Acot, P., 2006. *Catastrophes climatiques, désastres sociaux.* Paris: Presses Universitaire de France.

Agamben G., 2005. *State of Exception.* University of Chicago Press.

Anders, G., 2005. *L'uomo è antiquato. 1. Considerazione sull'anima nell'epoca della seconda rivoluzione industriale.* Trans. L. Dallapiccola. Torino: Bollati Boringhieri. Original title: *Die Antiquiertheit des Menschen.*

Beck, U., 1992. *Risk Society: Towards a New Modernity.* London: Sage.

Beck, U., 2003. Toward a New Critical Theory with a Cosmopolitan Intent, *Constellations*, 10 (4), 453-468.

Beck, U., 2009. *World at Risk*. London: Polity Press.

Blaikie P., *et al.*, 1994. *At Risk: natural hazards, people's vulnerability and disasters*. London: Routledge.

Bultrini, R., 2009. Il Sisma in Aula. *D la Repubblica delle Donne* [online], 2 May, 82-87. Available from: http://dweb.repubblica.it/dweb/2009/05/02/societa/societa/082qua64482.html [Accessed 5 March 2013].

Castel, R., 2003. *L'Insécurité sociale: que'est-ce-que etre protégé*. Paris: Seuil.

Chen, J., 2009. Law Among the Ruins. *In*: R.P. Malloy, ed. *Law and Recovery from Disasters: Hurricane Katrina*. Farnham: Ashgate, 1-5.

CRED Centre for Research on the Epidemiology of Disasters, 2013. *EM-DAT: The international Disaster Database* [online]. Available from: http://www.emdat.be/ [Accessed 5 March 2013].

Dombrowsky, W.R., 1998. Again and Again: is disaster what we call a disaster? In: E.L. Quarantelli, ed. *What is a disaster? Perspectives on the question*. London: Routledge.

Douglas, L., Sarat, A., Umphrey, M.M., 2007. A Jurisprudence of Catastrophe: An Introduction. *In*: A. Sarat, L. Douglas, M.M. Umphrey, eds. *Law and Catastrophe*. Stanford University Press.

Dupuy, J.P., 2002. *Pour un catastrophisme eclairé. Quand l'impossible est certain*. Paris: Seuil.

Farber, D.A., *et al.*, eds., 2010. *Disaster Law and Policy*. 2nd ed. New York: Aspen.

Green, S. P., 2007. Looting, Law and Lawlessness. *Tulane Law Review*, 81 (4), 1129-1174.

Klinenberg, E., 2002. *Heat Wave: A Social Autopsy of Disaster in Chicago*. University of Chicago Press.

Malloy, R., ed., 2009. *Law and Recovery from Disasters: Hurricane Katrina and Beyond*. Farnham: Ashgate.

Meyer, L.R., 2007. Catastrophe: Plowing up the Ground of Reason. In: A. Sarat, L. Douglas, M.M. Umphrey, eds. *Law and Catastrophe*. Stanford University Press, 19-32.

Miller, R.A., 2009. *Law in Crisis. The Ecstatic Subject of Natural Disaster*. Stanford University Press.

Neyrat, F., 2008. *Biopolitique des catastrophes*. Paris: Mf.

Oberdiek, J., 2009. Toward a Right Against Risking. *Law and Philosophy*, 28 (4), 367-392.

Oxfam International, 2009. *The Right to Survive. The humanitarian challenge for the twenty-first century*. Oxford: Oxfam.

Posner, R.A., 2004. *Catastrophes: Risk and Responses*. Oxford University Press.

Prieur, M., *et al.*, 2008. Projet de convention relative au statut international des déplacés environnementaux = Draft convention on the international status of environmentally-displaced persons. *Revue européenne de droit de l'environnement*, 4, 381-393, 395-406. Available in English: http://www.cidce.org/pdf/Draft%20Convention%20on%20the%20International%20Status%20on%20environmentally%20displaced%20persons.pdf [Accessed 5 March 2013].

Quarantelli, E.L., 2000. Emergencies, Disasters and Catastrophes Are Different Phenomena, *Preliminary Paper n. 304, University of Delaware—Disaster Research Center*. Available from: http://dspace.udel.edu:8080/dspace/bitstream/handle/19716/674/PP304.pdf?sequence=1 [Accessed 6 March 2013].

Roberts, J.T., and. Parks, B.C, 2007. *A climate of Injustice. Global Inequality, North-South Politics, and Climate Policy*. Cambridge (MA): MIT Press.

Santos, B. de Sousa, 2007. Beyond Abyssal Thinking: From Global Lines to Ecologies of Knowledges. *Review (Fernand Braudel Center)*, 30 (1), 45-89.

Sarat, A., Douglas L., Umphrey, M.M., eds. 2007. *Law and Catastrophe*. Stanford University Press.

Segal, H., 2001. *Environmental Refugees: A New World Catastrophe*. In: D.D. Caron and C. Leben, eds. *The International Aspects of Natural and Industrial Catastrophes*. The Hague: Martinus Nijhoff Publishers, 142-174.

Ségur, P., 1997. La catastrophe et le risque naturel. Essai de définition juridique. *Revue du Droit Public*, 4, 1693-1716.

Simon, J.S., 2007. Wake of the Flood: Crime, Disaster, and the American Risk Imaginary after Katrina. *Issues in Legal Scholarship*, Article 4, 1-19.

Somers, M.S., 2008. *Genealogies of Citizenship: Markets, Statelessness, and the Right to have Rights*. Cambridge University Press.

Sun, L. G., 2011. Disaster Mythology and the Law. *Cornell Law Review* [online], 96(5), 1131-1208. Available from: http://www.lawschool.cornell.edu/research/cornell-law-review/upload/Sun-final.pdf [Accessed 5 March 2013].

UNISDR—The United Nations Office for Dissaster Risk Reduction, 2009. *Terminology on Disaster Risk Reduction* [online]. Available from: http://www.unisdr.org/eng/terminology/terminology-2009-eng.html [Accessed 5 March 2013].

Veitch, S., 2007. *Law and Irresponsibility*. New York: Routledge-Cavendish.

Walter, F., 2008. *Catastrophes. Une histoire culturelle (XVI-XXI siecle)*. Paris: Seuil.

# 4

# THE COMPARATIVE JURISPRUDENCE OF WILDFIRE MITIGATION: MORAL COMMUNITY, POLITICAL CULTURE, AND POLICY LEARNING

## Lloyd Burton

**ABSTRACT**

The cultural and societal diversity in the jurisprudence of living dangerously reflects equally diverse views on the deeper question of law's moral purpose. What duty of care does (or does not) a community owe to those at the greatest risk of harm to their homes and persons? And is there also a right to be left alone—to assume all the risks and all the responsibilities for one's own well-being, neither helped nor hindered by the community of which one is a part?

This chapter reports comparative research being done on two states in the U.S. that have used the law to answer these morally freighted questions in very different ways, with specific regard to land use regulation in forested areas where wildfires have taken many lives and destroyed billions of dollars in residential property. It also suggests how this same analytic framework might be applied to transnational research in other legal cultures also endangered by catastrophic wildfires, such as Australia and Spain.

La diversidad cultural y social en la jurisprudencia de los lugares en los que se vive bajo un peligro refleja equitativamente diferentes opiniones sobre el propósito moral de la ley, un tema más profundo. ¿Qué obligación tiene (o no) una comuni-dad de ofrecer atención a aquellos individuos en mayor riesgo de sufrir daños sobre sus hogares o personas? ¿Y existe también el derecho a que cada uno asuma todos los riesgos y todas las responsabilidades sobre su propio bienestar, sin que le ayude, o le moleste, la comunidad de la que forma parte?

## INTRODUCTION AND OVERVIEW

Are catastrophic natural disasters really so 'natural' if the loss of life and property resulted from people choosing to live in dangerous places? Around the world each year, thousands perish and/or lose their homes and belongings to forest and bushfires, flooding, earthquakes, volcanic eruptions, tsunamis, tornadoes, and hurricanes. And all this loss of life and property takes place in locations where such events been happening regularly for millennia.

These cataclysmic events are not disasters. They are naturally occurring events. They are what the Earth's geosphere, hydrosphere, biosphere, and atmosphere sometimes *do*. What makes them disasters is us—our presence, and our perception of them. We call them disasters (from the Middle French and the Greek: "ill-starred") because in sufficient proximity and scope they threaten our estate, health, safety, social structure, and sometimes our very survival.

People move into harm's way for many reasons. The well-off live in aesthetically pleasing but disaster-prone natural environments such as beaches, coastal bluffs, steep canyons, and forested open space because they like the view and want to be "close to nature" (not nature as it is, of course, but as they wish it to be). The poor live in dangerous circumstances such as neighborhoods in the shadow of dangerous heavy industry, on reclaimed swampland, or in trailer parks in the path of tornadoes because they cannot afford to live anywhere else. Others make their homes in places that—due to factors such as overcrowding or climate change—are more dangerous now than they use to be, like 'one hundred-year' flood plains that now flood every three to five years.

Various cultures and societies use the law in various ways to adjudicate the relationship between at-risk populations and their perilous surroundings. Some lay no restrictions at all on where people can live or in what manner. Some impose absolute "hard law" prohibitions on living in some places and stringent structural and land management requirements for living in others. Some use "soft law" approaches such as public education and requiring full disclosure notice requirements to would-be residents of risky areas, but nothing more.

This cultural and societal diversity in the jurisprudence of living dangerously reflects equally diverse views on the deeper question of law's moral purpose. What duty of care does (or does not) a community owe to those at the greatest risk of harm to their homes and persons? Does this duty differ according to the volition of the residents—that is, between the relatively affluent who willingly move to beautiful but dangerous places, and the disadvantaged who cannot afford to live elsewhere? And is there also a right to be left alone—to assume all the risks and all the responsibilities for one's own well-being, neither helped nor hindered by the community of which one is a part?

In this chapter I describe a research framework for cross-cultural analysis of these questions, within the context of the first category— communities of residents who live in aesthetically pleasing (but relative dangerous) natural environments by choice. The specific environment in question is what in the United States is referred to as the "wild lands/urban interface" (WUI). These are the formerly open spaces sur- rounding major urban areas that are gradually being populated with residents intent on escaping the noise, pollution, pace, and density of urban life. Yet they also still want and to some extent expect amenities that cities offer, such as reliable and effective emergency services, and ease of access to the financial and cultural benefits of urbanity. Desiring neither city life nor the isolation and minimal infrastructure of true rural life, WUI residents live lives on the edge in more ways than one. In fire- prone landscapes, they also inhabit a danger zone.

Sadly, climatologist sand foresters are all telling us to prepare for more rather than fewer wildfire disasters in the future, even as the num- ber of people living in harm's way continues to grow. A 2011 report on climate change impacts prepared by the U.S. National Research Council predicts a 200-400% increase in forest acreage destroyed by wildfires in the United States over the course of this century if current global warming trends continue (U.S. National Research Council 2011).

It is not only the ecosystems, infrastructures, and economies of na- tion-states plagued by wildfires that will be subjected to greater stress by the growing scope of these disasters. Their legal systems will be stressed as well, as conflicts between communities seeking to minimize the conse- quences of disaster and individual community members' resistance to regulation of their land use continue to grow.

Given the scrutiny the law of living in dangerous places is now under, the time seems right to have a closer and deeper look at the moral ground- ing of this body of law, at how various cultures order competing moral claims within the jurisprudence of disasters, and at how this variety is expressed in specific policies and practices across these cultures in the specific context of mitigating death and destruction by wildfires in the WUI. That closer look is what this chapter provides.

Building on existing research in this area, this study first presents a descriptive theoretical construct for understanding the moral dimensions of wildfire mitigation law and policy. Second I apply this construct to the development of case studies of two states in the American West— California and Colorado—that to date have followed different policy paths toward the goal of more effective wildfire mitigation. And third, I suggest how this construct might be similarly applied to case studies of wildfire mitigation in other cultures that share a similar genealogical heritage regarding the moral foundations of law (in this instance, Australia and Spain).

## THE THEORETICAL CONSTRUCT

The construct consists of four related propositions, each flowing from the previous one. In order, they are that:

- *Moral purpose in the law* of modern western nation-states and the institutions that implement it is both discoverable and traceable to a common jurisprudential ancestry.

- *Political culture* is one means by which the polis orders its core values, for the determination of which moral claims will take precedence in the design and function of its laws and the institutions that implement them.

- *Catastrophic disasters challenge the status quo ante.* They may call into question the efficacy of pre-existing laws, policies, and institutions responsible for disaster management if they are perceived to have failed to honor their underlying moral duty to the polis.

- *The long-term sustainability* of both the political culture and the natural environment on which it depends will be determined in part by how flexible the culture is in re-ordering its value structure and its institutional behavior to accommodate changed environmental circumstances.

***Justice and Moral Purpose in Law.*** Since jurisprudence first emerged as a subject of public discourse in ancient times, one of its enduring themes has been articulation of the relationship between that which is legal and that which is just. In their writings on systems of governance and the role of law within them, the classical Greek philosophers did not begin with the question of "What form of government and laws should we have?" The question was instead, "What constitutes the good life?" And thus, "What forms and functions of government are most conducive to making the good life possible?" (Wills 2002).

Aristotle, the leading foundational thinker in the natural law tradition, posited that justice as a governing principle was derived from two interactive sources: an innate human tendency toward virtuous behavior as a necessary precondition to living in a safe and civil community, and social conventions intended to institutionalize virtuous behavior (*Nicomachean Ethics*, Book V, chp. 7). In his writings on the art of political persuasion in the *demos*, he characterized appeals to the virtuous *(ethos)* as one of three prime motivators to political action, along with appeals to reason *(logos)* and to sentiment or passion *(pathos)* (*Rhetoric*, Book I, chp. 2). What Aristotle apparently meant by ethos is a combination of the modeling of moral character on the part of the persuader and the evocation of the good—specifically including principles of justice and fairness—from within the value structure of the community being addressed.

Nearly a millennium later, Aristotle's views helped lay the intellectual foundation for the Emperor Justinian's *Corpus Juris Civilis*, the most comprehensive rendering of the laws of the state and the principles underlying them that the ancient western world ever produce. Within the

*Corpus*, the *Code* contains the substance of the laws governing the empire, while the *Institutes* provide the jurisprudential justification for the exercise of the powers of the state and the rights of its citizenry.

Two doctrines in the *Institutes* are central to understanding the moral underpinnings of modern public law: *jus regium* (law or rights of the regime); and *res publicum* (rights of the public). Both doctrines make clear that the sovereign's only justification for holding such plenary powers is that they be truly exercised on the public's behalf—to regulate private behavior (including land use) in the public interest; and to ensure that the rights of the public (including access to public resources) were protected. This moral imperative on the part of the sovereign to wield its power in the public interest and to honor publicly held rights in doing so found its first expression in English law in *Magna Charta* in 1215 (Patalano 2001).

When 13 of Britain's North American colonies revolted against the British Crown, their Declaration of Independence was in large part an indictment of the sovereign for failing in its moral duty to protect rather than oppress them, and to respect their rights as British subjects. The preamble to the new nation's constitution represents a promise to the American people that the federal government would use its powers for their benefit.

Most state government constitutions also made the same assurances to the public—to the polis. But state government's legal authority to govern on the public's behalf differs from that of the federal government as a matter of federal constitutional law. In 1824 in *Gibbons v. Ogden*, U.S. Supreme Court Chief Justice John Marshall was the first American jurist to use the term "police power" to describe the plenary powers state governments have to govern on behalf of their residents—powers reserved to the states by the 10th Amendment to the U.S. Constitution.

In *Martin v. Waddell's Lessee* in 1842, the high court also affirmed that state governments did indeed inherit both the powers and obligations of *res regium* from the British Crown upon victory in the American Revolution (Tribe 1988). The difference between the doctrine as originated in Roman jurisprudence and exercised as a God-given right by the sovereigns of western Europe was social contract theory holding that the powers of *res regium* emanated from the polis itself.

As American cities grew in size and population density in the late 19th century, so too did associated urban problems, such as frequent devastating fires and the prevalence of deadly infectious diseases. So among the most important early assertions of the municipal police powers were those associated with fire prevention and preventive public health protection (Hoffer 2006). State and federal courts steadily supported the use of these powers; in 1905 the U.S. Supreme Court upheld local government power to require immunization against some potentially fatal communicable diseases.

In the realm of land use regulation, a historic turning point was the Supreme Court's 1926 decision in *Euclid v. Ambler Realty*. Here for the first time the court affirmed the power of the state (and its subordinate local jurisdictions) to engage in comprehensive land use planning and zoning, for the purpose of protecting the "public health, safety, morals, and welfare."

While this decision affirmed state and local government's ability to regulate private rights and behavior in the interests of public health and safety, matters took a very different turn when it came to regulating public morals. As late as the mid-20th century, states in various regions of the country outlawed birth control, prohibited inter-racial marriage, segregated students by race in public schools, and criminalized a woman's efforts to end an unwanted pregnancy.

In each of these examples, the federal courts stepped in to void this use of state and local governments' police powers. Repeatedly, the U.S. Supreme Court ruled that such use of the police powers was itself morally compromised, in that it denied fundamental rights to privacy, personhood, individual dignity, due process and the equal protection of law assured in the federal constitution. Put another way, the national political culture asserted its values regarding such issues to be morally superior to those of state and local governments violating such rights.

As emperor of Rome, Justinian knew from the examples set by his predecessors in office how the power of the state could be used for good or ill, and how the very survival of any regime depends on the judgment of its subjects as to whether the laws of the state were being crafted and enforced in their best interest. The principles he spelled out on the obligations of the state to govern on behalf of the needs and rights of its citizenry may have come too late to save an empire dying from its neglect of such ideals, but they did provide a guiding light for future nation-states seeking moral legitimacy for their use of power.

***Political Culture.*** In the half-century since Almond and Verba's (1965) definitional work on the subject, the concept of political culture has taken on diverse meanings. Generally, it has to do with how the value structure of a given political community (polis) influences the form and function of its governing institutions. Daniel Elazar (1966) also did pioneering work on the subject, offering a 3-part typology of value structures within American states as determinants of political behavior and institutional function.

In one view, political culture is simply the observed variation in how different cultures and societies practice politics and make public policy—an interpretation in which the first word in the phrase carries more emphasis than the second. In Mishler and Pollack's (2003) distinction between "thick" and "thin" culture (in the context of understanding political culture), this view certainly falls into the thin category.

The alternative perspective sees culture as thick indeed (emphasis on the second word)—and in many ways determinative of political behavior. Culture in this view is a 'learned network of patterns of thought and behavior through which members of a defined community understand and relate to themselves, each other, their communities, and their environment' (per Geertz 1973; and Spradley and McCurdy, 1987). It is the community's collective consciousness, including the symbols and systems of meaning it uses to make sense of itself and its surroundings.

Several contemporary scholars of disaster law and policy in the United States allude to the role of culture in influencing how communities respond to past disasters and mitigate against future ones. Peter Schuck (2009) cites American political culture as preferring populism over technocratic expertise in disaster management policy making; federal appellate court judge Richard Posner (2004) goes further, indicting an anti-scientific bias in American popular political culture that too often thwarts the adoption and enforcement of science-based disaster management decision making. And Thomas Birkland (2006) identifies a positive association between the size and scope of a disaster and the likelihood of a realignment of values sufficient to instigate and support disaster policy reform.

If law's ability to fulfill its moral purpose depends in part on the value structure of the polis governed by that law (that is, its political culture), what we need is some sort of litmus test for determining which values support that fulfillment and which ones do not. In other words, with specific regard to the wielding of its police powers, what constitutes moral community?

In *The Moral Commonwealth*, Selznick (1992) proposed just such a normative theory of community, and provides a list of criteria for assessing the degree to which morality informs its use of power. Morally grounded community, he held, is recognizable by its simultaneous honoring of certain key values at some threshold level: historicity, identity, mutuality, plurality, autonomy, participation, and integration.

*Historicity* is both an understanding of and respect for a community's shared history as an important basis for wise decision making about its future. *Identity* derives from shared history (as well as from family lineage, ethnicity, religion, profession, or common purpose); this is the means by which one defines oneself in relation to community.

*Mutuality* connotes reciprocal obligation; it is the duty of care we owe to each other by virtue of community membership, as well as the community's medium for the expression of common purpose (including the making of public policy). *Plurality* refers to "intermediate associations" in the larger community within which individuals can more immediately experience connection with others who hold shared views, interests, and purpose. Without these, community becomes nothing more than the relationship between a collection of individuals and one central authority.

When the values of either mutuality or plurality are coercively enforced, it is nearly always at the expense of personal *autonomy* and liberty. The importance of respect for personal autonomy within community—in both theory and practice—is what most clearly distinguishes Selznick's "liberal communitarianism" from the earlier formative principles of earlier, more conservative communitarian theorists.

Regarding the value of *participation*, Robert Putnam and others' "social capital" and civic engagement are every bit as crucial to Selznick's concept of community as they are to that of either Putnam (1993) or Bellah *et al.* (1985). Personal, voluntary investment in the enterprise of community is ultimately what makes it possible. While autonomy respects the right to be left alone, participation respects equally the right of those who wish to participate to have the opportunity to do so.

Finally, *integration* refers to the "supportive institutions, norms, beliefs, and practices" required to actualize the foregoing values—to ensure that they are all honored simultaneously to some recognizable degree. In Selznick's view, the first six values and the community's ability to hold them all in balance via the seventh, comprise a metric: "the moral quality of a community is measured by its ability to defend all the chief values at stake, to hold them in tension as necessary, and to encourage their refinement and elaboration" (Selznick 1992, p. 364).

The research protocol described in this chapter does just that: it applies Selznick's metric to the study of moral aspects of the law of living in dangerous places as derived in diverse communities, cultures, and geographic environments. Though Selznick's work has been criticized for being somewhat over-reaching in its claims of objective measurability and general applicability, it certainly has relevance for the cultures and cases described in this research. And it is in applying Selznick's general principles to particular cases that the concept of political culture has proven useful.

As Selznick understood, his moral community can only exist within a specific cultural context. And each culture will order the values in his pantheon a little differently, as he also recognized. But to maintain its moral grounding, he argued, a community may not so privilege some values as to ignore or sacrifice others.

**Catastrophic Disasters and the Status Quo Ante.** In the political science policy process literature, considerable attention is devoted to the concept of a "focusing event" as a potential stimulus to policy change. In the specific context of disaster law and policy, authors such as Thomas Birkland (2006) have documented the circumstances under which catastrophic disasters either have or have not resulted in significant law and policy reform.

In most such cases, a popular call usually goes up for policy reform to mitigate against the negative consequences of such event happening in the future. However, only under some circumstances does such reform ensue. Those who benefit from the status quo tend to oppose reform. In order to overcome such resistance and bring about learning-based policy change, several factors must be present: (1) the scope and scale of the disaster must be sufficient in size to compel the attention of the public and policy makers alike, combined with public demand for policy change; (2) pre-existing or quickly assembled coalitions of policy actors (both inside and outside government) must have idea-based diagnoses of the disaster's causative factors as well as evidence-based prescriptions for effective future mitigation; and (3) they must keep public and policy maker attention focused on the issues long enough and intensively enough to achieve the desired reforms (Birkland 2006, at 13%).

***Cultural and Environmental Sustainability.*** In *Collapse*, Jared Diamond (2005) presents a series of cases studies of ancient societies which either came close to or actually did commit ecocide—the fatal degradation (through excessive and unrestrained exploitation) of the life-sustaining capacity of the environment on which their survival depended. As a result of such degradation, the society itself collapsed. Jared's work is a highly cautionary tale. In these cases, he demonstrates how the rigidity and inflexibility of a society's value structure (what today we might call its political culture) prohibited it from rapidly and effectively transitioning to more sustainable environmental management.

In contemporary terms, what the societies that collapsed failed to do was to engage in policy learning and learning-based policy reform that was timely enough and effective enough to stave off environmental doom. The two principal symptoms of impending societal demise were failure to timely acknowledge the severity of environmental disaster the society was bringing about (or at least contributing to); and an inability to realign its value structure sufficiently to adjust their expectations and behaviors to changed environmental realities.

Applied to the study of contemporary wildfire management and policy, Diamond's findings are eerie. The human population in the WUI in some of the world's most fire-prone landscapes goes up every year, as does the death and destruction occasioned by the fires that strike there. And all the climate change models that have been run so far point to the strong likelihood that the wildfire danger will only continue to worsen.

CASE STUDIES: APPLYING THE THEORETICAL
CONSTRUCT TO WILDFIRE MITIGATION

In a catastrophic WUI wildfire, many factors contribute to determining whether lives and properties will be saved or destroyed by the conflagration. These include the characteristics of the fire scene (weather conditions, terrain, vegetative structure), ease of ingress and egress at the fire scene, timely and adequate notice to residents in the fire zone, and interoperability (of communications and fire-fighting technology and lines of authority) among first responder agencies.

Yet fire science research—in both laboratory settings and post-conflagration fire zones—reveal one of the most significant determinants of private property survivability to be characteristics of what fire scientists call the *home ignition zone*. The U.S. Forest Service researchers define this as the area within a 100-foot radius of home (U.S. Department of Agriculture Forest Service 2012, p. 65). The design of structures and the materials of which they are made can make them either fire prone or fire-resistant, to varying degrees. And the relative presence or absence of fuel sources (trees, bushes, and flammable ground cover, as well as piles of firewood and other introduced fuel sources) within the HIZ, in combination with the fire resistance of the structure itself, constitute the most important determinants of whether a structure (and those who may be within it) will survive a major WUI wildfire. Research on Colorado's 2010 Fourmile Canyon fire provides recent compelling evidence that this is so.

It has now been well over a century since major American cities started using their police powers to enforce fire mitigation building construction and maintenance codes within their jurisdictions (Hoffer 2006). In some of America's western states, the same thing is beginning to happen with regard to defensible space ordinances in the WUI. So one goal in the development of these case studies was to learn how state and local government police powers are being deployed HIZ defensible space regulation.

For comparative assessment purposes, I gathered information on two dimensions of the defensible space regulation of private property in the WUI. One is the *locus of authority*—the level of political community at which primary authority for WUI regulation is vested: local, regional, or state. The other is the *form of authority* dimension. What is the mixture of "soft law" and "hard law" in the WUI wildfire mitigation policy? Does it consist primarily of public information and education programs, urging voluntary cooperation with optional mitigation standards? Or are there provisions that impose mandatory mitigation standards on property owners, on either newly built structure or all existing ones in the WUI? Is the severity of the mandate gradated in accordance with the perceived risks? Are there areas in the WUI deemed to be of such high risk that no permanent human habitation is permitted at all?

The case studies of California and Colorado presented here begin with a discussion of the historical roots of their respective political cultures (the second of the four theoretical propositions). I then use this perspective on the value structure of the polis (using Selznick's typology) to help explain differences between the two states in terms of locus and form of authority for land use regulation in the WUI (third proposition), followed by commentary on the moral dimensions of the use of police powers in these two states (first proposition). Then in the concluding section of the chapter I suggest ways this approach may be used to study other cultures and legal regimes located in similarly fire-prone regions of the world. I also stress the importance of searching community self-evaluation in the polis of its value structure relative to its WUI wildfire dangers and its use of *res regium* (in the U.S., state and local police powers) to mitigate those dangers (fourth proposition).

These case studies are like sketches on canvas, outlining the features of the painting that is coming more fully into being in the course of ongoing research. The cases are suggestive of rather than fully illustrative of the analytic framework being used. The U.S. interstate comparative study is ongoing, as data are still being collected and analyzed. The transnational comparative work remains to be done, informed by what has been and is being accomplished now.

***California, the "Bear Flag Republic."*** Archeological evidence indicates that humans have lived in present-day California for at least twelve thousand years, with the highest population concentrations being along the mild-weather, resource-rich coastlines. And when European explorers first ventured into the landscape, it was also mostly via the sea. Spanish colonial governance was seated in the sheltered harbor of Monterey, even as Catholic mission settlements developed there and elsewhere along the coastline, as well as inland.

When Mexico gained its independence from Spain in 1821, California became a Mexican province—though not for long. Just twenty-five years later the United States made war on the unstable and militarily weak Mexican government, and seized millions of acres of formerly Mexican land, including the entirety of California, which essentially became a prize of war (though the 1848 Treaty of Guadalupe Hidalgo along with a cash payment from the U.S. to Mexico put a post-hoc legal imprimatur on the outcome of this war of aggression and acquisition). Notwithstanding that the treaty called for equal treatment of formerly Mexican citizens, the reins of political power were firmly in the hands of the Anglo victors.

When rumors of impending war reached northern California in 1846, expatriate American settlers seized (with no armed resistance) the Mexican Army garrison at Sonoma, captured Commandant Vallejo, and declared California to be a free republic. They fashioned a flag with the words "California Republic" on it, along with a star, a stripe, and the image of a grizzly bear (which settlers were already busily hunting to extinction). Just a week later, a small U.S. Army contingent arrived—confirming the war rumors—and all of California was declared to be an American military protectorate. The republic may have been short-lived, but the banner was not; it remains today as California's official state flag.

At the war's conclusion, Congress failed to declare California an American Territory due to conflict over the question of whether slavery would be allowed there. When it failed to do so again in 1849 (as the Gold Rush was flooding California with new people), the ex-military governor summoned a constitutional convention, which was made up mostly of American settlers. They adopted a fairly liberal constitution (patterned largely on New York's) that established institutions of government, out-lawed slavery, and included a Bill of Rights. Residents governed them-selves as a state under this constitution until Congress finally granted California statehood in 1850 (Lloyd 2001).

So Californians (at least, those who held most of the political power) desperately wanted statehood, and arrogated to themselves that status in advance of congressional action. California was a state born out of war, the political culture of which included strong elements of self-identification as Californians—a short-lived republic, and then a self-declared state before the Congress would recognize it as such. With its fairly robust statewide institutions of government, the 1849 constitutional conventioneers were quite evidently opting for a system of governance that valued highly the principle of *mutuality* as well as unity—sensing the need for laws and institutions sufficiently empowered to forge a unified state out of the sprawling ethnically, geographically, and financially diverse landscape the Spanish and then Mexican governments had never proved capable of governing effectively. Respect for the value of *autonomy*—for individual rights—(though not so much for ethnic diversity) was written into this document as well, but the early history of this constitution's implementation clearly put more emphasis on *unum* than *e pluribus*.

The 1849 Gold Rush catapulted San Francisco into the status of California's pre-eminent city, as nearly all the supplies necessary to support the burgeoning mining and milling industry as well as the railroads and northern California agriculture flowed into the state from the city's deepwater port. And the wealth flowed from the hinterland back into the city, to fuel commerce, banking, manufacture, and communications.

So San Francisco's sudden major-city status owed far more to circumstance than anything resembling rational planning or adequate urban infrastructure. The city burned down five times in the first three years of the Gold Rush, and its criminal laws were enforced mostly by vigilantes (Rubin 2005). It was nearly the end of the nineteenth century before San Francisco came to resemble a fully structured city in the same sense of those in the eastern United States.

And then in 1906 it burned down again, the fire this time being started by a huge earthquake. Nearly every major structure in the city was damaged or destroyed by the combined effects of the earthquake and fire. In the wake of this unprecedented disaster, there were calls for rational urban planning, building codes to make structures safer, and limitations on what could be built where. But all of these efforts were successfully resisted by the city's moneyed commercial, financial, and real estate interests, who spoke only of the great San Francisco fire and minimized the role of the earthquake's devastation. Even though most of the deaths and injuries were caused by collapsing structures rather than fire, city leaders feared that if San Francisco came to be known as a place where devastating "acts of God" could again level the city, real estate investors and property insurance companies might decide to take their business elsewhere.

Geologists at the University of California immediately undertook a seismic survey of the city in response to the 1906 event, and founded the seismological society that would soon document the fact that nearly every city of any size in the state was built on or near a major earthquake fault. Their findings went unheeded by civic and government leaders at the time, but highly destructive earthquakes in Santa Barbara in 1925 and Long Beach in 1933 (along faults the scientists had already located) prompted the California Legislature to enact the first statewide mandatory seismic safety building codes. It turned out that *not* having such as code was more discouraging to investors and insurers than having one.

Protecting public health and safety is one of the prime legal as well as moral rationales for empowering governments to articulate and enforce our mutual commitments to our own well-being, even if it is at the partial expense of the autonomy of those resisting regulation. In California, science, historicity, and a sense of common purpose in its political culture dating back to the founding of the state made statewide disaster mitigation through land and property use regulation a reality.

This precedent having been established, other disaster mitigation laws followed. They addressed some of the other deadly environmental events to which the state is prone, such as landslides, flooding, and wildfires at the WUI. By the 1970s, the WUI had grown so dramatically throughout the state (along with the incidence of wildfires within that zone) that the leadership combined fire services at the local, regional, and statewide levels met to develop their own integrated disaster management system. These meetings, in turn, informed creation of the all-hazards, all-phases disaster management framework set forth in the National Governors' Association 1979 report on integrated emergency management.

The history of the evolution of California WUI wildfire law and policy is intertwined with the history of ever-more deadly and disastrous fires at the WUI (Lundberg 2009). In reviewing news accounts of major WUI California wildfires over the last three decades, the phrase "worst wildfire in California history" appears frequently. This is because in every drought cycle, the fires that raged through the WUI were larger, more deadly, and more destructive because the perimeter of the WUI itself had expanded. So every three to five years, the state would suffer another, larger Worst Fire in State History. The forests were not moving down into the cities and setting them ablaze. The cities were moving up into the forests, and into the deadly gears of the seasonal wildfire cycle that is a defining characteristic of much of California's open space.

The first policy response was to better coordinate multi-jurisdictional firefighting efforts (the all-hazards, all-phases framework for unified command of major wildfire suppression efforts). While a necessary measure, it proved to be an insufficient one. So just as fire departments in municipalities have the authority to enforce building and maintenance codes for the prevention of fires, so too did the California Legislature empower the state fire marshal and fire service to adopt mandatory statewide regulations for wildfire prevention.

Nearly all of California's deadly WUI fires rise in the parched landscapes of the southern chaparral regions in the mountains above urban centers such as San Diego, San Bernardino, and Los Angeles. But in 1991, the Tunnel Fire flaring up suddenly in the hills above Berkeley and Oakland killed 25 people and destroyed 3,500 residences collectively worth more than $1.6 billion. Then two years later the Laguna Beach fire and others back in southern California destroyed over 1,600 homes.

In keeping with the policy learning/policy reform model described by Birkland (2006), in 1993 the California Legislature adopted the "Bates Bill." This amendment to Government and Natural Resources Codes represented a fundamental reform of WUI wildfire mitigation law. It directed the state fire marshal to create two kinds of maps: one to divide the entire state into zones based on their degree of vulnerability to catastrophic wildfires; and the other to demarcate what firefighting service (local, state, or federal) at the WUI had fiscal responsibility for wildfire mitigation and suppression in what specific areas of the state: State Responsibility Areas (SRAs) and Local Responsibility Areas (LRAs).

The law also empowered the state fire marshal to write a model code containing mitigation requirements for adoption and enforcement by local government in areas for which they have fire management responsibilities. City and county governments could avoid adopting such a code only if they had substantial evidence showing that the fire marshal was incorrect in designating lands within their borders as high-hazard zones—a daunting burden of proof. In essence, what the Bates Bill did was to grant to the state fire marshal many of the same science-based discretionary authorities to mitigate against WUI wildfires that had been held by municipal fire marshals since the beginning of the 20th century.

As the code is written, the greater the wildfire hazard in a given zone, the more stringent the property management requirements. For instance, the more hazardous, the greater the space around a structure that must be clear of flammable vegetation and other materials, and the more fire-resistant the materials comprising such structures must be.

Since this regulatory framework was adopted, it has been amended several times in response to lessons learned from ensuing catastrophic wildfires—each time in the direction of more stringent regulations to close loopholes in the previous ones. In October of 2003, for example, the Cedar Fire—the latest Worst Fire in California's History—broke out in San Diego County, eventually burning over 270,000 acres and destroying over two thousand homes. Fourteen people died, including one firefighter. Over 60 local, state, and federal fire service agencies were eventually mobilized, putting into the field more than 15,000 firefighters. Other large fires in San Diego County simultaneously burned with equal ferocity, but were smaller in scope.

Up until that time, new subdivisions built in San Diego County were allowed to include homes with highly flammable wooden shake shingle roofs. And haphazard residential land development on steep hillsides in narrow canyons with equally narrow roads proved to be a deadly combination: thirteen of the deaths in what was to become known as the "San Diego Firestorm" were among residents trapped in one subdivision in just such circumstances (Lundberg 2009). As a result, WUI building codes in high-risk areas in California no longer allow the use of flammable roofs in new construction, and ingress and egress requirements in newly build neighborhoods have also been employed.

How one defines a "worst fire" or "worst fire season" depends on how the word "worst" is defined. The southern California season of 2007, which included hundreds of fires throughout the region (the largest ones again in San Diego County) created nearly one million fire refugees, which comprised the largest peacetime movement of displaced persons in the history of the United States. State legislation the following year moved the defensible space perimeter in very high-hazard WUI zones from thirty out to one hundred feet, and enhanced the state's efforts to control tree-killing bark beetle epidemics in its forests.

As in Colorado, there is a strong "home rule" clause in the California

Constitution that gives incorporated cities in the state a great deal of autonomy in crafting policies and ordinances that do not directly conflict with state law and constitutional authority. Thus, the *plurality* and *autonomy* values of local communities are recognized in the California Constitution, as are the autonomy values of individuals in the protection of rights in private property.

When it comes to wildfire mitigation at the WUI, however, the California Legislature was very explicit in terms of the assertion of the *mutuality* value at the level of statewide political community. In setting forth the rationale for the 1993 Bates Bill, legislators declared, "The prevention of wildland fires is not a municipal affair, as that term is used in . . . the California Constitution, but is instead, a matter of statewide concern" (Cal. Govt. Code 51175).

The rationale for this assertion of plenary state authority over wildfire mitigation at the WUI exemplifies the very essence of the mutuality value. It avails a local community at the WUI little if it does everything possible to mitigation wildfire devastation, but its neighboring communities do little or nothing. They will all be destroyed by the same fire. Uneven, inconsistent, or non-existent patchwork regulation at the local level has cost Californians billions of dollars in property losses, and several hundred of them their lives. It was the intent to the legislature to ensure that no one lose their lives or property by reason of their neighbor's failure to maintain a fire-safe property.

California's centralized, state-driven system of wildfire mitigation regulations in high-risk areas of the WUI, where an estimated forty percent of all homes in California are located, certainly does represent the subordination of individual and local government autonomy to the authority of the state. But it rests on the understanding that everyone living in and every community located in the WUI bears a reciprocal duty to each other—a mutually held obligation—to manage their own property not just to protect their own well-being, but that of their neighbors as well.

**Colorado, Where Home Rule Rules.** Each U.S. state has its own official nickname, or self-descriptor. California is the "Golden State." Colorado is the "Centennial State," since Congress granted it statehood in 1876, just a century after the founding of the United States. But Colorado might just as well have been named the "Reluctant State," or the "Ambivalent State." For in marked contrast to California's eagerness to assume statehood, it was seventeen years from the time that residents of present-day Colorado first voted on statehood (against it) until the "Centennial State" was born.

In 1859, residents voted by a ratio of three to one against statehood and in favor of becoming a federal territory instead. The argument that carried the day against statehood was that if Coloradans voted themselves into statehood, they would also have to tax themselves to finance the state government. However, as long as the area remained a federal territory, it was the federal government that would bear fiscal responsibility for administering it (Abbot, Leonard, Noel 2005).

Coloradans voted against statehood again in 1864. In 1865, they voted in favor, but President Andrew Johnson vetoed the bill. He also vetoed later attempts; historians suspect it was because the Democratic president did not want to see two senators from a strongly Republican new state seated in the Congress (Abbott, Leonard, Noel 2005). It took several more votes and petitions and a more welcoming president to usher Colorado into the union in 1876.

It has since been argued, and with substantial historical evidence, that the strong libertarian influence on Colorado politics and public discourse today can trace its roots back to these very early attitudes favoring either no government or as little government as possible—and preferably one that someone else has to pay for. As contrasted with California, from its very inception, the political culture of Colorado has been one that places a much higher premium on the values of autonomy and plurality (in this case, empowering local and intermediate levels of government at the expense of the state—and empowering them no more than absolutely necessary) than on the mutuality value at the state level that is the ultimate source of moral authority for stronger state laws.

A comparative look at environmental management generally in the two states illustrates the very different approaches they have taken in terms of institutional design. For example, the federal Clean Air Act and Clean Water Act devolve very substantial implementation authority to state (and in some cases regional and local) governments, should those governments wish to assume such powers. When Congress was first crafting these laws, representatives from California and some other populous states argued successfully for the inclusion of provisions empowering the states to establish more stringent environmental protection regulations than the federal ones if they wished to do so, and still have those regulations enforceable as federal law. And California subsequently did just that. Clean air and clean water standards in California are substantially stronger with regard to certain pollutants and regional environments.

As in California, Colorado legislators also adopted clean air and clean water legislation in order to enable state regulators to enforce federal law. The difference in Colorado is that—instead of adopting stricter standards—the legislator forbade state regulators from enacting environmental health protection standards that are any more stringent than the federal ones. The contrast in political cultures between the two in this regard is fairly stark; Colorado simply favors weaker state governmental institutions in the realm of environmental management and environmental protection generally than does either California or some other states in the Mountain West.

So it should come as no surprise that while California has among the strongest statewide mandatory WUI wildfire mitigation laws in the nation, Colorado has none. It has adopted some aspects of the California approach, including the mapping of WUI fire hazard levels statewide, and differentiating areas for which the state and local governments, respectively, have fiscal responsibility for fire suppression. But there is no mandatory WUI wildfire mitigation law in the state, and most such regulation at the local level applies only to new construction.

Colorado law does go as far as far as requiring that counties with high-risk WUI zones adopt community wildfire protection plans. But the law does not specify specific defensible space measures to be taken, nor does it mandate their inclusion in county plans. It only directs that county governments shall "take into consideration" recommendations from the state forester regarding WUI mitigation measures.

As a result, some counties have developed fairly rigorous WUI mitigation regulations at least with regard to newly built or newly remodeled structures, while other high-risk jurisdictions have done little or nothing. So the state has a patchwork of uneven local regulation, which has led to equally uneven levels of protection from wildfire. Some landscapes are considerably more at risk than others not by reason of natural conditions alone but also by a lack of attention to forest fire fuels management on private property.

To compound the situation, the U.S. Forest Service has also been compelled by budget constraints to make some hard choices as to which forests it will expend funds to clear of excess fuels along the WUI, and which ones it will not. No matter how hard a mountain community works to make itself fire-safe, if the surrounding national forest has not been thinned of excess trees and undergrowth and succumbs to a racing crown fire, the community can still be at peril.

Colorado is no stranger to destructive WUI wildfires. In the 21st century alone, the state has experienced a series of increasingly destructive—and very recently, deadly—conflagrations. Colorado's two Worst Fires in State History (depending again on the definition of "worst") both occurred in the century's first decade. The greatest acreage burned was in the 2002 Hayman Fire in the Pike National Forest in the mountains ninety miles southwest of Denver. About 138,000 acres of forest on both public and private lands burned down, but only 132 homes (about 600 structures total). No human lives were directly lost in the fire (Kent *et al.* 2003). Property insurance claims totaled $46 million (Bounds and Snider 2010).

The 2010 Fourmile Fire (in Fourmile Canyon, five miles north of Boulder, Colorado) was quite another story. Though it burned only 6,000 acres of public and private forestland, it destroyed 169 homes, resulting in $217 million in insurance claims. Reasons for this contrast to the Hayman fire include the fact that Fourmile Canyon is much more densely populated, the terrain is steeper and less accessible, and the assessed value of the homes was much higher. In Colorado, about 14% of the WUI has been subjected to exurban residential development; in Boulder County, over 60% of the WUI is now residentially occupied. This makes Boulder County home to the most densely populated WUI in the state, and the tenth densest in the entire Mountain West (Bounds and Snider 2010). Fortunately, no one died in the Fourmile Fire.

However, as of the end of 2011, this fire history appears to have had little meaningful effect on the process of either policy learning or policy reform. No state legislative measures similar to California's Bates Bill arose during the 2011 law-making session. And in fact, there is some evidence that at least at the local level, the policy process is moving in the other direction.

Summit County, Colorado sits atop the Continental Divide, and within it are some of the state's most popular ski resort towns. The county has no mandatory WUI mitigation requirements for pre-existing structures, but does require that in high-hazard areas all new construction and major remodeling work be done with fire-resistant materials, and that a defensible space perimeter be created.

Prior to the 2009 fire season, the city council in the Summit County resort community of Breckenridge decided to go further, and adopted an ordinance requiring all homeowners within the city limits (which extend well up into the forested hillsides) to create defensible space around their existing homes and other structures. But within two months, the ordinance itself had gone up in smoke. A local real estate agent organized an initiative to rescind the ordinance on the argument that "thinning vegetation to create fire breaks around mountain homes 'should be a homeowner's choice'" (Finley 2009). The city council then voted to make defensible space activities voluntary, leaving other resort community governments in the mountains very reluctant to adopt any form of mandatory mitigation regulation.

During an unseasonably hot, dry, windy spell in March of 2012, the deadly Lower North Fork WUI wildfire broke out in the mountains west of Denver in suburban Jefferson County, killing three residents and destroying over two dozen homes. Interestingly, in the immediate aftermath of the fire, press coverage of the three lives and homes lost focused only on an out-of-control prescribed burn and a faulty phone warning system as causative factors. There was no mention made at all of the defensible space status of the homes destroyed—including those residents received no warning to flee.

***Comparing the Cases.*** California is only a third larger than Colorado in geographical area, but it has six times more residents. Forty per cent of California's housing stock (and thus, a relatively high percentage of its population) is in the WUI. By contrast, over eighty percent of Colorado's population lives in towns and cities along the Front Range, the seam where the state's eastern prairies meet the base of the Rocky Mountains. And while the population is definitely growing along the WUI interface as the cities' exurbs move up into the foothills, the great majority of Front Range residents live down in the cities of Denver, Boulder, Aurora, Fort Collins, Colorado Springs, and Pueblo. Generally, the WUI in the high country along the Continental Divide and in the mountains to the west is much less populated than the Front Range, although that is changing. Thus, California's wildfires are generally deadlier because its WUI is far more vast and much more densely populated.

There is occasional public debate in Colorado over whether it would be wise for the state to adopt some form of mandatory WUI wildfire mitigation statute, like California's or Nevada's. So far, the sentiment against such a law has prevailed, based mostly on two arguments. The first is that such a statute represents an unwarranted intrusion into the realm of private property rights, on the view that it should be an individual property owner's choice whether to mitigate against the threat of wildfire, or take the risks associated with doing nothing.

The second argument is that since Colorado has never experienced anything approximating the massive, costly, deadly fires that commonly strike California, such a law is not needed. As of this writing, it remains to seen whether the fatalities in the 2012 Lower North Fork fire will make such mandatory state regulation more likely.

What this raises is the larger question of law's moral purpose, and the competing arguments over that purpose—specifically, in this instance, the debate over preventive versus reactive regulation (Burton and Egan 2011). Colorado is now rapidly doing the same thing that California did in the 1970's—filling its fairly inaccessible, fire-prone mountain canyons and ravines with housing, and thus inviting those who can afford to do so to move directly into harm's way. In so doing, however, neither growth-hungry Colorado counties nor the state is so far applying any of the tragic lessons California has learned from its wildland/urban interface residents assume such terrible risks and suffer such profound losses.

Reactive regulation means not employing the regulatory authority of the state until repeated catastrophes have demonstrated an undeniable need for such regulation. At that point, regulation can consist of only remedying the specific causes of the past disaster (reactive), or it can be transmuted into a more preventive form—anticipating the likelihood of similar future events, and proactively regulating in a way that mitigates against the likelihood of a catastrophe of similar scope and harm occurring in the future.

California started making the move from reactive to proactive statewide regulation in the realm of seismic safety as early as the 1930's, and in WUI wildfire mitigation nearly two decades ago. Policy learning of the sort described by Birkland (2006) was very much in evidence in the steadily shifting WUI wildfire mitigation law in California. Each new wildfire catastrophe in the WUI gave rise to more stringent statewide mitigation measures. Given Colorado's political culture, however, it may be that effective, preventive WUI wildfire mitigation law and policy must await more uncontrolled residential infilling in the WUI, and then uncontrollable wildfires that may take lives as well as property.

WUI defensible space regulation is a means, not an end. The end is to mitigate against the loss of lives and property in WUI wildfires. Colorado may indeed figure out a way to use its relatively soft-law, local control approach to achieve these ends. The stakes are high in this experiment, however. Colorado continues to rapidly populate its WUI, just as are other states in America's Mountain West. More and more people are moving into harm's way, making the question of what duty of care its government may or may not owe them ever more urgent.

IMPLICATIONS FOR A TRANSNATIONAL COMPARATIVE RESEARCH AGENDA

In-depth research on the comparative law and policy approaches to WUI wildfire mitigation in California and Colorado is already under way, and will continue for some time—probably encompassing some other fire-prone states in the American West, such as New Mexico and Arizona. But just as this work may help provide a framework within which various states can learn more of each other's approach to WUI mitigation, so too can comparison with other nation states enhance that learning potential for all concerned. Scholars and regulators from the Common Law countries of Australia and the United States may have a lot to learn from each other, regarding how the local, state, and national governments of each has accommodated common law principles of the jurisprudence of property into their respective regulatory regimes, and addressed the moral arguments raised for and against WUI wildfire mitigation.

And comparing these regimes with the regulatory approach to mitigation taken in the equally fire-prone landscapes of a European Union member country such as Spain can make for an even richer learning experience, especially when all three of these bodies of law and policy are viewed through the common framework of something like Selznick's criteria for the constitution of moral community. In addition to the policies of its autonomous regions and national government, regulators in Spain must also factor in the general directives of the European Commission, which has already taken a heavily mutualistic stance in its adoption of the precautionary principle in the area of public health and safety regulation (Ponce 2013).

Research applying the four descriptive theoretical propositions set out in this paper to transnational studies involving nations such as Australia and Spain might yield some important insights into the methods these nations and the U.S. do and don't use to mitigate the dangers to populations in a given political community who live in harm's way. More specifically, a great deal might be revealed in terms of policy learning and values realignment by comparing the substance of wildfire mitigation law before and after the February (summer), 2009 "Black Friday" fires that engulfed vast swaths of residential landscape and took 178 lives in the Australian State of Victoria.

In the northern hemisphere, the hot, dry, windy summer of 2009 saw similarly devastating wildfires devour as much landscape and take lives in Mediterranean Europe. Spain and Greece were especially hard-hit. A before-and-after search for wildfire mitigation policy reform in Spain's local and national levels of government as well as that of the European Commission could yield valuable insights into whether policy learning and any degree of wildfire mitigation law reform has occurred there as well.

All of Britain's former colonies around the Pacific Rim—including Australia and the United States—share with the civil law nations of Europe a common ancient intellectual heritage on the subject of law and moral community. It dates back to Aristotle and to Justinian's *Institutes*.

It has since been explicated by an array of Enlightenment, Romantic, Modern, and post-Modern political and legal philosophers.

This heritage is also an important basis for studying the comparative jurisprudence of wildfire mitigation. From these shared origins, we may be able to discern a common moral purpose in the goal of protecting ourselves from catastrophic harm, even if we use different means.

A lot depends on our ability to learn from our own and each other's experience in trying to mitigate against the effects of major natural disasters such as WUI wildfires. As Jared Diamond demonstrated in *Collapse*, our ability to save ourselves, our estates, our communities, and the integrity of our own cultures and institutions is in the balance.

Nature's four archetypical elements of earth, water, wind, and fire will continue to do what they have always done: burn, shake and split, storm, and flood. These are not "ill-starred" events except to the extent that we choose to live in harm's way oblivious to what Nature is up to. Perhaps Shakespeare was on to something, when in the voice of Cassius in *Julius Caesar*, he observed, "The fault, dear Brutus, lies not in our stars, but in ourselves."

## Bibliography

Abbot, A., Leonard, S. and Noel, T., 2005. *Colorado: A history of the centennial state.* 4th ed. Boulder, CO: Univ. Press of Colorado.

Almond, G. and Verba, S., 1965. *The civic culture.* Boston, MA: Little, Brown and Co.

Aristotle. *Nicomachean Ethics.*

Aristotle. *Rhetoric.*

Bellah, R., *et al.,* 1985. *Habits of the heart.* Berkeley, CA: Univ. of California Press.

Birkland, T., 2006. *Lessons of disaster—policy change after catastrophic events.* Washington, D.C.: Georgetown Univ. Press.

Bounds, A. and Snider, L., 2010. At $217M in damage, fourmile fire most expensive in Colorado history. *Boulder daily camera* [online], 20 Sep. Available from: http://www.dailycamera.com/fourmile-canyon-fire/ci_16124907 [Accessed 25 February 2013].

Burton, L. and Egan, M., 2011. Courting disaster: systemic failures and reactive responses in Railway Safety Regulation. *Cornell journal of law and public policy* [online], 20 (3), 533-569. Available from: http://www.lawschool.cornell.edu/research/JLPP/upload/Burton-Egan-final.pdf [Accessed 25 February 2013].

Diamond, J., 2005. *Collapse: How societies choose to succeed or fail.* New York: Penguin Group.

Elazar, D., 1966. *American federalism: a view from the states.* New York: Thomas Y. Crowell.

Finley, B., 2009. Breckenridge's widlfire-safety law rescinded. *Denver Post* [online], 1 Aug. Available from: http://www.denverpost.com/news/ci_12970233 [Accessed 25 February 2013].

Geertz, C., 1973. *The interpretation of cultures: selected essays.* New York: Basic Books.

Kent, B., *et al.*, 2003. Social and economic issues of the hayman fire. *In*: R.T. Graham, Technical Ed. *Hayman Fire Case Study. Gen. Tech. Rep. RMRS-GTR-114.* Ogden, UT: U.S. Department of Agriculture, Forest Service, Rocky Mountain Research Station, 315-396. Available from: http://www.fs.fed.us/rm/pubs/rmrs_gtr114.pdf [Accessed 25 February 2013].

Hoffer, P., 2006. *Seven fires: the urban infernos that reshaped America.* New York: Penguin.

Kuh, K., 2012. When government intrudes: regulating individual behaviors that harm the environment. *Duke law journal* [online], 61 (6), 1111-1181. Available from: http://scholarship.law.duke.edu/dlj/vol61/iss6/1/ [Accessed 25 February 2013].

Lloyd, G., 2001. Nature and convention in the creation of the 1849 California constitution. *Nexus, a Journal of opinion,* 6, 23-42.

Lundberg, K., 2009. The San Diego firestorm. *In*: A. Howitt and H. Leonard, eds. *Managing crises.* Washington, DC: CQ Press.

Mishler, W. and Pollack, D., 2003. On culture, thick and thin: toward a neo-cultural synthesis. *In*: D. Pollack, ed. *Political culture in post-communist Europe.* Burlington, VT: Ashgate.

Patalano, D.J., 2001. Note: police power and the public trust: prescriptive zoning through the conflation of two ancient doctrines. *Boston college environmental affairs law review* [online], 28, 683-718. Available from: http://www.bc.edu/content/dam/files/schools/law/lawreviews/journals/bcealr/28_4/11_FMS.htm [Accessed 25 February 2013].

Ponce, J., 2013. Land Use Planning and Disaster: A European Perspective From Spain. *Oñati Socio-legal Series* [online], 3 (2), 196-220 (Chapter 2 of this book). Also available from: http://ssrn.com/abstract=2221235 [Accessed 28 April 2013].

Posner, R., 2004. *Catastrophe.* Oxford, New York: Oxford University Press.

Putnam, R., 1993. The prosperous community: social capital and public life. *American prospect* [online], 4. Available from: http://prospect.org/article/prosperous-community-social-capital-and-public-life [Accessed 25 February 2013].

Rubin, C., ed., 2005. *Emergency management: the American experience 1900-2005.* Fairfax, VA: Public Entity Risk Institute.

Schuck, P., 2009. Crisis and catastrophe in science, law, and politics. *In*: A. Sarat and J. Lezaun. *Catastrophe: law, politics, and the humanitarian impulse.* Cambridge, MA: University of Massachusetts Press, Chp. 1.

Selznick, P., 1992. *The moral commonwealth.* Berkeley, CA: University of California Press.

Somers, M., 1995. What's political or cultural about political culture and the public sphere? Toward an historical sociology of concept formation. *Sociological theory*, 13 (2), 113-144.

Spradley, J. and McCurdy, D., 1987. *Conformity and conflict*. 6th ed. Boston: Little, Brown.

Tribe, L., 1988. *American constitutional law*. 2nd ed. Mineola, NY: Foundation Press.

U.S. Department of Agriculture Forest Service, 2012. *Fourmile canyon fire preliminary findings Gen. Tech. Rep. RMRS-GTR-289* [online]. Fort Collins, CO: U.S. Department of Agriculture, Forest Service, Rocky Mountain Research Station. Available from: http://www.fs.fed.us/rm/pubs/rmrs_gtr289.pdf [Accessed 25 February 2013].

U.S. National Research Council, 2011. *Climate stabilization targets: emissions, concentrations, and impacts over decades to millennia*. Washington, D.C.: National Academies Press

Wills, G., 2002. *A necessary evil: a history of American mistrust of government*. New York: Simon and Schuster.

# 5

# TRANSBOUNDARY IMPACTS OF THE 2010 HAITI EARTHQUAKE DISASTER: FOCUS ON LEGAL DILEMMAS IN SOUTH FLORIDA

Alka Sapat and Ann-Margaret Esnard

**ABSTRACT**

Catastrophic disasters affect not just the areas/regions and countries where they strike, but also have transboundary effects and repercussions on neighboring countries, which often serve as receiving areas for displaced survivors. South Florida, for example, served as a receiving area for earthquake survivors after the 2010 Haiti earthquake. To understand the transboundary sociolegal impacts on host communities, we draw theoretical insights from research on transboundary crises and interviewed key members of school districts, city and county governments, non-profit organizations, relief task forces, the Haitian-American diaspora, and local government agencies. We also looked at relevant plans/policies modified by governmental and non-governmental institutions in response to the legal issues that arose. The findings highlight the manner in which street-level workers in state and non-state organizations deal with legal complexities and ramifications, along with the role played by the Haitian-American diaspora actors and their networks.

Los desastres por catástrofes no afectan solo a las áreas/regiones y países a los que golpean, sino que también tienen efectos transfronterizos y repercuten en los países vecinos, que a menudo sirven como áreas de recepción para los sobrevivientes desplazados. El sur de Florida, por ejemplo, sirvió como área de acogida para los supervivientes del terremoto de Haiti de 2010. Para entender el impacto sociojurídico a nivel transfronterizo en las comunidades de acogida, se trazan nuevas percepciones teóricas a partir de la investigación de crisis transfronterizas, y mediante entrevistas a miembros clave de distritos escolares, gobiernos de ciudades y condados, organizaciones sin ánimos de lucro, grupos de trabajo de auxilio, la diáspora haitiano-estadounidense, y agencias del gobierno local. También se estudian los planes/políticas relevantes, modificados por las instituciones gubernamentales y no gubernamentales para responder a las cuestiones jurídicas que se plantearon. Los resultados destacan cómo se enfrentan los trabajadores a nivel de calle de las organizaciones estatales y no estatales a las complejidades y consecuencias legales, junto con el papel desempeñado por los protagonistas de la diáspora haitiano-estadounidense y sus redes de contactos.

## INTRODUCTION

Crises and catastrophic disasters in today's globalized world can affect not just the areas/regions and countries where they strike, but may also have transboundary effects and repercussions on neighboring countries, and nations which serve as receiving areas and host communities for displaced survivors. These transboundary effects may have legal, social, political, and economic implications for home and host countries. While disaster research and scholarship has steadily grown in the last few decades (e.g. Dynes 1970, Quarantelli 1983, Mileti 1999, Rodriguez, Quarantelli and Dynes 2006, Oliver-Smith 2009, Smith 2011), more insights are needed on the transboundary nature of disasters and related social and legal issues that affect host countries. For instance, host communities often have to deal with immigration issues related to the medical treatment of displaced survivors. At other times, they need to navigate intergovernmental complexities in the interpretation of national or state statutes applicable to displacees. While there have been some studies on the role of first responders in dealing with disasters, these studies have, however, typically focused on domestic disasters (Schneider 1992, 1995, 2011, Flynn 2007, Dearstyne 2007). We know much less about the role played by state and non-state agencies in responding to transboundary disasters or about the legal complexities engendered by the latter.

This chapter seeks to address such issues and dilemmas by focusing on the 2010 earthquake in Haiti. This catastrophic magnitude 7 earthquake and its aftermath highlighted inherent but understudied legal and related social complexities of disaster recovery and displacement on a national and transnational level. South Florida, home to an estimated 263,000 Haitians, served as a receiving area for severely injured earthquake survivors and for school-aged displacees. In doing so, host communities and state and non-state agencies had to deal with several issues for which the legal solutions were not clearly defined. This chapter attempts to shed light on the transboundary effects of disasters and more specifically on the legal issues that can arise from cross-boundary displacement of disaster survivors. Our main research questions for this chapter are as follows:

1. What were the transboundary legal ramifications of the Haiti earthquake?

2. How did state and non-state organizations at the frontlines of response within Florida deal with these legal complexities arising from the transboundary effects of the earthquake and the resulting influx of displacees who came into Florida?

3. What role did diaspora actors and their networks play in aiding institutional responses to the Haiti earthquake?

To address these questions, we examined four key issues: 1) terminology and definitions used for displacees; 2) immigration and citizenship issues; 3) regulations and policy practices; and 4) compensation, federalism and implementation of laws. In exploring these issues and their management, we also focus on how transnational actors such as diasporas can play a role in the framing and interpretation of legal issues. Our contention here is that these groups can be critical players in dealing with the legal and related social ramifications of transboundary crises and disasters.

We begin by discussing theories and past research about transboundary crises that are relevant to this paper. Next, we provide information on our study area, data sources and methodology which include primary data from interviews with key members of the Haitian-American diaspora, school districts, city and county governments, non-profit organizations, relief task forces, and local government agencies. We also looked at relevant plans and policies modified or adopted by governmental and non-governmental institutions in response to the sociolegal issues that have arisen as part of our analysis and when referred to by our interviewees. Based on these data, in the third section of the chapter, we analyze key legal issues discussed above in the context of South Florida, which serves as our case study. In the fourth section of the chapter, we discuss the importance of street-level bureaucrats and the role of formal and informal networks as related both to inter-agency coordination and diaspora actors; we analyze some of our findings with regard to the role of these actors in responding to legal and other transboundary issues that emerged after the earthquake. We conclude with some recommendations for future research on the legal and other transnational effects of disasters, their implications for street-level bureaucrats, and the role of diaspora (or immigrants) actors in transnational displacement.

## TRANSBOUNDARY CRISES AND DISASTERS

In an increasingly globalized world, crises or disasters have repercussions not just within the nation-states in which they occur; their impacts may be felt beyond nation-state boundaries. For instance, the 2004 Indian Ocean Tsunami affected thousands of people in coastal communities and tourists, businesses, and other groups around the world. More recently, the 2011 Tohoku earthquake in Japan and its effects within Japan disrupted supply chains around the world and spread fears of nuclear radiation far beyond its borders. Similarly, the focus of the research in this study, the 2010 earthquake in Haiti resulted in the displacement of survivors across Haiti and into the United States and other countries.

Despite the disruptive nature of such crises and the ways in which they are perceived, framed, and managed by policy-makers, leaders, and citizenry of affected nation-states, there has been relatively little attention paid to transboundary crises in disaster and policy research (Boin, Groenleer and Sundelius 2007, Clifford 1956, Rosenthal and Hart 1998, Wachtendorf 2000). Only recently has greater attention been paid to the transboundary nature of disasters and its implications particularly in the context of crises and disasters that extend beyond politically and socially constructed borders (Boin 2009a, 2009b, Boin and Rhinard 2008, Ansell, Boin and Keller 2010, Wachtendorf 2000, 2009).

Some part of this scholarly work has focused on defining the concept of crises that cross boundaries; for instance, the term "trans-system social ruptures" (TSSR) was coined by Quarantelli, Lagadec and Boin (2006) to refer to events that reach beyond societal boundaries and disrupt multiple social systems. Characteristics of TSSRs by this definition are that they spread quickly, initially have no known central or clear point of origin, and have impacts that extend across national political boundaries, potentially impact a large number of people, lead to emergent behavior, and do not lend themselves to local-level solutions (Quarantelli, Lagadec and Boin 2006, pp. 25-27).

Wachtendorf (2009) extends research on TSSRs to looking at the effects of them not only on national systems as envisaged by Quarantelli, Lagadec and Boin (2006), but also on the transnational systems. She discusses transnational systems as mutually dependent cross-border systems such as healthcare, trade, and transportation using the example of such systems between Canada and the U.S., and also argues that the extent of the linkages between national and transnational systems and TSSRs impact the vulnerability and resilience of the systems themselves (Wachtendorf 2009, pp. 380-384). In discussing areas for future theoretical development, Wachtendorf (2009, p. 390) points out that "TSSRs are about significant cross-system disruption and about the people who occupy distinct national or transnational systems."

Boin (2009b, p. 203) and Ansell, Boin and Keller (2010) also further our understanding in this area by defining transboundary crises as those that cross different types of boundaries such as: political (affecting different political jurisdictions vertically and horizontally), geographical (such as pandemics and the fiscal crisis), and functional (from the private to the public realm, such as the BP oil spill). These transboundary crises overwhelm organizations that are designed with traditional crises and disasters in mind. Tighter linkages between countries and systems (economically, politically, and technologically) tend to exacerbate the potential impacts of transboundary crises (Boin and Rhinard 2008, Boin 2009a). In exploring this concept within the context of the European Union (EU), Boin and Ekengren (2009) studied the capacity of institutions to deal with transboundary crises. They noted that while capacities to deal with transboundary crises have grown within the EU, this development has also been marked by fragmentation and many obstacles. Similarly, Herman and Dayton (2009) analyze the decision-making challenges that transboundary crises pose to crisis leaders and argue that the manner in which decision makers perceive unfolding events informs the crisis-decision making process. In addition to decision-making challenges, transboundary crises also render it difficult for policy-makers to 'make sense' of events due to ambiguity and uncertainty (Weick 1993, Ansell, Boin and Keller 2010). These issues are relevant to the analysis here; state and non-state organizations in South Florida found themselves having to process and deal with an influx of displacees and the legal complexities and ambiguities that emerged with their ingress.

In summary, past research on transboundary and trans-system ruptures and crises has examined the impacts of these on systems (national and transnational) (Quarantelli, Lagadec and Boin 2006, Wachtendorf 2009), on leaders and institutions (Boin 2009a, Boin and Ekengren 2009), and on capacities and tools (Santella, Steinberg and Parks 2009) to respond to these crises. However, knowledge of transboundary crises and their impacts is still an area that remains, as described by Boin (2009a), *terra incognita*. The aim of this study is to use understandings of transboundary crises to gain more insight into the linkages between disasters and crises and their transnational and transboundary effects such as occurred with the Haiti earthquake, including their legal and associated social ramifications on host communities; there is still a lacuna in research on these phenomena. The transboundary effects of the Haiti earthquake were different from other transboundary crises, as defined in past research, in that it was not a crisis like a pandemic that spread across geographic boundaries; its occurrence was local, but its effects and impact extended beyond its boundaries. These transboundary effects were due to the displacement of people that occurred, the close geographic proximity to the U.S., and because of the history and past relations between the two countries. Current research on transboundary crises has not paid much attention to how potential displacement and the subsequent legal challenges it creates affects host communities. Also, there is only a limited understanding of the role played by transnational actors and diasporas and their networks in responding to the issues associated with transboundary crises and disasters.

## STUDY REGION AND METHODOLOGY

We focused on the South Florida region of the United States, which includes Miami-Dade, Broward, and Palm Beach counties for the following four main reasons, also documented in Esnard and Sapat (2011), and Sapat and Esnard (2012a, 2012b). First, the South Florida region immediately served as a receiving area for school-aged displacees and for severely injured earthquake survivors (Bushouse and Freeman 2010, Baker and Berger 2010). Several schools absorbed these children, including Toussaint L'Ouverture High School for Arts and Social Justice which is a charter high school in Palm Beach County. Second, Florida is also the nation's largest refugee[1] resettlement state. While a majority of the refu-

---

[1] Refugee Services is a program within Florida's Department of Children and Families (DCF). That agency defines a refugee as "someone who has fled his/her country be-

gees who resettle in Florida live in Miami-Dade County, there are significant refugee populations in Broward, Palm Beach, and other counties (Florida Department of Children and Families). Third, South Florida already serves as a gateway to the Caribbean and Latin America and is home to many immigrants from Haiti, both legal and illegal. The region is home to more than 250,000 Haitians, many of whom have family in Haiti. Population estimates based on the 2010 American Community Survey estimates for Haitian ancestry are 116,137 in Miami-Dade County, 116,334 in Broward County, and 76, 134 in Palm Beach County.[2] According to Fagen *et al.* (2009, p. 24), Haitians make up 4.2 percent of the population of Miami-Dade County, which now has the largest concentration of Haitians in the U.S.[3] Thirty percent of the residents of the City of North Miami are Haitian and this is evident in the high number of Haitian-born politicians in that city. Fourth, South Florida is home to several Haitian-American organizations (with some whose mission has broadened since the earthquake crisis), and home to activists who have for decades been fighting causes of immigration equality for people of Haitian descent (Burch and Brecher 2010, Zezima 2010) and who play an active role in the community.

## *Methodology*

The research design for this study was based on a qualitative approach blending in-depth semi-structured interviews along with secondary data. The secondary data (coalition documents, reports, newspaper articles, website information and prior research) were used to understand the history and missions of the groups and agencies being interviewed, to generate a purposive sample of experts, and to start a snowball sample of respondents for in-person interviews (Singleton and Straits 1999).

Since qualitative research and snowball sampling has its limitations including problems of generalizability/external validity, in order to minimize the limitations of this method, we used the following as key guidelines (Miles and Huberman 1994) in setting up our interviews. The sampling method and strategy: (i) allowed a valid means by which to answer the research questions under study; (ii) provided rich and textured data given the descriptive nature of the study; (iii) was ethical and followed all the required approvals and consents; and (iv) the results generated allow transferability and generalizability to other Haitian enclaves beyond our study area.

---

cause of a well-founded fear of persecution based on their race, religion, nationality, social group or political opinion, and has been granted refugee status in a country of asylum." See http://www.dcf.state.fl.us/contact/contact_Refugee.shtml

[2] It should be noted that margins of error range from 7,618 to 11,353.

[3] The second largest concentration of Haitians is King's County (Brooklyn) and the third largest is in Broward County, immediately to the North of Miami-Dade.

Interviews were conducted with representatives from Haitian organizations and professional coalitions, other non-profits (e.g. the United Way), faith-based organizations, government agencies, school districts, school principals, media, immigration advocates, Florida Department of Children and Families Refugee Services, hospitals and health care administrators, Haitian diplomats and other Haitian American representatives on special task forces and commissions.

The findings presented herein are based on thirty semi-structured interviews (lasting an average of 45 minutes) conducted within the timeframe of June 2010 to March 2011. The number of interviewees by category is as follows: Haitian diaspora professional advocacy coalitions (n = 10); other non-profits (n = 4); schools and school districts (n = 4); state and local government agencies (n = 4); social service agencies (n = 3); hospitals (n = 2); faith-based organizations (n = 1); Haitian government official (n = 1); and the Haitian media (n = 1). All but one of the interviews was conducted in person, the one exception being interviewed by telephone. Some interviews were conducted partly in Creole with the help of a Haitian student translator. Some interviewees received draft questionnaires upon request. All interviewees were provided with a short description of the project and a consent form and all of the recorded interviews were fully transcribed and returned to the interviewees for clarifications and edits. We used interview data as the primary source for our findings as the perceptions of front-line workers, host-community organizations, and diaspora actors and their networks are critical to understanding how they interpreted statutory requirements to deal with the legal issues explored in this paper. In doing so, we reviewed interview transcripts to select appropriate interviewee quotes that dealt with how these issues perceived by our interviewees. Interview data were then triangulated with secondary data obtained from websites and other documents where appropriate to substantiate the findings. The methodology employed in this study also follows a combination of deductive and inductive reasoning. While we use theoretical understandings of transboundary crises to understand the legal issues that arose following the Haiti earthquake, our interview data also led to us to link the issues faced by front-line workers to theories of street-level bureaucracy.

Overall, these mixed methods, particularly the interviews, lend themselves to one of the strengths of qualitative research espoused by Miles and Huberman (1994, p. 10), i.e. "richness and holism, with strong potential for revealing complexity; such data provide 'thick descriptions' that are vivid, nested in real context."

## TRANSBOUNDARY LEGAL ISSUES

As discussed, we focus on key legal issues that arose in the aftermath of the 2010 earthquake which are as follows: 1) terminology and definitions used for displacees; 2) immigration and citizenship issues; 3) regulation and practice; and 4) compensation, federalism, and implementation of laws. As we analyze these issues using the data collected from the interviews, we also discuss how diaspora groups and actors played a role in framing and understanding the legal complexities that arose.

### Terminology and definitions used for displacees

One of main issues that arise from displacement of peoples following crises and disasters is with respect to terminology, particularly when cross-boundary migration takes place. Terminologies used for people displaced after disaster range from 'refugee' to 'Internally Displaced Persons' to Disaster Induced Displaced Persons and these definitions remain imprecise (Mitchell, Esnard and Sapat 2012). Yet, these definitions are not merely semantic in nature; using a particular definition carries with it certain rights to and expectations for services. As scholars of social construction and policy design have pointed out, the social construction of certain populations and the language used to describe them greatly influence the kind of policies that are subsequently adopted to deal with their problems (Berger and Luckman 1966, Schneider and Ingram 1993, Donovan 1993, 2001, Stone 2001). Terminology and designations play an important role in policy design and determine who benefits and loses from policies that get adopted (Schneider and Ingram 1993). When terminology fails to acknowledge the existence of a social group, such as displaced persons, then policy and practice are unlikely to address their needs (Mitchell, Esnard and Sapat 2012).

It was for this reason that children who came from Haiti after the earthquake and who were living with family members were classified as "homeless" by the Broward and Palm Beach county school districts. This allowed the school districts to keep track of and identify the students displaced by the earthquake, which would facilitate possible reimbursement for educational costs, along with the costs for transportation, translation, curriculum support and other services that the school districts incurred. Thus, the terminology and definitions used in the aftermath of the quake were important for monetary reasons, a lesson local governments had learned after Hurricane Katrina, when close track was not kept of the number of school children who came into the South Florida school system temporarily because they had to relocate after Katrina. To deal with the absence then of formal, legal definitions of displacees, administrators within the school districts dealing with the displacees used past knowledge and practice in a pragmatic fashion to provide assistance within the limitations they faced.

### Immigration and citizenship issues

Along with terminology, the Haiti earthquake also brought immigration issues back into the limelight. Within the domain of immigration, several legal complexities and concerns arose, of which the primary ones were: a) management of potential mass migration; b) Temporary Protection Status; and c) family reunification.

**Potential mass migration**

In the immediate aftermath of the earthquake, fears arose about a mass influx of immigrants coming to South Florida (Hsu 2010). The responses were reflective of a two-pronged approach reflecting tensions between adhering to immigration laws and regulations on the one hand, and providing humanitarian aid to the disaster on the other. The political responses to immigration concerns were reflective of the former, more formalistic approach to adhere to immigration rules; it took the form of an immediate crackdown on a potential exodus from Haiti at the federal level. A federal mass migration plan, known as Operation Vigilant Sentry, was activated to stop a mass exodus of refugees. This plan had been initially put in place in 2003 because of experiences with Caribbean migrations by the Homeland Security Task Force Southeast (HSTF-SE) under the premise that "a mass migration has the potential to overwhelm independent agency action, and threaten the safety and security of the United States. Since no single agency has the capability or resources to respond effectively to this contingency, an organizational plan and structure that can rapidly and effectively combine DHS forces with those of other federal, state and local agencies is necessary" (Department of Homeland Security (DHS) 2007). News reports surfaced about how immigration authorities were clearing space in a 600-bed detention center in Miami and about the preparation of detention centers to turn away and repatriate illegal immigrants who might attempt crossing the "Miami river" (Hsu 2010). The media also reported on how South Florida counties such as Miami-Dade were refining their contingency plans to accommodate thousands of Haitian refugees (Fausset 2010).

However, perhaps due to the legal crackdown or also due to the vast devastation in Haiti itself, the initially-expected mass exodus of refugees did not occur. There were fewer displacees than expected. Apart from those who needed medical help, the first wave of survivors who came were the ones who were already either American citizens or permanent residents and were fortunate in having the means to travel back to the U.S. Those following this first wave included families and children who came in on tourist visas. While official counts are not available, a number of children were sent to South Florida to be able to continue with their studies, sometimes with or without one or both parents. Many of these children came to finish the school year, often to stay with relatives or friends they barely knew.

**Temporary Protection Status (TPS)**

TPS is a temporary immigration status granted to eligible nationals of a certain country designated by the Secretary of Homeland Security because that country has experienced temporary negative conditions, such as armed conflict or an environmental disaster, that prevent nationals of the country from returning safely or for the country to handle their return adequately; it allows qualified individuals from designated countries (or parts of those countries) who are in the United States to continue to legally reside here for a limited time period (DHS 2010).

In 2008, Haiti was struck by four hurricanes and tropical storms: Fay, Gustav, Hanna and Ike. The entire country was severely damaged (800 dead, 600,000 houses damaged and more than 3 million persons affected); floods and mudslides wiped out most of the food crops and millions faced the prospect of acute hunger (Lacey 2008, p. 1). However, whether it has been political conflict or natural disasters during the last thirty years that have prevented Haitians living legally or illegally in the United States from returning home, successive US administrations have refused to grant TPS to Haitians. After the devastating hurricanes of 2008, even concentrated lobbying efforts, letter campaigns, marches or protests did not change the administration's position. It was only after the January 12, 2010 earthquake that TPS was granted to allow immigrants already in the United States to continue living and working in the country for 18 months following the earthquake. TPS benefits were extended following this initial period. On May 17, 2011, DHS Secretary Janet Napolitano announced an 18-month extension of TPS for Haitians. Effective July 23, 2011, this allowed TPS beneficiaries to remain in the United States through January 22, 2013. Another major change that was made was that Secretary Napolitano also *redesignated* TPS for Haiti, advancing the eligibility date by a year, meaning that eligible Haitians who had continuously resided in the U.S. since January 12, 2011 could also apply for TPS (Institute for Justice and Democracy in Haiti (IJDH) 2011). As noted, after the first wave of medical parolees, citizens, and permanent residents who came into the U.S., there were hundreds of other post-quake arrivals described above, who came on temporary and tourist visas and the implications of the redesignation were that these individuals could also apply for TPS.

During the first application period for TPS registration which expired on January 18, 2011, Semple (2011) reported that 53,000 individuals applied. This number was much lower than the 100,000 ballpark number estimated by the United States Citizen and Immigration Services back in early 2010 (Forry 2010). Several of our interviewees indicated that these low numbers of TPS applications were most likely due to a number of factors. Some of these were the monetary and procedural costs of the applications itself: the application fee for those between the ages of 14 to 65 applying for TPS and the ability to apply for employment that accompanied it was $515 (United States Citizenship and Immigration Services 2012). The application also requires a number of supporting documents and certified English translations of all forms. Apart from cost factors, interviewees also indicated that other major deterrents were the potential fear of discovery and of future immigration possibilities, lack of knowledge of the process, lack of necessary and available documents, and uncertainty about the extension of application deadlines. As Coutin (2000) notes in her study of the quest by Salvadoran immigrants for legalized immigrant status, U. S. law makes immigrants simultaneously present and absent and the way in which official and unofficial law are intertwined challenge the authority of law itself. Illegal aliens cannot work, but to regularize their status through programs (such as TPS), they must show that they have been present and contributed to society; so at a time when they are not "officially" present, they must still produce bills, contracts, leases, receipts, and records that attest to their social participation in the United States. The TPS program for Haitians, who were in the country illegally but could apply for temporary legal status, required for instance, that they show proof of being present in the U.S. prior to the earthquake, presenting a legal contradiction, as noted by Coutin (2000) in her work. Further as she points out, these contradictions can lead to confusion and opportunities for fraud and being defrauded in concerns about immigration status.

Some Haitian organizations did try to help TPS applicants, as discussed later in this chapter; nonetheless, since these organizations were limited by their resources, the obstacles discussed above still prevailed, preventing a number of potential applicants from utilizing the program. The same socio-politically rooted obstacles that hindered more TPS applications in the first round, are also likely to affect applications by those eligible under redesignation; legal issues are likely once again to be affected by social factors. Law as practiced on the ground is likely to be affected by both those administering the law and those affected by it.

### Family reunification

Another major issue related to immigration that arose was a family reunification program. After the 2010 earthquake, Haitian diaspora advocacy groups advocated more strongly for the adoption of a Family Reunification Parole Program (FRPP) as a possible way to help in the recovery process. This program would waive the waiting period for approximately 55,000 Haitians who already have approved visa petitions and whose family members are U.S. citizens or permanent residents; it would allow them to join their families in the United States quickly (IJDH 2011). For most Haitians, as for other nationalities, the waiting period for the legal immigration is a long period of time; adult children of U.S. citizens must wait six years to immigrate if they're single and nine years if they're married; siblings of citizens face an eleven-year wait; for spouses and minor children of U.S. permanent residents, the wait is about four years (Washington Post 2010).

The arguments being made by diaspora advocates for a FRPP are that: a) it would provide for a more humanitarian and orderly procedure for quicker legal migration, rather than push people to try more illegal forms of migration that are hazardous. As Laguerre has pointed out, over the years, the "tragic results of American policy *vis-à-vis* Haitian refugees has turned "the sea corridor between Haiti and Florida" into a cemetery for thousands of Haitians (Laguerre 1998, p. 85); (b) it would reduce the numbers who need aid and financial help from the U.S., other countries, and NGOs within Haiti; (c) it would increase the flow of cash remittances by increasing the pool of Haitians working in the United States (who currently provide an estimated one-third of Haiti's gross domestic product) sending cash remittances to their families (Orozco 2006); advocates point to estimates that a Haitian working in the United States can support as many as 10 relatives at home (IJDH 2011); and (d) it would not be an unusual or unprecedented policy, as it would be similar to the Cuban FRPP created in 2007 and similar to programs created for other refugees such as the Vietnamese and Kosovar Albanians; it would also, as noted by advocacy groups and in a number of editorials posted in the Miami Herald, Palm Beach Post, Boston Globe, Lost Angeles Times, Chicago Tribune (Haitian Advocacy Working Group 2011), help mitigate 'double standards' in immigration treatment for Haitians as compared to Cubans.

As noted by one of our interviewees,

> There's all kinds of reasons, this (the FRPP) is a no brainer. The administration can do it, no congressional action is needed, it helps Haiti recover, there is a precedent because of the Cuban program, the remittances; the remittances equal to all kinds of reasons, it's a no brainer (Source: Interviewee code 028).

As discerned from our interview data, while the FRPP would be a humanitarian solution and aid Haitian recovery, objections to the FRPP stem from concerns raised by anti-immigrant groups about more immigrants coming in, the potential drain on public services, and the potential precedent for other disasters and other immigrant groups. Objections to the FRPP are also rooted in negative social constructions of Haitian groups about Haitian immigrants bringing in crime, draining social resources, and being uneducated and unskilled; ironically however, based on past studies (Stepick *et al.* 1982) and our interview data, these perceptions are not supported by reality in terms of utilization of services. For instance, DCF reported on an extremely low utilization of the public services, (even after the earthquake) and noted that this was not a surprise to them since Haitians are probably the lowest users of services within the refugee program.

Like TPS, the calls for FRPP were increased in the aftermath of the earthquake; the transboundary effects of the quake helped strengthen the legitimacy of the immigration reform arguments made by Haitian-American diaspora groups. As a focusing event, the earthquake provided advocacy groups with an opportunity to push for their issues (Sapat and Esnard 2012b). The mobilization of these groups also exemplifies the manner in which such transnational advocacy groups can affect legal responses to transboundary crises, both within their host and their home countries.

### Regulations and practices

As a transboundary crisis, the earthquake also prompted host communities and agencies in South Florida to enact some changes in their regulations and practices to adapt to certain cultural concerns of displaced survivors, illustrating how institutions and front-line workers within them dealt with the repercussions of the earthquake. Examples of such changes could be found in the way that the school systems dealt with school requirements such as immunizations. A number of displaced children who came over to South Florida after the earthquake did not have the necessary paperwork or documentation on immunization records. Since that is a legal requirement for schools, school district officials dealt with the problem by making appointments for students on the first day they came in to get their immunization shots. They also resorted to non-traditional ways to reach out to families hosting displaced children attending their schools by setting up KONBIT[4] socials. Using knowledge gleaned from Haitian diaspora members who were working for school districts and other non-profits who aided school districts in dealing with displaced Haitian children who came into the local school system, these KONBIT socials were organized with a cultural flavor that included Haitian music and food. Haitian speaking social workers and psychologists were also available to work with the families who attended, and explain to them what was available and how to get it, such as immunization shots. Other measures included setting up a website for schools and teachers on the process, procedures, and protocols that they needed to follow when they received new students from Haiti. A directory of services that a post-earthquake student could benefit and receive was also compiled, along with the adoption of other measures such as sensitivity training. For instance, as noted by one of our interviewees,

> Also ... we developed and pulled together a group of our staff and we developed a sensitivity training. And we did this by podcast so our schools could just dial in on their computers and see the whole thing and ask questions. That kind of stuff ... it was really very excellent ... we dealt with things that schools need to be aware of, as they work with students. Simple things that you wouldn't think of, for example ... many of our schools have uniforms and some schools have red uniforms ... and children are grieving ... red for them is a problem. They are used to wearing black or gray during the grief period ... the colors are a problem ... part of the importance of cultural awareness. But I am very proud to say that is the system we thought of those things and put that out so that our families and the schools could really be more sensitive to the needs of the kids (Source: Interviewee Code 05).

These insights into Haitian culture led to minor yet important changes then in certain regulations and practices; school children were allowed to wear the darker-colored uniforms. So while existing regulations and practices were adhered to by school officials, such as the requirement for immunizations and school uniforms, the manner in which those policy goals were accomplished were influenced by knowledge about and information provided by the Haitian community members who were either

---

4 *Konbit* is a word in Haitian Kreyol for gathering, collaborating and cooperation for the greater good.

working within school bureaucracies or actively involved with school policies through non-profit and other agencies.

## Compensation, federalism, and implementation of laws

Following the earthquake, issues related to compensation for services rendered to displaced survivors brought into South Florida was an issue that providers of those services had to deal with. This was complicated by the question of which level of government was responsible for covering those expenses, along with the interpretation, implementation, and even suspension of relevant laws and regulations to render assistance swiftly. These issues arose primarily for school children and for those with medical needs.

As previously mentioned, school districts had kept records of students displaced by the Haiti earthquake to facilitate reimbursement for educational costs, along with costs for other additional services that the schools and school districts had to provide. As of July 2010, the number of children who were enrolled in the tri-county area were as follows: ~1147 in Miami-Dade County; ~ 1200 in Broward County; and ~ 654 in Palm Beach County.[5] Given these numbers, there was a push by Florida's legislators to get reimbursement for these students: according to Olmeda and Freeman (2010), United States Congresswoman Wasserman-Shultz announced in July of 2010 that "the U.S. House of Representatives had approved an emergency spending measure that among other things, repaid Florida school districts approximately $12 million for taking in 3700 students for half a year without asking for money upfront."

In terms of medical needs, there were many more complex circumstances and issues. For instance, a number of injured survivors were brought into the country by both government ships and planes and by non-profit groups and private individuals. Local hospitals in South Florida hospitals such as Broward Health, Jackson, and at Palm Beach county had to deal not only with the medical needs of the injured, but also with the legal issues that arose in the provision of medical treatment. First, they needed to deal with the immigration status of those who had been injured. A number of the seriously and critically injured patients had to be cleared by Immigration authorities before they could be brought to the hospital and as noted by one of our interviewees, for the first time, immigration work was done on the tarmac as planes landed with patients to expedite their transport into waiting ambulances that took them to various area hospitals equipped to deal with their injuries. State-level agencies like the Agency for Healthcare Administration (AHCA) and the Division of Children and Families (DCF) also helped the hospitals ensure that the immigration paperwork was correctly filled out and the American Red Cross

---

[5] Based on our interview data, we found that schools only kept the data on the children who came into the school system for around 6 months as they were not sure whether they would be reimbursed for any additional children coming into the school system.

and other non-profits such as Catholic Charities helped the families of survivors. The hospitals also had to work closely with the U.S. Citizen and Immigration Services once patients who were of Haitian nationality had to be discharged, while balancing medical concerns. Other issues that were legal in nature arose due to the lack of records, identification of survivors, and even with in translation issues. One of the healthcare providers we interviewed noted that even though there were already a number of Kreyol speaking personnel at the hospitals,

> In healthcare you cannot use an employee to translate because of HIPAA (The Health Insurance Portability and Accountability Act) federal law. Red Cross has certified translators and they have to sign to protect information of the patient. On the floors where we had a Haitian patient that came from Haiti we had a translator there 24/7. It was part of American Red Cross... (Source: Interviewee Code 18).

Other legal complications that pertained to U.S. regulations were issues related to funding and assistance from the federal government via activation of the National Disaster Medical System (NDMS). The NDMS is a federally coordinated system that temporally augments the Federal, Tribal, State and Local medical response capability, by funding, organizing, training, equipping, deploying and sustaining a specialized and focused range of public health and medical capabilities. The NDMS was activated to provide services through its field care component through which 270 health and medical personnel were deployed to Haiti as part of the international medical response in the first week following the earthquake. In response to a request from then Florida Governor Charlie Christ, the NDMS was also used to reimburse U.S. hospitals that provided care to critically ill patients (http://www.hhs.gov/haiti/ndms _ushospitals.html); this was the first time that this system was activated for an international disaster, which may have set an important precedent for the future. Activation of the NDMS in instances when the disaster does not impact the U.S. mainland has legal and political implications that have yet to be explored. While the activation of the NDMS following the Haiti earthquake helped, the funds, however, only covered acute care and were available only from the date of activation of the NDMS.

The fact that the NDMS only covered acute care and not rehabilitation, along with the difficulties of tracking patients led to problems in reimbursements for hospitals, prompting Charlie Christ, then Governor of Florida to declare to the U.S. Department of Health and Human Services, that Florida would have to stop taking in more patients if it was not reimbursed for these expenses (Hundley 2010). While hospitals and other medical professionals were finally eligible for reimbursement months later,[6] what drove hospitals and other agencies however, to continue to immediately treat and serve patients were the humanitarian issues, their

---

[6] See http://haiti.apprio.com/news-release.php?m3=on for more details.

concern for their Haitian employees, and their ability to help given the geographic proximity to Haiti. This occurred despite the lack of financial reimbursement or of state/federal assistance in the months following the earthquake. As pointed out by one of our interviewees:

> From a business standpoint it is a no-win. Financially it is a loss no matter how to put it. There is nothing good, financially, that is going to come from it. ... We sat down and had the heart to heart talks, and we had to convince the financial folks that this is a financial write-off and it the right thing to do. The other side is that so much of our population and so many of our employees are Haitian and Haiti it is 150 miles away (Source: Interviewee Code 01).

Given the legal complexities they faced in dealing with displacees from another country and in managing transboundary issues on a vertical dimension (between the federal, state, and local level), street-level workers in state and non-state organizations as indicated by our data appear to have yielded to humanitarian impulses, along with a pragmatic approach dictated by the constraints they faced. Caseworkers and agencies made decisions that were not always tightly linked to a statute; this was similar to the manner in which housing policy was handled for Katrina displacees (Sterett 2009). As Sterett (2009, p. 87) notes, "After Katrina, the state ... allowed general rules to continue while suspending them in the instance or it extended relief in a wholly discretionary way, both of which disaster relief had done before." Agencies dealing with the aftermath of the Haiti earthquake also had to use their discretion and judgment to make changes in rules and practices to accommodate displacees and provide services at times without clarity on compensation or about applicable rules.

## DISCUSSION OF FINDINGS: INSTITUTIONAL RESPONSES, STREET-LEVEL BUREAUCRATS AND FORMAL AND INFORMAL NETWORKS

The discussion above highlights some of main legal issues that emerged due to the transboundary effects of the 2010 earthquake. What also emerges as being crucial to understanding these legal issues are the institutional responses, particularly those by street-level workers in state and non-state institutions. As theories of street-level bureaucracy suggest, these street-level workers did not work in isolation—rather the formal and informal networks they operated in were critical to understanding how they dealt with the transboundary legal issues they faced. As noted earlier, diaspora groups and actors were also embedded in these networks, both within government and outside of it and they did affect legal and other policy responses to the issues that emerged.

We discuss the role of street-level workers and the role of formal and informal networks more explicitly here, as follows: 1) the role of street-level workers; 2) the importance of formal networks and prior collaboration; and, 3) informal networks among diaspora groups and diasporic identities.

### Street-level workers

The findings in this study indicate that street-level workers were critical to understanding institutional responses to transboundary issues that emerged after the Haiti earthquake. This is consistent with past research on street-level bureaucracy which has argued that street-level bureaucrats play important policy-making roles owing to the relatively high degrees of discretion and relative autonomy from organizational authority that they enjoy; while goal expectations tend to ambiguous, conflicting, and difficult to measure and their resources are chronically inadequate, street-level bureaucrats deal with these problems by developing patterns of practice and routines to simplify their tasks (Lipsky 2010). Also as noted by Maynard-Moody and Musheno (2003, p. 4), street-level bureaucrats bring their own views of fairness into assessments of clients, they exercise discretion subjectively and variably, and see themselves as citizen-agents, even while they act inherently as state-agents (Maynard-Moody and Musheno 2012, p. S21).

Our findings support this literature; street-level workers positively constructed displaced people, giving particular weight to images of family unification and school children needs and with this positive judgment, engaged in pragmatic improvisation of legal complexities to the benefit of this population while skirting anti-immigrant sentiments.[7] As discussed by Maynard-Moody and Musheno (2003, 2012), street-level workers used moral norms to deal with the issues that faced them and law was put to work in a pragmatic way to serve a population that was constructed as worthy of services under conditions of humanitarian crisis. Critical to achieving this stance towards displaced people was the bridging work of NGOs and their formal and informal networks between the Haitian diaspora living in South Florida.

### Importance of networks and prior collaboration

Our interview data indicate that prior interactions in the form of formal networks among agencies were critical during the short- and long-term recovery period and helped to resolve some of the main legal issues that emerged in South Florida. There were a number of agencies and organizations some of which were already used to working with each other: the Florida Department of Children and Families Refugee Services; United Way of Broward and Palm Beach counties; Broward Health Emergency Preparedness Department, the Palm Beach County Disaster Coalition, school district representatives from Palm Beach, Broward, and Miami-Dade counties, and the Florida Department of Emergency Management (FDEM). Fortunately, there were also planning efforts that

---

7 The importance of street-level bureaucrats emerged as a major finding rather than a starting point for our study and we revised and reorganized the paper accordingly. We thank anonymous reviewers and Susan Sterett for their feedback in that regard.

among other things addressed issues of mass migration, as well as repatriation. For instance, there was a State Emergency Repatriation Plan which is housed within FDEM, as well as a state comprehensive emergency plan that addresses repatriation, mass migration, hurricanes and other hazards. While FDEM was the lead agency, DCF received funding as well. They worked very closely with emergency management and all of the agencies that are part of emergency management process. New networks, partnerships, and organizations, such as the Broward Haiti Relief Task Force and Konbit for Haiti, were also forged to deal with a large spectrum of the sociolegal issues discussed above.

Prior exercises and discussions among these groups helped. For instance, as noted by one of our interviewees from the medical profession:

> About 5 years ago, we did a mass migration exercise and we looked at what if Castro dies and Cuba empties out—how many would come to South Florida? So what would we do with mass immigration as far as health care, law enforcement, boarder control etc. One of the things that came up is that if you have someone that comes to your doorstep with no record, SSN, what do you do with them? Do you think immigration will come for one person when they have tens of thousands more? We knew there was a hole there and the feds knew it and of course we did not have an action plan for this. Changing laws and going through legislation at the state and federals levels would take years... We have been working for a while on a catastrophic plan. What do we do when the cat 4/5 hurricane takes out South Florida (Source: Interviewee Code 18).

However, there were issues that were not foreseen by some of these prior exercises. For instance, despite these plans, the scenario played out much differently after the Haiti earthquake since according to one of our interviewees, the emergency plan primarily focused on a large number of arrivals, not a significant number of the severely injured people. On the other hand, the interviewee commented that:

> We were lucky; honestly, that this happened in Haiti because of the unique situation of Haitian parolees in that many are able to get some medical assistance. If that had not been the case, there would have been even greater concerns about the immediate and long-term medical needs of these individuals. We know that the impact on our Refugee Medical Assistance program, which is a 100% federally funded program, exceeded 6 million dollars, because the people who came in as parolees were the most severely injured (Source: Interviewee Code 21).

Thus, plans were important; but the exercises, existing networks, and prior collaboration among street level bureaucrats in local and state agencies and organizations turned out to be critically important.

### Informal networks among diaspora actors and groups

In addition to these formal networks, as noted in our discussion above, there were a number of informal networks among a number of Haitian-American diaspora non-profit organizations and faith based groups, such as Haitian Lawyers Association, FANM, SantLa, the Haitian-American Emergency Relief Committee, Haitian-American Nurses Association, Haitian-American Grassroots Coalition, Haitian-American Professional Coalition, Haitian-American Leadership Organization, Haitian-American Association of Engineers and Scientists, Radio TeleAmerica, and the Notre Dame d'Haiti Catholic Church. Some of these were umbrella organizations. Familial and social networks among the Haitian diaspora themselves, as well as between the Haitian diaspora and their relatives and families in Haiti also helped in the other issues that arose in the aftermath of the quake and in tracking displacees and survivors coming in. They assisted with the flow of earthquake survivors and displacees who came for medical help, schooling, and other reasons, including helping with immigration issues. Churches and religious institutions were another major source of support in both South Florida and Haiti. The Notre Dame d'Haiti Catholic Church, based in Little Haiti in South Florida is especially noteworthy in regard. As reported by Esnard and Sapat (2011), their activities are both short term (i.e. organizing container shipments of food and medical supplies; organizing medical missions; helping with the placement of kids at Catholic schools) as well as long-term (e.g. fundraising for eventual reconstruction of places of worship, and establishment of medical establishments).

Unity among diaspora groups was also a key factor. Prior to the earthquake, this had been most apparent in the context of immigration. Several diaspora groups and coalitions have advocated for TPS and for legal and political rights of the Haitian American community, particularly for comprehensive immigration reform in the U.S. and even in the broader Caribbean region where Haitians have taken refuge over the decades. In fact, coalitions such as the Haitian American Grassroots Coalition were born out of the struggle of Haitian immigrants to improve their condition of life and also to be able to have a foothold in America. According to one of our interviewees:

> I don't think we had really a common denominator in the last forty years and the only fights that we've been fighting is immigration, immigration, immigration then this came up (Source: Interviewee code 23).

The reality though is that immigration and citizenship issues continue to be a unifying issue for Haitian diaspora organizations. The Haitian consulate played a critical role with documentation such as passports and birth certificates that were damaged/lost in the earthquake. The Haitian Lawyers Association, hosted a radio program called 'KOZE Legal,' a legal talk show in Creole, which was one of several media avenues through which the community was educated on TPS issues. As noted earlier, a number of Haitian organizations also helped in the TPS process; they did this through holding free legal clinics and information sessions and through general education and outreach activities. According to one of our interviewees:

> Now following the earthquake ... that same TPS issue ... we actually had three successful TPS drives where we assisted hundreds of Haitians complete their TPS applications free of charge. We did two TPS drives in the city of North Miami, which has the largest concentration of Haitian Americans in the country. ... We also did one in the city of Miami Gardens, and have weekly TPS drives on Fridays where we assist Haitians free of charge in completing their TPS applications. (Source: Interviewee Code 002)

In March 2010 (two months after the catastrophic earthquake), the Haitian diaspora had two unprecedented opportunities to provide input on a broader range of issues: (i) at the Haitian Diaspora Forum held at the Organization of American States (OAS) Headquarters in March 21-23, 2010; and (ii) at the Haiti Donors Conference held at the United Nations Headquarters in New York on March 31, 2010. The OAS Forum focused on a strategic plan for reconstruction and development in Haiti and specifically how the Haitian Diaspora will engage in capacity and nation building (OAS 2010). The Forum was co-organized by the OAS and Haitian Diaspora organizations (several based in South Florida), and the outcome and results were presented to the Haiti government at the March 31st donors conference in New York. According to one member of the diaspora, "this was the first time in the annals of the diaspora, that the diaspora had been considered as an institution versus a separate entity of one to one" (source: Interviewee code 007).

## CONCLUSION

The earthquake in Haiti had repercussions not just in Haiti, but transnationally in other countries such as the United States. The objectives of this chapter were to analyze the transnational ramifications, in particular the legal issues that emerged after this disaster for displaced survivors and receiving host communities in South Florida. Host communities and agencies within them, such as school districts and hospitals, had to deal with these issues for which the legal solutions were not clearly defined.

In dealing with these issues, we find that results from our interviews of agencies in host communities in South Florida supports prior research on street-level bureaucrats and the patterns of practice they develop to deal with uncertainties and ambiguities (Lipsky 2010, Maynard-Moody and Musheno 2003). In the absence of formal, legal definitions of displacees, organizations dealing with the displacees used past knowledge and practice in a pragmatic fashion to provide assistance within the limitations they faced. This was particularly evident in school districts, hospitals, and within non-profit organizations who were helping several schools and hospitals in dealing with the displacees and their families. The findings here also add to the literature on the role of street-level bureaucrats, in that the focus in this paper is on how street-level workers in state and non-state organizations respond to transboundary effects and legal complexities following a disaster in another country; a dimension that has hitherto been neglected in extant studies.

Additionally, we also find that transnational actors, their formal and informal networks, and particularly the Haitian-American diaspora played a critical role in assisting Haiti with relief and recovery efforts and served as an invaluable post-earthquake conduit for Creole-speaking doctors, nurses, engineers, educators, advisers, and reconstruction planners (Newland 2010). They were also critical players in framing and understanding of the legal complexities that arose, and in dealing with sociolegal ramifications of transboundary crises. Long-standing formal and informal networks, as well as diaspora identity formation and history (especially with regard to immigration rights and reform) provided both a context to understand legal responses and it conditioned the nature of these responses. The accommodation of displacees was managed in a way that reflected to some extent the disaggregated nature of the American state; as Slaughter (2005) points out states relate to each other not only through centralized foreign policy offices, but also through formal and informal networks that transcend national borders.

In addition, the presence of diaspora members who worked within the government and non-profit agencies on the frontlines played a critical role in framing the response and decision making process. This helped to increase 'situational awareness' or 'sense-making' (Weick 1993), which is particularly difficult in a transboundary crisis, when there is "incomplete, often contradictory information that is distributed over a large and shifting number of actors" (Ansell, Boin and Keller 2010). This finding also affirms the arguments made by theorists of street-level bureaucracy who argue that street-level bureaucrats "draw significantly on their general, religious, class, physical, ethnic, racial, and sexual, and gender identities" (Maynard-Moody and Musheno 2003, p. 52). Since there are a number of Haitian-Americans working as nurses, social workers, lawyers, and school district administrators in South Florida, they were able to use their knowledge and personal concerns about the Haiti earthquake to not only counter negative stereotypes of Haitians, but also to frame the response to legal dilemmas in a humanitarian light.

However, while our study does help shed light on the how street-level workers in state and non-state organizations and diaspora networks deal with legal dilemmas arising from transboundary disasters, there are several limitations as well: the research here is based on data from one geographical area and related to one diaspora group, which is subjective and subject to various other limitations of qualitative and case study research. Survey or other types of quantitative data and a broader discussion of diaspora groups may present a different picture.

The subjects of our study are also primarily from social service organizations. Future work on the legal and other transnational effects of disasters could examine bureaucratic responses by non social-service organizations (such as the police, coast guard, or immigration services); their responses are arguably likely to indicate a greater need for conformance to the rules as compared to focusing only on humanitarian assistance. More understanding is also needed of the effects of other kinds of transboundary crises that may differ in terms of the type of disaster (i.e. flooding, tornadoes, terrorism) or degrees of geographic proximity. Finally, in light of our research and findings, we conclude that future research on disasters and policy practices in disaster management needs to pay attention to diaspora (or immigrants) groups and their role in transnational displacement. This is particularly important given the potential number of refugees fleeing climate-change related events and other disasters and the effects of globalization; how these issues will be addressed by policies will have implications for disaster management.

## Bibliography

Ansell, C., Boin, A., and Keller, A., 2010. Managing Transboundary Crises: Identifying the Building Blocks of an Effective Response System. *Journal of Contingencies and Crisis Management*, 18 (4), 195-207. doi: 10.1111/j.1468-5973.2010.00620.x.

Baker, P., and Berger, J., 2010. U.S. Will Reimburse Hospitals That Treat Haitians. *The New York Times* [online], 1 Feb. Available from: http://www.nytimes.com/2010/02/02/world/americas/02airlift.html?pagewanted=2&emc=eta1 [Accessed 23 March 2013].

Berger, P., and Luckmann, T., 1966. *The Social Construction of Reality: A Treatise in the Sociology of Knowledge*. Garden City: Anchor Books.

Birkland, T., 2006. *Lessons of Disaster: Policy Change after Catastrophic Events*. Washington, D.C.: Georgetown University Press.

Boin, A., 2009a. The new world of crises and crisis management: implications for policymaking and research. *The Review of Policy Research*, 26 (4), 367-377. doi:10.1111/j.1541-1338.2009.00389.x

Boin, A., 2009b. Meeting the Challenges of Transboundary Crises: Building Blocks for Institutional Design. *Journal of Contingencies and Crisis Management*, 17 (4), 203-205. doi: 10.1111/j.1468-5973.2009.00591.x.

Boin, A.R., Groenleer, M.L.P., and Sundelius, B., 2007. Managing European emergencies: Considering the pros and cons of a European Union agency. *In: 4'h ECPR General Conference*, 6-8 September 2007 Pisa, Italy [online]. Available from: http://www.essex.ac.uk/ecpr/events/generalconference/pisa/papers/PP746.pdf [Accessed 17 March 2008].

Boin, A., and Rhinard, M., 2008. Managing Transboundary Crises: What Role for the European Union?. *International Studies Review*, 10 (1), 1-26. doi: 10.1111/j.1468-2486.2008.00745.x.

Boin, A., and Ekengren, M., 2009. Preparing for the World Risk Society: Towards a New Security Paradigm for the European Union. *Journal of Contingencies and Crisis Management*, 17 (4), 285-294. doi: 10.1111/j.1468-5973.2009.00583.x.

Burch, A.D., and Brecher, E.J., 2010. South Florida key to recovery in Haiti, but road is long and uncharted. *The Miami Herald*, 31 Jan.

Bushouse, K., and Freeman, M., 2010. Palm Beach county schools open door to 157 Haiti earthquake survivors. *The Sun Sentinel* [online], 2 Feb. Available from: http://www.sun-sentinel.com/news/haiti/fl-palm-schools-haiti-20100131,0,5279783.story [Accessed 26 March 2013].

Clifford, R.A., 1956. *The Rio Grande flood: A comparative study of border communities in disaster. Publication 458*. Washington, DC: National Academy of Sciences, National Research Council. Available from: http://openlibrary.org/books/OL7201623M/The_Rio_Grande_flood [Accessed 26 March 2013].

Coutin, S.B., 2000. *Legalizing Moves: Salvadoran Immigrants Struggle for U.S. Residency*. Ann Arbor, MI: University of Michigan Press.

Dearstyne, B., 2007. The FDNY on 9/11: information and decision-making in crisis. *Government Information Quarterly*, 24 (1), 29-46.

Department of Homeland Security, 2007. *Fact Sheet—Operation Vigilant Sentry*. Washington: Department of Homeland Security.

Department of Homeland Security, 2010. *Statement from Homeland Security Secretary Janet Napolitano on Temporary Protected Status (TPS) for Haitian Nationals*. 15 Jan. Washington: Department of Homeland Security. Available from: http://www.dhs.gov/ynews/releases/pr_1263595952516.shtm [Accessed 26 March 2013].

Department of Homeland Security, 2011. *Secretary Napolitano Announces the Extension of Temporary Protected Status for Haiti Beneficiaries*. 17 May. Available from: http://www.dhs.gov/ynews/releases/pr_1305643820292.shtm [Accessed 26 March 2013].

Dewan, S., 2010. Scattered Émigrés Haiti Once Shunned Are Now a Lifeline. *The New York Times* [online], 3 Feb. Available from: http://www.nytimes.com/2010/02/04/us/04diaspora.html?scp=1&sq=Haitian%20expatriates&st=cse# [Accessed 23 March 2013].

Donovan, M., 1993. The social construction of people with AIDS: Target populations and U.S. policy 1981-1990. *Policy Studies Review*, 12 (3/4), 3-29.

Donovan, M., 2001. *Taking Aim*. Washington DC: Georgetown University Press.

Dynes, R. 1970. *Organized Behavior in Disaster*. Lexington, MA: D.C. Health.

East, G., and Fleshler, D., 2010. Earthquake could mean major changes for South Florida Haitians. *The Sun Sentinel* [online], 19 Feb. Available from: http://articles.sun-sentinel.com/2010-02-19/news/fl-haitian-communities-20100219_1_haitian-american-south-florida-haitians-haitian-communities [Accessed 26 March 2013].

Esnard, A.-M., and Sapat, A., 2011. Disasters, Diasporas and Host Communities: Insights in the Aftermath of the Haiti Earthquake. *Journal of Disaster Research*, 6 (3), 331-342.

Fagen, P.W., *et al.*, 2009. *Haitian Diaspora Associations and their Investments in Basic Social Services* [online]. Washington: Inter American Development Bank. Available from: http://www.iadb.org/en/publications/publication-detail,7101.html?id=7303%20&dcLanguage=en&dcType=All [Accessed 26 March 2013].

Fausset, R., 2010. U.S. to change illegal Haitian immigrants' status. *Los Angeles Times* [online], 16 Jan. Available from: http://articles.latimes.com/2010/jan/16/nation/la-na-haiti-refugee16-2010jan16 [Accessed 26 March 2013].

Flynn, S.E., 2007. *The edge of disaster: Rebuilding a resilient nation.* New York: Random House: in cooperation with the Council on Foreign Relations.

Forry, B., 2010. Immigration chief pushes eligible Haitians to apply for legal status. *Dorchester Reporter* [online], 23 Apr. Available from: http://www.dotnews.com/2010/immigration-chief-pushes-eligible-haitians-apply-legal-status [Accessed 26 March 2013].

Haitian Advocacy Working Group, 2011. *Immigration: Create a Haitian Family Reunification Parole Program to Increase Remittances to Haiti Permit Applications to Waive the Humanitarian Parole Fee* [online]. Available from: http://ijdh.org/wordpress/wp-content/uploads/2010/07/HAWG_Immigration_FINAL.pdf [Accessed 15 May 2011].

Herman, M.G., and Dayton, B., 2009. Transboundary Crises through the Eyes of Policymakers: Sense Making and Crisis Management. *Journal of Contingencies and Crisis Management*, 17 (4), 233-241.

Hsu, S., 2010. Officials Try to Prevent Haitian Earthquake Refugees From Coming to the U.S. *The Washington Post* [online], 18 Jan, A08. Available from: http://www.washingtonpost.com/wp-dyn/content/article/2010/01/17/AR2010011701893.html?hpid=topnews&sid=ST2010011703508 [Accessed 26 March 2013]

Hundley, K., 2010. Gov. Crist: Florida hospitals can't take more Haitian quake victims. *Tampa Bay Times* [online], 28 Jan. Available from: http://www.tampabay.com/news/health/gov-crist-florida-hospitals-cant-take-more-haitian-quake-victims/1068952 [Accessed 26 March 2013].

Institute for Justice and Democracy in Haiti, 2011. *Haitian TPS Extended and Redesignated* [online]. South Boston: Institute For Justice and Democracy in Haiti. Available from: http://ijdh.org/wordpress/wp-content/uploads/2011/05/TPS-extension-and-redesignation-press-release.pdf [Accessed 26 March 2013].

Lacey, M., 2008. Meager Living of Haitians Is Wiped Out by Storms. *The New York Times* [online], 10 Sep. Available from: http://www.nytimes.com/2008/09/11/world/americas/11haiti.html [Accessed 22 May 2011].

Laguerre, M., 1998. *Diasporic Citizenship: Haitian Americans in Transnational America*. New York: Palgrave Macmillan.

Lipsky, M., 1980. *Street Level Bureaucrats: Dilemmas of the Individual in Public Services*. New York: Russell Sage.

Lipsky, M., 2010. *Street Level Bureaucrats: Dilemmas of the Individual in Public Services*. 3rd ed. New York: Russell Sage.

Martin, L., 2010. Haitians in U.S. feeling the pull of home. *Miami Herald* [online], 23 Feb. Available from: http://www.tnj.com/news/african-and-caribbean/haitians-us-feel-pull-home [Accessed 22 March 2013].

Maynard-Moody, S., and Musheno, M., 2003. *Cops, Teachers, Counselors: Stories from the Front Lines of Public Service*. Ann Arbor: Univ. Michigan Press.

Maynard-Moody, S., and Musheno, M., 2012. Social Equities and Inequities in Practice: Street-Level Workers as Agents and Pragmatists. *Public Administration Review*, 72 (S1), S16-S23. doi: 10.1111/j.1540-6210.2012.02633.x.

Miles, M.B., and Huberman, A.M., 1994. *Qualitative Data Analysis: An Expanded Sourcebook*. Thousand Oaks: Sage Publications.

Mileti, D., 1999. *Disasters by Design: A Reassessment of Natural Hazards in the United States*. Washington, DC: Joseph Henry Press.

Mitchell, C.M., Esnard, A.M., and Sapat, A., 2012. Hurricane Events and the Displacement Process in the United States. *Natural Hazards Review*, 13 (2), 150-161.

Newland, K., 2010. *Voice After Exit: Diaspora Advocacy* [online]. Washington, DC: Migration Policy Institute. Available from: http://www.migrationpolicy.org/pubs/diasporas-advocacy.pdf [Accessed 26 March 2013].

Oliver-Smith, A., 2009. Development-Forced Displacement and Resettlement: A Global Human Rights. *In*: A. Oliver-Smith, ed. *Development & Dispossession: The crisis of forced displacement and resettlement*. Santa Fe: SAR Press.

Olmeda, R.A., and Freeman, M., 2010. South Florida schools may be reimbursed for Haitian evacuees. *The Sun Sentinel* [online], 19 July. Available from: http://articles.sun-sentinel.com/2010-07-19/news/fl-broward-schools-reimbursed-20100719_1_haitian-evacuees-haitian-students-school-districts [Accessed 2013 March 2013].

Organization of American States (OAS), 2010. *Haitian Diaspora Forum: Contributing to a Strategic Plan for Reconstruction and Development in Haiti*. Washington, DC, 21-23 March. Available from: http://www.oas.org/en/ser/dia/docs%20PO/Program_Haitian_Diaspora_Forum.DOC [Accessed 26 March 2013].

Orozco, M., 2006. *Understanding the remittance economy in Haiti*. Inter-American Dialogue paper commissioned by the World Bank. Available from: http://ww.thedialogue.org/PublicationFiles/Understanding%20the%20remittance%20economy%20in%20Haiti.pdf [Accessed 26 March 2013].

Quarantelli, E.L., 1983. *Emergent citizen groups in disaster preparedness and recovery activities. Final Project Report #33.* Newark, DE: Disaster Research Center, University of Delaware. Available from: http://www.cridlac.org/digitalizacion/pdf/eng/doc3742/doc3742.htm [Accessed 26 March 2013].

Quarantelli, E.L., Lagadec, P., and Boin, A., 2006. A heuristic approach to future disasters and crisis. *In*: H. Rodriguez, E.L. Quarantelli and R.R. Dynes, eds. *Handbook of disaster research.* New York: Springer, 16-41.

Rodríguez, H., Quarantelli, E.L., and Dynes, R.R., eds., 2006. *Handbook of Disaster Research.* New York: Springer.

Rosenthal, U., and Hart, P.'t, 1998. *Flood response and crisis management in Western Europe: A comparative analysis.* Berlin: Springer-Verlag.

Santella, N., Steinberg, L.J., and Parks, K., 2009. Decision making for extreme events: modeling critical infrastructure interdependencies to aid mitigation and response planning. *The Review of Policy Research,* 26 (4), 409-422.

Sapat, A., and Esnard, A.-M., 2012a. Displacement and Disaster Recovery: Transnational Governance and Sociolegal Issues following the 2010 Haiti Earthquake. *Risk, Hazards and Crisis in Public Policy,* 3 (1), Article 2. Available from: http://onlinelibrary.wiley.com/doi/10.1515/1944-4079.1095/pdf [Accessed 26 March 2013].

Sapat, A., and Esnard, A.-M., 2012b. The Transnational and Transboundary Effects of Focusing Events: Diasporas, Disasters, and the Policy Process. *Annual Meeting of the Midwest Political Science Association,* Chicago, Illinois, 31 March-2 April 2012.

Semple, K., 2011. U.S. Sees Success in Immigration Program for Haitians. *The New York Times* [online], 19 Jan. Available from: http://www.nytimes.com/2011/01/20/nyregion/20haitians.html [Accessed 26 March 2013].

Schneider, A., and Ingram, H., 1993. Social Construction of Target Populations: Implications for Politics and Policy. *The American Political Science Review,* 87 (2), 334-347.

Schneider, S., 1992. Governmental Response to Disasters: The Conflict Between Bureaucratic Procedures and Emergent Norms. *Public Administration Review,* 52 (2), 135-145.

Schneider, S., 1995. *Flirting with Disaster: Public Management in Crisis Situations.* Armonk, NY: M.E. Sharpe.

Schneider, S., 2011. *Dealing with Disaster: Public Management in Crisis Situations.* Armonk, NY: M.E. Sharpe.

Singleton, R.A. Jr., and Straits, B.C., 1999. *Approaches to Social Research.* 3rd ed. New York: Oxford University Press.

Slaughter, A-M., 2005. *A New World Order.* Princeton University Press.

Smith, G., 2011. *Planning for Post-Disaster Recovery: a Review of the United States Disaster Assistance Framework.* Fairfax, VA: Public Entity Risk Institute.

Stepick, A., *et al.*, 1982. Haitians in Miami: An Assessment of Their Background and Potential, Dialogue #12. *LACC Occasional papers series, Dialogues 1980-1994,* Paper 32. Available from: http://digitalcommons.fiu.edu/laccopsd/32 [Accessed 26 March 2013].

Sterett, S., 2009. New Orleans Everywhere: Bureaucratic Accountability and Housing Policy After Katrina. *In*: A. Sarat and J. Lezaun, eds. *Catastrophe: Law, Politics, and the Humanitarian Impulse.* Amherst, MA: University of Massacheusetts Press, 83-115.

Stone, D., 2001. *Policy Paradox: The Art of Political Decision Making.* New York: W.W. Norton and Company.

Terrazas, A., 2010. *Haitian Immigrants in the United States* [online]. Washington, D.C.: Migration Policy Institute. Available from: http://www.migrationinformation.org/USfocus/display.cfm?id=770 [Accessed 26 March 2013].

United States Citizenship and Immigration Service (USCIS), 2012. *18-Month Extension and Re-designation of Haiti for Temporary Protected Status: Fact Sheet* [online]. Washington: USCIS. Available from: http://www.uscis.gov/portal/site/uscis/menuitem.5af9bb95919f35e66f614176543f6d1a/?vgnextoid=c8514b9594900310VgnVCM100000082ca60aRCRD&vgnextchannel=8a2f6d26d17df110VgnVCM1000004718190aRCRD [Accessed 26 March 2013].

Wachtendorf, T., 2000. When disasters defy borders: What we can learn from the Red River flood about transnational disasters. *The Australian Journal of Emergency Management*, 15 (3), 36-41. Available from: http://www.em.gov.au/Documents/AJEM_Vol15_Issue3.pdf [Accessed 26 March 2013].

Wachtendorf, T., 2009. Trans-system social ruptures: exploring issues of vulnerability and resiliency. *The Review of Policy Research*, 26 (4), 379-393.

The Washington Post, 2010. The U.S. Should Welcome Haitians. Editorial. *The Washington Post* [online], 29 Jan. Available from: http://www.washingtonpost.com/wpdyn/content/article/2010/01/28/AR2010012803513.html [Accessed 15 April 2011].

Weick, K. 1993. The collapse of sensemaking in organizations: The Mann Gulch disaster. *Administrative Science Quarterly*, 38 (4), 628-652.

Zezima, K., 2010. Running for President of Haiti, but Stumping in U.S. *The New York Times* [online], 12 Nov. Available from: http://www.nytimes.com/2010/11/13/us/13campaigns.html?scp=1&sq=haitian%20candidates%20Boston%20New%20York&st=cse# [Accessed 26 March 2013].

# 6

## DISASTER MYTHOLOGY AND AVAILABILITY CASCADES

### Lisa Grow Sun

**ABSTRACT**

Sociological research conducted in the aftermath of natural disasters has uncovered a number of "disaster myths"—widely shared misconceptions about typical post-disaster human behavior. This chapter discusses the possibility that perpetuation of disaster mythology reflects an "availability cascade," defined in prior scholarship as a "self-reinforcing process of collective belief formation by which an expressed perception triggers a chain reaction that gives the perception increasing plausibility through its rising availability in public discourse" (Kuran and Sunstein 1999). Framing the spread of disaster mythology as an availability cascade suggests that certain tools may be useful in halting the myths' continued perpetuation. These tools include changing the legal and social incentives of so-called "availability entrepreneurs"—those principally responsible for beginning and perpetuating the cascade, as well as insulating decision-makers from political pressures generated by the availability cascade. This chapter evaluates the potential effectiveness of these and other solutions for countering disaster mythology.

Las investigaciones sociológicas realizadas tras los desastres naturales han hecho evidentes una serie de "mitos del desastre", conceptos erróneos ampliamente compartidos sobre el comportamiento humano típico tras un desastre. Este artículo analiza la posibilidad de que la perpetuación de los mitos del desastre refleje una "cascada de disponibilidad", definida en estudios anteriores como un "proceso de auto-refuerzo de la formación de una creencia colectiva, a través del que una percepción expresada produce una reacción en cadena que hace que la percepción sea cada vez más verosímil, a través de una mayor presencia en el discurso público" (Kuran y Sunstein 1999). Enmarcar la propagación de los mitos del desastre como una cascada de disponibilidad sugiere que ciertas herramientas pueden ser útiles para parar la continua perpetuación de los mitos. Estas herramientas incluyen el cambio de los incentivos legales y sociales de los llamados "emprendedores de la disponibilidad", los principales responsables del inicio y la perpetuación de la cascada, además del aislamiento de quienes toman las decisiones de las presiones políticas generadas por la cascada de disponibilidad. Este artículo evalúa la efectividad potencial de estas y otras soluciones para contrarrestar los mitos del desastre.

## INTRODUCTION

In the aftermath of Hurricane Katrina, both public officials and the mainstream media painted a dramatic and deeply disturbing picture of violence and looting in devastated New Orleans. The New Orleans Police Superintendent asserted that "little babies [were] getting raped" in the Superdome, a shelter where hurricane survivors took refuge (Oprah 2005). As a guest on the Oprah Winfrey Show, New Orleans Mayor Ray Nagin reported that Katrina's survivors were sinking into an "almost animalistic state" after days of "watching hooligans killing people, raping people" (Thevenot 2006, p. 34).

Similar accounts dominated newspaper headlines and TV coverage of Katrina for days. Post-Katrina New Orleans was consistently depicted both as a city descending into anarchy and violence, and as a war-zone in which Katrina's victims attacked those who had come to their aid. A *New York Times* editorial reported that New Orleans was "a snake pit of anarchy, death, looting, raping, marauding thugs, suffering innocents, a shattered infrastructure, a gutted police force, insufficient troop levels and criminally negligent government planning" (Dowd 2005). The *Financial Times* of London asserted that, at the Convention Center, another shelter of last resort for New Orleans' besieged citizens, "girls and boys were raped in the dark and had their throats cut and bodies were stuffed in the kitchens while looters and madmen exchanged fire with weapons they had looted" (Dinmore 2005). The lead news story in the *Los Angeles Times* described National Guard troops taking "positions on rooftops, scanning for snipers and armed mobs as seething crowds of refugees milled below, desperate to flee"(Barry *et al.* 2005). TV coverage likewise asserted that looting had overtaken New Orleans, playing clips of Katrina survivors taking goods from deserted stores in a seemingly never-ending 24-hour loop.

These unrelenting tales of anarchy, violence, and chaos in post-Katrina New Orleans proved to be, at best, greatly exaggerated, and, at worst, utterly false. Nearly a month after Katrina struck New Orleans, major news outlets retracted many of their previous reports of widespread violence and crime in Katrina's wake (Dwyer and Drew 2005, Rosenblatt and Rainey 2005, Thevenot and Russell 2005). Unfortunately, the early reports have proved resilient, and the truth has never fully overtaken the myth.

## DISASTER MYTHOLOGY AND ITS CONSEQUENCES

The myths about post-disaster human behavior that took hold in the aftermath of Katrina were not unique to that catastrophe. Disaster sociologists long ago identified several important public misconceptions about typical human behavior in disaster's aftermath (Quarantelli and Dynes

1972). These misconceptions—also called "disaster myths"—include (1) the myth that widespread antisocial behavior, such as violence and looting, is common after disasters; (2) the myth that most disaster survivors will panic and engage in irrational flight behavior; and (3) the myth that disaster survivors commonly suffer a shock reaction that paralyzes them and interferes with their ability to respond to the disaster and care for themselves and others (Quarantelli and Dynes 1972).

Understanding how these myths gain traction during disasters is important because the existence of these misconceptions distorts our legal and policy framework for disaster response and recovery (Sun 2011). The myth of widespread antisocial activity, for example, has resulted in a U.S. legal system of disaster response that overemphasizes security risks at the expense of humanitarian efforts to rescue and care for survivors (Sun 2011). First, exaggerated reports of looting and violence post-disaster make the President more likely to deploy federal troops in a law enforcement, rather than humanitarian, capacity and less likely to deploy troops at all if the President decides for legal or political reasons not to invest federal troops with law enforcement authority (Sun 2011). Second, such exaggerated reports also tend to delay aid to survivors (Sun 2011). After Katrina, Mayor Nagin reacted to exaggerated reports of violence and looting by diverting 1,500 New Orleans police officers from search and rescue missions to anti-looting patrol (NBC News 2005). Officials also delayed delivery of desperately needed food, water, and sanitation supplies to shelters of last resort until massive military escorts could be assembled to accompany the deliveries and respond to the looting and gangs that the shipments were expected to encounter (Reckdahl 2006). Third, public officials may respond to inflated fears of looting and violence by implementing restrictions on freedom and freedom of movement— such as roadblocks, curfews, and vague declarations of "martial law"—that may risk excessive use of force by police, interfere with response efforts, delay evacuated residents' return to their homes, and violate basic rights (Sun 2011). Private citizens may likewise react to the myth by engaging in vigilante behavior to protect themselves and their property from perceived, but largely imaginary, threats (Sun 2011). Fourth, the prevalence of the disaster myth of looting and violence convinces us to squander post-disaster political capital on the passage of unnecessary looting laws, often at the expense of passing hazard mitigation measures that might protect lives and property during the next hazard event (Sun 2011).

In addition to these concrete, detrimental effects on our legal and policy framework for disaster response, exaggerated reports of widespread looting and violence can also stigmatize disaster victims (Garfield 2007). That stigma can make other communities less receptive to taking in disaster survivors, in both the short and long term. In the short term, communities may balk at setting up evacuation centers and shelters for displaced survivors. In the long term, those survivors who choose to permanently relocate to another community may face discrimination in employment and other opportunities.

Katrina survivors from New Orleans faced this kind of stigma in cities such as Houston, Texas, where they took refuge. Many New Orleans residents relocated, at least temporarily, to Houston. During that time, it was widely reported in both the local and national news that Katrina survivors were responsible for a wave of crime in the Houston area (Bustillo 2006). Studies later disproved the existence of a "Katrina crime wave," ushered in by evacuees from New Orleans, but the stigma remains (Pinkerton 2010). Of course, Katrina evacuees were stereotyped, in part, because of the high crime rates that plagued New Orleans prior to the storm (Gelinas 2006), but the reports of widespread looting and violence in Katrina's aftermath contributed to the public perception that Katrina evacuees were criminals (Vergano 2010). Moreover, reports suggesting that disaster evacuees spawned a crime wave are likewise "typical of 'disaster myths' seen after catastrophes" (Vergano 2010 cited Trainor). The stigmatization of Katrina survivors as violent criminals has also resulted in employment and housing discrimination against survivors (Reckdahl 2006).

## DISASTER MYTH PERPETUATION AS AN AVAILABILITY CASCADE

These detrimental consequences of the disaster mythology of widespread violence and looting demonstrate the necessity of finding political and legal tools to counter the myth's perpetuation and its effects on our framework for disaster response and recovery (Sun 2011). Considering the perpetuation of disaster mythology as an "availability cascade" may be helpful in understanding the myth's spread and in generating possible options for countering the myth and its consequences.

Timur Kuran and Cass Sunstein (1999) have defined an "availability cascade" as "a self-reinforcing process of collective belief formation by which an expressed perception triggers a chain reaction that gives the perception increasing plausibility through its rising availability in public discourse." More simply, an availability cascade results from the "interaction of the 'availability heuristic'—a mental shortcut by which an individual judges the probability of an event by his or her ability to conjure up examples of that event—and the social mechanisms through which risk perceptions are propagated" (Kuran and Sunstein 1999 quoted Sun 2011).

The mental "availability" of violence and looting as disaster risks is amplified in the United States by a popular culture of disaster movies and by media reporting of disasters, both of which—not surprisingly—focus on such antisocial behavior in disasters' aftermath:

> [T]he calm, helping behaviors typically exhibited by disaster survivors are hardly the fodder of either attention-grabbing headlines or fast-paced entertainment. Those portrayals of disaster increase the mental "availability" of violence and looting as disaster risks by proliferating examples of disaster-related violence and looting (even if those examples never, in fact, occurred) (Kuran and Sunstein 1999, cited Sun 2011).

A disaster risk that has a human component—like looting and vio- lence—may also be more "available" mentally than the underlying risks posed by the natural hazard event itself because manmade risks tend to be more salient in people's minds than those that appear to be naturally created (Kuran and Sunstein 1999, Sjoberg 1999). Of course, Kuran and Sunstein are likely to view this tendency to focus on and react more strongly to manmade risks than "natural risks" as a cognitive error, whereas others like Dan Kahan (2008) might view this tendency as a "culturally mediated value judgment." Regardless of how one characteriz- es this tendency, the consequence is that at least some members of the public may be predisposed to believe that violence and looting are com- mon reactions to disasters because of the salience of those manmade risks (Sun 2011).

Sunstein and Kuran's work on availability cascades focuses on the role of two (often interrelated) social mechanisms that produce and amplify availability cascades: "informational cascades" and "reputational cascades" (Kuran and Sunstein 1999). An informational cascade—or "bandwagon or snowballing process"—arises when individuals "base their own beliefs on the apparent beliefs of others" because those individuals lack complete information about the relevant issues (Kuran and Sunstein 1999). Informational cascades occur, in part, because of the "bounded rationality" of human beings: individuals necessarily lack the time, re- sources, and mental energy to gain perfect information on every matter; therefore, individuals may be inclined to accept a particular view "simply [because] of its acceptance by others" (Kuran and Sunstein 1999). Infor- mation cascades may be particularly likely to occur in the aftermath of disasters, which often curtail access to information by disrupting commu- nication networks and which also bring basic survival needs to the fore- front, perhaps crowding out some attempts to verify the accuracy of information received from fellow survivors and other sources. Hurricane survivors, for example, "may be inclined to believe that looting is likely to occur simply because their neighbors post signs declaring that 'Looters will be shot,' reflecting the neighbors' apparent belief that looting is a serious problem" (Sun 2011). They may also be inclined to believe word- of-mouth reports from fellow survivors that looting and violence are occurring because they lack adequate means and time to verify the stories and believing a false report is likely to appear less personally costly than disbelieving a report that turns out to be true.

The second social mechanism for spreading availability errors is a reputational cascade, which occurs when an individual embraces a certain view in their public dealings (a view which may conflict with the person's own privately held view) to garner public approval or forestall public criticism or censure (Kuran and Sunstein 1999). A state governor might, for example, call out the state National Guard to police a disaster- devastated area, not because she believes that looting and violence are likely to occur, but because she believes her constituents are concerned about those risks and will criticize her for failing to take action to counter those risks (Sun 2011). Similarly, a state legislator might propose passing or strengthening a state looting law after a serious disaster in his state, not because he believes the law is necessary to deal with disaster-looting, but because he believes he can score political points with his constituents who worry about looting of their homes.

Observations gleaned from the perpetuation of disaster mythology suggest that perhaps "reputational cascades" should be viewed as a subset of a broader category we might term "false acquiescence cascades." Individuals may have various motivations, aside from reputational interests, for "false acquiescence"—acting and speaking as though they hold a particular view, when in fact they do not—including motivations that are more public regarding. (These "false acquiescence cascades might also be termed "preference falsification cascades"; however, Kuran defines "preference falsification" primarily as misrepresentation of private preferences induced by "social pressures" such as reputational interests, (Kuran 1995, ix)). For example, during Hurricane Gilbert, one city emergency manager, who knew that "looting rarely occurs," "took very public precautions to prevent looting" in order "to convince citizens that it was safe to evacuate" (Fischer 2008). This example suggests that once a risk assessment has achieved a certain threshold of acceptance, individuals may acquiesce in, and even participate in, the perpetuation of that assessment, even if they disagree with it, for fear that the assessment is too widely held to be effectively countered and that failure to respond to that assessment will produce adverse social consequences. We might call this subset of false acquiescence cascades "futility cascades."

Scholars have thus far given insufficient attention to the possibility that public officials (or other individuals) might acquiesce in—and even promote—a particular conception of risk for reasons that are less about bounded rationality or reputational interests and more grounded in that individual's desire to further the public good in the face of substantial and intractable opposition to what the individual views as the "correct" assessment of risk.

## POTENTIAL TOOLS FOR COUNTERING DISASTER MYTH PERPETUATION

Framing the perpetuation of disaster mythology as an availability cascade may be helpful in addressing the problems created by disaster myths because scholars have already identified some tools to reduce the deleterious effects availability cascades can have on risk regulation. These tools include altering the incentives of so-called "availability entrepreneurs" and insulating decisionmakers from political pressures generated by availability cascades.

The first of these ideas suggests that availability cascades might be addressed by changing the incentives of those who are principally responsible for both setting the cascade in motion and perpetuating its spread. Kuran and Sunstein (1999, p. 733) posit the existence of "availability entrepreneurs," who are "instigators and manipulators of availability campaigns," often to achieve some political end. In the disaster myth context, at least some of those most directly involved in myth perpetuation—Hollywood producers and media—seem driven less by political aims and more by commercial and other concerns. These myth perpetuators seem to be unwitting "entrepreneurs" at best, at least in terms of the political and social effects of disaster mythology.

Even the incentives of some of these accidental entrepreneurs potentially could be altered, however, by imposing penalties for the perpetuation of availability cascades based on false premises. For example, Kuran and Sunstein (1999, pp. 749-751) discuss the possibility of product defamation laws as one way to deter availability cascades that exaggerate the dangers posed by particular products. The parallel remedy for disaster myths might be group libel suits brought by disaster survivors. In the case of post-Katrina New Orleans, there is evidence that the false media reporting permanently stigmatized New Orleanians, as a group, as dangerous, violent people undeserving of our assistance (Garfield 2007, p. 58). As suggested earlier, that stigma has followed many displaced Katrina survivors to their new homes (whether temporary or permanent) in other cities, making it more difficult for Katrina survivors to find both housing and jobs (Reckdahl 2006). The stigmatization of New Orleans Katrina survivors may also have influenced the amount of money the country has been willing to commit to rebuilding New Orleans (Reckdahl 2006).

Group libel is no remedy for these potential harms in the U.S., however, nor is it an effective deterrent of similar myth-perpetuation in the future, as group libel suits have been all but eliminated by the U.S. Supreme Court on First Amendment grounds. Although the Supreme Court upheld the constitutionality of a statute making it unlawful to engage in group libel against a "class of citizens" in *Beauharnais v. Illinois*, this holding has been severely undermined by the Court's subjection of defamation law to First Amendment inquiry under *New York Times v. Sullivan*. Nevertheless, given that the media have no obvious political motivation for perpetuating disaster mythology and have at least an aspirational commitment to truth, a targeted information campaign that exposes disaster mythology and suggests other attention-grabbing headlines (like dramatic rescues) might have some success in decreasing media reporting of disaster myths. For example, Fischer (2008) reported that education in disaster myths improved the accuracy of two reporters' coverage of a local disaster.

Disaster sociologists Kathleen Tierney and Christine Bevc (2007, p. 39) have perhaps identified a more purposeful "availability entrepreneur" of looting and violence mythology when they write that those who favor militarism in society will tend to perpetuate mythology that sets the stage for militarized disaster response. Other potential myth perpetuators include law enforcement agencies in the affected areas, who might fear losing control and might hope that rumors of looting and violence will result either in outside reinforcements or loosening of constitutional or other restraints on law enforcement activities (as under the popular conception of "martial law") (Sun 2011). Local public officials (as well as business owners and disaster survivors in affected areas), desperate for a quick influx of outside aid, might also exaggerate law-and-order difficulties on the ground in an effort to spur faster state and federal response (Sun 2011). The same officials might exaggerate law-and-order difficulties for an entirely different reason: to justify and excuse slow or inept governmental response (Sun 2011). Conversely, political opponents of current officeholders might attempt to get a jump-start on the "blame game" that often follows natural disasters (Picou and Marshall 2007, p. 13) by exaggerating the prevalence of looting and violence in the disaster's aftermath. More fundamentally, emphasizing that disaster-induced governmental breakdown or incapacity results in a kind of Hobbesian state of nature among survivors may serve to justify more mundane, everyday governmental exercises of power outside the disaster context, as well, by reaffirming that only government stands between us and chaos.

Some of these incentives to perpetuate the myth can perhaps be countered by amending disaster laws and plans to preclude the outcomes the "availability entrepreneurs" seek. For example, the Insurrection Act (10 *United States Code* 2006) which allows the President to invest federal military troops (or federalized National Guard troops) with law enforcement powers during, *inter alia*, "insurrections," (10 *United States Code* 2006) could be interpreted narrowly to preclude the President from deploying federal military as disaster police absent clear evidence of widespread rebellion against government authority (Sun 2011). Making clear that there is a substantial threshold that must be met before investing military with law enforcement authority during natural disasters might convince would-be availability entrepreneurs who favor militarization of disaster response that exaggerating law-and-order difficulties to force the militarization of the federal response would likely be futile. Similarly, if the relevant state and local disaster laws preclude the imposition of "martial law" during a disaster (or the suspension of federal constitutional rights), local police may be less likely to exaggerate rates of looting and violence because they know that such rumors cannot be invoked to justify restrictions on basic rights (Sun 2011). Making clear to local officials that, historically, attempts to speed aid by overplaying law enforcement concerns have often backfired, slowing the delivery of aid and interfering with recovery efforts, might also mitigate public officials' incentives to perpetuate inflated rumors of violence and looting (Sun 2011). These mechanisms for disincentivizing myth perpetuation may thus be important tools for countering disaster mythology. Moreover, if public officials are perpetuating the myths not to achieve particular political or legal outcomes, but because they are themselves swept up by the myths and exhibiting what Lee Clarke and Caron Chess have called "elite panic" (Clarke and Chess 2008), then these same legal limitations on official discretion to act on those fears may help mitigate the deleterious effects of official panic on disaster response.

The second of Kuran and Sunstein's (1999, pp. 752-58) ideas suggests reliance on politically insulated, deliberative expert decisionmakers as a solution to the arguably irrational risk regulation spurred by availability cascades. In particular, they recommend that these politically insulated decisionmakers employ cost-benefit analysis. Dan Kahan (2008) criticizes this proposal, arguing that emotional assessments of risk reflect cultural value judgments that may be entitled to some weight in policy-making, which therefore should be democratically accountable rather than insulated from politics.

What kinds of cultural value judgments might contribute to a heightened willingness to believe that post-disaster looting and violence are serious disaster risks that should be prioritized over other risks that exist in disaster's aftermath? Perhaps some individuals believe that it is worse to have their property stolen by looters than to have it destroyed by the hazard itself. Similarly, some individuals might believe that it is worse to be injured or killed in post-disaster violence than by either the hazard event or the humanitarian crisis the disaster may provoke. While it is possible that such cultural commitments exist, these commitments may do substantial harm (for example, by delaying aid) to others who do not share these commitments.

Moreover, it seems equally—if not more—likely that the myth of post-disaster violence has found a warm reception with at least some audiences because of racism and classism (Sun 2011) or because of a propensity to blame the victims in order to justify the status quo (Napier, *et al.*, 2006, p. 64)—cultural commitments that clearly should not be given weight in policy making. Kahan himself acknowledges that not all value judgments are entitled to weight in the democratic process, particularly if imposing those judgments on others "exposes [them] . . . to significant physical harm or restrictions on liberty" (Kahan and Slovic 2006). Indeed, disaster mythology may be problematic, in part, because it provides a more culturally acceptable narrative and framework for playing out age-old stereotypes about minorities and the poor. There seems to be little doubt, for instance, that preexisting racism played an important role in the initiation and propagation of the looting and violence rumors that plagued post-Katrina reporting. Disaster availability cascades focused on survivor looting and violence, then, seem likely both to entrench preexisting racism and further stigmatize already disadvantaged groups.

Although Kahan's concerns do not seem particularly weighty in this context, assigning disaster decisionmaking to politically insulated experts would nonetheless be problematic. The decisions made in a disaster's immediate aftermath about response priorities, curfews, etc. seem like particularly poor candidates for insulated, deliberative expert decision-making. First, in contrast to most risk regulation that Congress undertakes, lives at stake in disaster decisionmaking are not vague, unidentifiable victims reduced to statistics, but concrete, more easily identifiable individuals whose lives and well-being are immediately affected. Local citizens, rightly, will demand that their elected officials make such critical decisions. Second, all the planning in the world cannot anticipate the precise problems, demands on resources, and trade-offs that will have to be considered in a particular disaster situation. Much of the critical information will not be available until the disaster occurs (and even then serious information gaps will likely exist), and decisions will have to be made under tremendous time pressure in order to minimize deaths, injuries, and property damage. These circumstances will generally require quick executive action rather than deliberative decisionmaking by some politically insulated body. Third, most disaster decisionmaking occurs at state and local levels. Given this multiplicity of decisionmakers, it is difficult to imagine that each state or locality would have the political will or the resources to employ insulated expert decisionmakers for disaster decisionmaking, particularly since it is often uncertain which localities will actually suffer major disasters and have to call upon those decisionmakers.

Nonetheless, there is significant value in ensuring that disaster decisionmakers have access to advice and counsel from emergency managers educated in the pitfalls of disaster mythology. Thus, a first step toward countering disaster mythology may be legally requiring (*Georgia* 2007, *Connecticut* 2007) or otherwise incentivizing (*Alabama* 2006) states and local governments to hire emergency managers who have at least some college education or experience in managing disasters. Insisting that state and local emergency managers fulfill continuing education requirements would also be valuable, particularly if the curriculum specifically requires education about disaster mythology.

Similarly, the relatively new requirements for the Federal Emergency Management Agency (FEMA) administrator, imposed by the Post Katrina Emergency Management Reform Act of 2006, (Public Law 2006) are an important step toward ensuring that federal decisionmakers have more expert input. These new requirements establish that the FEMA administrator must have "a demonstrated ability in and knowledge of emergency management and homeland security" and "not less than 5 years of executive leadership and management experience in the public or private sector" (6 *United States Code* 2006). These requirements were imposed largely in reaction to President Bush's appointment of Michael Brown, who lacked any significant emergency management experience, as FEMA Director—an appointment widely viewed as political cronyism that cost Katrina victims dearly (Krugman 2005). In contrast, the current FEMA Administrator, Craig Fugate, is widely regarded as a capable and experienced emergency manager (Thompson 2009). The Post-Katrina Act "also aims to increase the professionalism and expertise of FEMA staff by requiring FEMA to develop a 'strategic human capital plan,' and establish 'appropriate career paths'—including requisite training, education, and experience—for agency personnel" (5 U.S.C. §§ 10102, 10103 (2006) quoted Farber *et al.* 2010).

Some empirical evidence supports the conclusion that education of local emergency managers would be beneficial in counteracting disaster mythology. Although local emergency managers are more aware of disaster myths than the general public (Fischer 2008), research suggests that many still believe important components of disaster mythology. In a recent survey of local emergency managers, an overwhelming majority (85%) of local emergency managers "understood that survivors usually are the first to engage in search and rescue activities" (Fischer 2008, p. 125), but only half (50%) of the surveyed emergency managers realized that victims generally do not panic during a disaster (Fischer 2008, p. 126). "Less than half (46%) knew that survivors usually do not behave irrationally due to the shock of the experience" (Fischer 2008). Thirty-nine percent believe that residents will engage in looting (Fischer 2008).

Those local emergency managers who had taken more training courses, experienced at least two disasters, worked as emergency managers for more than five years, or had additional education had more accurate views of post-disaster human behavior (Fischer 2008, pp. 127-28). Neither general work experience in the disaster field nor participation in disaster drills was positively correlated with more accurate views (Fischer 2008, p. 128). "Education had a greater impact than disaster experience, or any of the job experience variables (training seminars, drills, years on the job, and years in the field)" (Fischer 2008, p. 128). The survey results suggest that "hiring individuals with a college degree and then involving them in an on-going [emergency management] training program is optimal" (Fischer 2008, p. 129). Requiring that emergency managers be college-educated may pay dividends in other respects, as well. Evidence suggests that the only factor positively correlated with an emergency manager's adoption of mitigation measures (to prevent future disaster costs) is increased education (Fischer 2008, pp. 149-152).

Of course, having more educated, informed decisionmakers is not a full solution to the problems created by disaster mythology. Indeed, as discussed earlier, even the best-educated decisionmakers may feel that they have little choice but to indulge the general public's fear of violence and looting by taking very public steps to reassure people in harm's way that they can safely evacuate their homes because the National Guard or police stand ready to thwart potential looters. Decisionmakers may reasonably fear that, without such reassurances, many will fail to evacuate.

For example, Thomas Drabek, a groundbreaking disaster sociologist, has suggested that the best approach to dealing with the disaster myth of extensive post-disaster looting is to allay public fears by creating an "impression" that law enforcement is prepared to prevent looting by heavy policing of the disaster area (Drabek 2010, p. 97). Drabek suggests that local officials should "emphasize security" when dealing with the public and should "communicate loudly and clearly that security will be tight" (Drabek 2010, p. 97). In addition, Drabek suggests that local law enforcement should "buttress[]" its forces with a "citizens' patrol" (Drabek 2010, p. 97).

Unfortunately, however, these solutions are prime examples of false acquiescence futility cascades that perpetuate both the myth itself and the deleterious consequences the myth engenders. While Drabek warns against "overallocat[ing] resources" to looting patrols, official announcements that such patrols are necessary are likely to prompt additional media reporting of the myth and to bolster the public's belief that looting and violence are typically serious problems in disaster's aftermath. Those heightened public fears, in turn, may increase public demand for excessive security measures that divert resources from other, more pressing needs. Law enforcement may also rely on those public fears to justify unnecessary restrictions on freedom and freedom of movement post-disaster. Moreover, Drabek's suggestion that a citizens' patrol be assembled to police for looting may well risk the kind of vigilante violence that was observed after Katrina. Indulging and reinforcing public fears of looting seems unlikely to be the right answer.

The need for effective public education to counter the disaster myth of pervasive looting and violence is evident. Unfortunately, the challenges facing successful education campaigns are both real and difficult to surmount. Sunstein, for example, is sufficiently skeptical of the value of public education in countering overblown risk assessments that he asserts that the best solution is often to "[c]hange the subject" (Sunstein 2005, p. 125). Despite Sunstein's well founded skepticism, well designed disaster-public-information campaigns—like environmental education and youth anti-smoking campaigns—may nonetheless be among the most effective tools for countering disaster mythology (Farrelly *et al.* 2005, Vandenbergh, Brakenbus and Gilligan 2008). Public information campaigns could, for example, publicize the real tradeoffs that occur when the myth encourages public officials to prioritize law enforcement needs over search and rescue and other basic humanitarian relief. A greater public understanding of the costs of disaster myth perpetuation—including the real risks that aid will be delayed to those in need—might help halt the spread of information cascades during disasters as individuals will have a better sense that crediting and spreading "false positive" reports of violence and looting has real costs, costs that might affect them individually or their family, friends, and neighbors. Dampening information cascades would, in turn, likely diminish the strength of false acquiescence cascades, including both the reputational cascades identified by Kuran and Sunstein and the futility cascades identified in this chapter.

Moreover, emotional risk assessments that reflect value judgments of the type identified by Kahan are most likely to be reshaped by public information campaigns that focus on altering the social meaning of disasters and reframing the values at stake. While the exact content of such campaigns would probably vary from community to community (Kahan 2008), if public information campaigns can help reconceptualize natural disasters as events that generally bring out the best in both people and communities, those campaigns might increase public skepticism about rumors of disaster atrocities and about the need for draconian military and police intervention after natural disasters.

One substantial obstacle that public information campaigns will likely encounter in altering people's conception of natural disasters is the phenomenon of "biased assimilation":

> Biased assimilation refers to the fact that people assimilate new in-
> formation in a biased fashion; those who have accepted false ru-
> mors do not easily give up their beliefs, especially when they have a
> strong emotional commitment to those beliefs. It can be exceedingly
> hard to dislodge what people think, even by presenting them with
> the facts (Sunstein 2009, p. 9).

"Biased assimilation" thus encapsulates the common-sense notion that people tend to process new information in light of their preexisting beliefs; their precommitments are particularly likely to influence their assimilation of new information if they have a strong emotional attach-ment to, or other investment in, those preexisting beliefs (Sunstein 2009).

News coverage of Japan's March 2011 earthquake and tsunami pro-vided an interesting illustration of biased assimilation in the context of the disaster myth of widespread looting and violence. In the aftermath of the devastating earthquake and tsunami, news sources reported—often with surprise—that there was very little looting taking place in Japan (James and Goldman 2011). Rather than entertaining the possibility that the lack of looting in Japan might reflect a broader truth about human nature that should cause us to reconsider our deeply held (and mistaken) beliefs about post-disaster human behavior, newspapers and pundits sought to "explain away" the lack of looting in Japan as the result of some unique characteristic of Japanese society or culture (Beam 2011, Chuensuksawadi 2011, Stuart 2011, cited Sun 2011). Indeed, rather than prompting recon-sideration of the Katrina news coverage or discussion of the fact that much of the early Katrina reporting was overblown and inflammatory, many media reports on the Japan earthquake simply resuscitated and repeated the exaggerated claims of looting and violence perpetuated in Katrina's immediate aftermath, contrasting the calm, orderly behavior of Japanese survivors with the imagined behavior of Katrina's survivors (Chuensuksawadi 2011, Stuart 2011).

The difficulties of rooting out firmly entrenched beliefs about looting and violence after disasters suggest that public education campaigns might be most effective if they are focused on the youngest citizens. Many elementary schools provide children with basic information about disas-ters (by, for example, conducting earthquake drills). Education campaigns aimed at children that teach that while disasters are tragedies, they are tragedies that usually bring communities together, rather than tearing them apart in chaos and crime, might be effective in creating a less jaun-diced view of post-disaster human behavior among individuals who have yet to form strong opinions about the likelihood of looting and other criminal behavior in disasters' aftermath. Any such campaigns should, of course, be subjected to empirical analysis to evaluate their effectiveness over time.

## CONCLUSION

Disaster myths—particularly the myth of widespread looting and violence—interfere with effective disaster response and recovery. The spread of disaster myths can be usefully analyzed as an availability cascade. Although there is certainly no panacea for the problem of disaster mythology, that analysis suggests that the spread of disaster mythology can perhaps be mitigated by changing the incentives of availability entrepreneurs who might otherwise perpetuate the myth, by hiring more educated emergency managers to advise local officials in disaster decisionmaking, and by creating targeted public information campaigns—particularly campaigns aimed at young people—that will help alter the social meaning of disasters. While these approaches are unlikely to completely halt the perpetuation of disaster mythology, they are important first steps in promoting a more accurate understanding of typical post-disaster behavior and designing the most effective policy and legal framework for disaster response and recovery.

## *Bibliography*

*United States Code*, 2006. Title 6, § 313.

*United States Code*, 2006. Title 10, §§ 331–335.

*Alabama Code*, 2006. §31-9-61 to -62, LexisNexis.

Barry, E., *et al.*, 2005. New Orleans Slides into Chaos; U.S. Scrambles to Send Troops. *Los Angeles Times*, 2 Sep, p. 1.

Beam, C., 2011. Stop, Thief! Thank You: Why so little looting in Japan? It's not just about honesty. *Slate* [online], 16 Mar. Available from: http://www.slate.com/id/2288514/ [Accessed 27 October 2011].

Beauharnais v. Illinois, 343 U.S. 250 (1952).

Bustillo, M., 2006. Houston Grumbles as Evacuees Stay Put. *Los Angeles Times* [online], 21 Aug. Available from: http://articles.latimes.com/2006/aug/21/nation/na-evac21 [Accessed 26 October 2011].

Chuensuksawadi, P., 2011. Stoic Calm in the Face of Utter Calamity. *Bangkok Post* [online], 15 Mar. Available from: http://www.bangkokpost.com/opinion/opinion/226703/stoic-calm-in-the-face-of-utter-calamity [Accessed 27 October 2011].

*Connecticut General Statutes Annotated*, 2007. § 28-1a, West.

Clarke, L., and Chess, C., 2008. Elites and Panic: More to Fear than Fear Itself. *Social Forces*, 87 (2), 993-1014.

Dinmore, G., 2005. City of Rape, Rumour and Recrimination. *Financial Times*, 5 Sep, p. 7.

Dowd, M., 2005. United States of Shame. *New York Times* [online], 3 Sep, p. A21. Available from: http://www.nytimes.com/2005/09/03/opinion/

03dowd.html?scp=1&sq=Maureen%20DoDo%20United%20States%20of%20S
hame&st=cse [Accessed 26 October 2011].

Drabek, T.E., 2010. *The Human Side of Disaster*. Boca Raton: CRC Press.

Dwyer, J., and Drew, C., 2005. Fear Exceeded Crime's Reality in New Orleans. *New York Times* [online], 29 Sep, p. A1. Available from: http://www.nytimes.com/2005/09/29/national/nationalspecial/29crime.html?scp=1&sq=Fear%20Exceede d%20Crime%27s%20Reality&st=cse [Accessed 26 October 2011].

Farber, D.A., *et al.*, 2010. *Disaster Law and Policy*. 2nd ed. Frederick, MD: Aspen; Austin: Wolters Kluwer Law & Business.

Farrelly, M.C., *et al.*, 2005. Evidence of a Dose-Response Relationship Between "Truth" Antismoking Ads and Youth Smoking Prevalence. *American Journal of Public Health* [online], 95 (3), 428-430. Available from: http://ajph.aphapublications.org/doi/full/10.2105/AJPH.2004.049692 [Accessed 7 March 2013].

Fischer, H.W. III, 2008. *Response to Disaster: Fact Versus Fiction and Its Perpetuation*. Lanham, Md.: University Press of America.

Garfield, G., 2007. Hurricane Katrina: The Making of Unworthy Disaster Victims. *Journal of African American Studies*, 10 (4), 55-74.

Gelinas, N., 2006. Katrina Refugees Shoot Up Houston. *City Journal* [online], 4 Jan. Available from: http://www.city-journal.org/html/eon2006-01-04ng.html [Accessed 26 October 2011].

*Georgia Code Annotated*, 2007. § 38-3-27(a)(3)(F)-(G).

James, S.D., and Goldman, R., 2011. Japanese, Waiting in Line for Hours, Follow Social Order After Quake. *ABC News* [online], 15 Mar. Available from: http://abcnews.go.com/Health/japan-victims-show-resilience-earthquake-tsunami-sign-sense/story?id=13135355 [Accessed 27 October 2011].

Kahan, D.M., and Slovic, P., 2006. Cultural Evaluators of Risk: "Values" or "Blunders"? *Harvard Law Review*, 119 (4), 166-172.

Kahan, D.M., 2008. Two Conceptions of Emotion in Risk Regulation. *University of Pennsylvania Law Review*, 156 (3), 741-766. Available from: https://www.law.upenn.edu/journals/lawreview/articles/volume156/issue3/Kahan156U.Pa.L.Rev.741%282008%29.pdf [Accessed 7 March 2013].

Krugman, P., 2005. All the President's Friends. *New York Times* [online], 12 Sep. Available from: http://www.nytimes.com/2005/09/12/opinion/12krugman.html [Accessed 7 March 2013].

Kuran, T., 1995. *Private Truths, Public Lies: The Social Consequences of Preference Falsification*. Cambridge: Harvard University Press.

Kuran, T., and Sunstein, C.R., 1999. Availability Cascades and Risk Regulation. *Stanford Law Review*, 51 (4), 683-768.

Napier, J.L., *et al.*, 2006. System Justification in Responding to the Poor and Displaced in the Aftermath of Hurricane Katrina. *Analyses of Social Issues and Public Policy*, 6, 57-73.

NBC News, 2005. New Orleans Mayor Orders Looting Crackdown. *NBC News* [online], 1 Sep. Available from: http://www.msnbc.msn.com/id/9063708/ [Accessed 26 October 2011].

New York Times v. Sullivan, 376 U.S. 254 (1964).

*Oprah Reports* [online], 2005. Available from: http://www.oprah.com/slideshow/ oprahshow/oprahshow1_ss_20050906/2 [Accessed 26 October 2011].

Picou, J.S., and Marshall, B.K., 2007. Introduction: Katrina as Paradigm Shift: Reflections on Disaster Research in the Twenty-First Century. *In*: D.L. Brunsma, D. Overfelt and J.S. Picou, eds. *The Sociology of Katrina: Perspectives on a Modern Catastrophe*. Lanham, Md.: Rowman & Littlefield Publishers, 1-20.

Pinkerton, J., 2010. Katrina's Impact on Crime Questioned. *Houston Chronicle* [online], 15 Feb. Available from: http://www.chron.com/news/houston-texas/article/Study-Katrina-crime-wave-nonexistent-in-Houston-1715592.php [Accessed 26 October 2011].

Public Law Number 109-295, §§ 689b(b)-689c, 120 Stat. 1394, 1449 (codified at 6 U.S.C. §§ 774-75 (2006)).

Quarantelli, E.L., and Dynes, R.R., 1972. When Disaster Strikes (It Isn't Much Like What You've Heard & Read About). *Psychology Today*, 5 67-70.

Reckdahl, K., 2006. The Myths of New Orleans. *Tucson Weekly* [online], 24 Aug. Available from: http://www.tucsonweekly.com/tucson/the-myths-of-new-orleans/Content?oid=1085005 [Accessed 26 October 2011].

Rosenblatt, S., and Rainey, J., 2005. Katrina Takes a Toll on Truth, News Accuracy. *Los Angeles Times*, 27 Sep, p. A16.

Sjoberg, L., 1998. Risk Perception: Experts and the Public. *European Psychologist*, 3 (1), 1-12.

Stuart, E., 2011. Discipline in the Face of Disaster: No Looting in Japan. *Deseret News* [online], 14 Mar. Available from: http://www.deseretnews.com/ article/700118414/Discipline-in-the-face-of-disaster-no-looting-in-Japan.html?pg=1 [Accessed 27 October 2011].

Sun, L.G., 2011. Disaster Mythology and the Law. *Cornell Law Review* [online], 96 (5), 1131-1208. Available from: http://www.lawschool.cornell.edu/ research/cornell-law-review/upload/Sun-final.pdf [Accessed 7 March 2013].

Sunstein, C.R., 2005. *Laws of Fear: Beyond the Precautionary Principle*. Cambridge University Press.

Sunstein, C.R., 2009. *On Rumors: how falsehoods spread, why we believe them, what can be done*. New York: Farrar, Straus and Giroux.

Thevenot, B., and Russell, G., 2005. Rape. Murder. Gunfights. *Times Picayune (New Orleans)* [online], 26 Sep, p. A1. Available from: http://www.nola.com/katrina/ pages/092605/0926PAGEA01.pdf [Accessed 7 March 2013].

Thevenot, B., 2006. Myth-Making in New Orleans. *American Journalism Review* [online], 27(6), 30-37. Available from: http://www.ajr.org/Article.asp?id=3998 [Accessed 7 March 2013].

Thompson, G., 2009. Emergency Manager Chosen for FEMA. *New York Times* [online], 5 Mar. Available from: http://query.nytimes.com/gst/ fullpage.html?res=9401EEDD113DF936A35750C0A96F9C8B63 [Accessed 7 March 2013].

Tierney, K., and Bevc, C., 2007. Disaster as War: Militarism and the Social Construction of Disaster in New Orleans. *In*: D.L. Brunsma, D. Overfelt and J.S. Picou, eds. *The Sociology of Katrina: Perspectives on a Modern Catastrophe.* Lanham, Md.: Rowman & Littlefield Publishers.

Treaster, J.B., and Goodnough, A., 2005. Powerful Storm Threatens Havoc Along Gulf Coast. *New York Times* [online], 29 Aug, p. A1. Available from: http://www.nytimes.com/2005/08/29/national/29storm.html?scp=1&sq=Powerf ul%20StoSt%20Threatens%20Havoc%20Along%20Gulf%20Coast&st=cse [Accessed 26 October 2011].

Vandenbergh, M.P., Barkenbus, J., and Gilligan, J., 2008. Individual Carbon Emissions: The Low-Hanging Fruit. *UCLA Law Review*, 55 (6), 1701-1758. Available from: http://www.uclalawreview.org/?p=384 [Accessed 7 March 2013].

Vergano, D., 2010. No Crime Wave Among Hurricane Katrina Evacuees. *U.S.A. Today* [online], 15 Feb. Available from: http://www.usatoday.com/weather/ storms/hurricanes/2010-02-12-hurricane-katrina-crime_N.htm [Accessed 26 October 2011].

# 7

# THE ROLE OF LAW IN ENGINEERING "NATURAL" DISASTERS

## Arthur F. McEvoy

### ABSTRACT

What people perceive as "natural disasters" typically take place when extractive industries operate at levels high enough that the ecological systems from which they draw resources lose their ability to buffer transient shocks, whether of environmental or technological origin. Legal institutions whose purpose it is to prevent such disasters from taking place may in fact encourage them, insofar as they must also broker competing demands for greater access to resources. Legal institutions may adapt to ecological instability in the wake of such disasters, "learning" from the experience more or less successfully depending on the conditions under which the disaster takes place. This chapter will develop these ideas in the context of a number of noteworthy disasters, including the sinking of the *Deepwater Horizon* in 2010.

Lo que se percibe como "desastres naturales" suelen ocurrir cuando las industrias extractivas operan a niveles tan elevados que los sistemas ecológicos de los que extraen los recursos pierden su capacidad para amortiguar las sacudidas transitorias, sean éstas de origen ambiental o tecnológico. Las instituciones legales, cuya finalidad es prevenir que ocurran estos desastres, puede en realidad promoverlos, desde el momento en que tienen que negociar las demandas de las partes interesadas en obtener un mayor acceso a los recursos. Las instituciones legales pueden adaptarse a la inestabilidad ecológica como consecuencia de tales catástrofes, "aprendiendo" de la experiencia de forma más o menos exitosa, dependiendo de las condiciones bajo las que ocurre el desastre. Este artículo va a desarrollar estas ideas en el contexto de una serie de desastres destacados, entre ellos el hundimiento de la plataforma petrolífera *Deepwater Horizon* en 2010.

## INTRODUCTION

The law takes particular interest in disasters, whether of the "environmental" or "technological" kind, because they involve society at large in a way that personal accidents or, indeed, trees falling in forests with no one to hear them do not. Lawrence Friedman and Joseph Thompson (2003, p. 251) noted that the distinction between man-made and "natural" disasters is an artificial one because what counts is the harm to people rather than the source: we reserve the term "disaster," moreover, for events so large as to require some kind of organized social response. Legal agencies concern themselves at different times with preventing disasters that might happen, with preparing for ones that seem certain to happen, with responding to them when they do happen and, finally, with assessing the effectiveness of whatever responses society makes to them once they have passed. Less obvious, perhaps, are situations in which legal agencies themselves contribute to conditions under which disasters (technological or natural) take place. The notion is a little odd because we usually think of the law as dedicated to the public good, however imperfectly. Still, if legal agencies—singly or collectively, inadvertently or by design—generate circumstances that precipitate catastrophe, the ways in which they do so might be worth investigating.

There is a well-developed literature that analyzes the ways in which the legal system responds to disasters, whether "natural" or anthropogenic. Friedman and Thomson (2003) compared different kinds of disasters, from the Johnstown Flood of 1889 to the attacks of September 11, 2001, to show how patterns of attributing causes to disasters and of government's willingness to relieve victims changed over time. Michele Landis (1999) analyzed the way in which the New Deal administration overcame political resistance to poor relief by rhetorically equating the Great Depression with a "natural" disaster for which unemployed workers and displaced farmers were not at fault. Fiona Haines (2009) showed how the socio-political contexts in which different disasters take place (in her case, an industrial accident, a financial collapse, and a series of terrorist attacks) can influence regulatory responses to them and, therefore, the system's relative ability to prevent similar incidents from taking place in the future. All of these studies pointed to the important influence that legal institutions and legal culture have over the ways in which society responds to disaster.

A related question is the role that legal agencies can play in permitting disasters to occur in the first place. The "disasters" in this group are usually though not necessarily of the technological kind. A report to the Governor of West Virginia on a deadly explosion at the Upper Big Branch coal mine in 2010 criticized the government agencies for their less-than-diligent oversight of the facility, but concluded that "responsibility for the explosion [lay] with the management" for its egregious disregard of worker safety (McAteer *et al.* 2001, p. 108). At the other end of the scale,

156

the distinguished commission that analyzed the loss of the Space Shuttle *Columbia* ascribed blame for the loss to "the failure of NASA's organizational system" (Columbia Accident Investigation Board [CAIB] 2003, p. 195). NASA had failed to correct the institutional problems that had led to the *Challenger* disaster in 1986. Indeed, in her contribution to the *Columbia* report, the sociologist Diane Vaughan concluded that the *Challenger* accident had actually enhanced political pressures that had from the beginning encouraged NASA officials to discount known risks. At the same time, NASA had done nothing to reform long-standing practices by which the agency "normalized" potential risks over time so that "[a]nomalies that did not lead to catastrophic failure" became "valid engineering data that justified further flights," rather than drawing attention to potentially dangerous problems with the orbiters (CAIB 2003, 99-102, 195-197). The commission that investigated the *Deepwater Horizon* oil spill in 2010 analyzed its subject in similar terms: it cited the *Columbia* report to the effect that "complex systems almost always fail in complex ways" and went on to describe the interaction between the inherent complexity of the oil rig itself, British Petroleum's notoriously risk-insensitive culture, and significant shortcomings in regulatory oversight of the enterprise (National Commission on the BP Deepwater Horizon Oil Spill and Offshore Drilling 2011, p. viii).

Insofar as law regulates the ways in which people develop natural resources, it plays a role in the collapse of ecological systems as much it does of mechanical ones. The Dust Bowl of the 1930s, for example, was as much a creature of public policy as it was of the cyclical droughts that have visited the Great Plains since long before people did. From public land law to military procurement, government at all levels had for nearly a century encouraged farmers to harness the Plains to high-yield agriculture, with the result that when drought did arrive it did incalculably more damage to nature and economy than it likely would have otherwise. "The Dust Bowl," wrote the environmental historian Donald Worster, "was the inevitable outcome of a culture that deliberately, self-consciously, set itself [the] task of dominating and exploiting the land for all it was worth." The disaster, Worster concluded, "came about because the culture was operating in precisely the way it was supposed to" (Worster 1979, p. 4). The legal historian J. Willard Hurst told a similar story of the nineteenth-century Wisconsin lumber industry, which cleared thirty million acres of timber in the space of a generation and left in its wake a depauperate waste of sand farms and cutover land (Hurst 1964). Hurst showed how people at all levels of the legal system—from judges and legislators to entrepreneurs and landowners—used law deliberately, inventing new institutions as they went and making new rules where necessary, to increase the flow of resources into the market: to "release creative economic energy," as Hurst (1956, p. 5) put it. Development trumped whatever normative obligations government might have had to manage the resources for long-term public benefit: "We would realize the greatest present production we could from the land," Hurst concluded, even if "this meant throwing away much that a broader future development could use" (Hurst 1956, p. 70).

Just as there is no such thing as a "natural" disaster in which people are not involved in some way (if only as casualties), there is no such thing as economic development without law: from common-law rights to property and contract to government-funded research and development to intensive environmental and safety regulation. This chapter discusses three instances in which people used law and legal institutions to engineer natural disasters, however inadvertently, by intensifying the development of resources to the point where catastrophic failure became sooner or later inevitable. The examples—chosen for illustrative value rather than statistical significance—all come from the state of California, although they took place at different times and involved different resource industries. The first is the collapse of the California sardine fishery in the 1940s, which, in terms of sheer value lost, ranks as one of the great natural disasters in our history. The second concerns the Sacramento Valley floods of the late nineteenth century, which grew out of the interaction between law, gold mining, the hydrology of the Sierra Nevada, and changing weather patterns. The last and most recent took place along the Southern California coast in 2005 and had to do with interactions between weather, coastal geology, real estate, avocados, and water law. All three examples involved interactions between natural and economic forces, but in each case people used legal agencies and legal tools to drive those interactions to the point of catastrophe.

## THE CALIFORNIA SARDINE FISHERY

My first story of engineered disaster concerns the fishery for sardine that developed off the coast of California early in the twentieth century and collapsed, spectacularly, in the years following World War II. At its peak in the 1930s, this was the most intensive fishery in the world and one of the few profitable industries in Depression-era California; its collapse is one of the great environmental calamities in the nation's history although its loss has not been much remarked, perhaps because the sardine is an uncharismatic animal whose fate played out underwater. A fishery is a renewable resource, to be sure, and its relevance to petroleum exploration might not seem obvious at first glance. It is also true, for one thing, that this fishery was entirely a creature of fossil fuels: it became feasible only when gasoline engines became available for small boats and it grew into a major industry only when the energy-intensification of farming in the Midwest generated a demand for the fish as feed for livestock. More important, the sardine fishery became part of a complex, tightly-coupled, high-flux food system and succumbed to cascading failure once it grew beyond its capacity to buffer random fluctuations in its environment (Ueber and Macall 1992, McEvoy 1986).

The first decade of the twentieth century was an opportune time to fish sardine in California. Boats, workers and cannery gear had fallen idle as overfishing and mining pollution destroyed the once-bountiful Central Valley salmon fishery; gasoline engines became practical about the same time, as well, which made it possible to harvest a schooling fish like sardine in coastal waters. Oceanographic data indicate that the biological productivity of California coastal waters, which could vary significantly over time, was also very high at the time: fish were visibly abundant and, once people matched the right tools to the resource, easy to catch (Soutar and Isaacs 1969, Smith 1978). The problem was the limited market for canned sardine; even export markets in Asia could support only part of what the fishery could produce. Military procurement generated a substantial burst of demand during World War I, but disappeared as soon as the war was over. Chronic overproduction thus kept everyone in the industry teetering on the edge of bankruptcy almost from the beginning (McEvoy 1986).

One problem that limited the potential growth of an industrial fishery for sardine was the enormous volume of waste that canneries produced. California processors sold the waste to Chinese gardeners for use as fertilizer or, more typically, dumped it at sea. Pressed to remove water and oil and then dried, cannery waste was a high-value, easily transportable feedstock for animals, and the U.S. Department of Agriculture began promoting it for poultry and hogs during World War I (Turrentine 1915, Weber 1916, US Department of Agriculture [USDA] 1922). It caught on in California soon thereafter; canned fish for food rapidly became a sideline and fishmeal the industry's main product (Thompson 1919, Scofield 1921). Like sardine fishing, intensive hogs and poultry were new industries at the time, made possible by electric power for farms and gasoline trucks for distribution. Fishing, then, became coupled not only to the marine ecosystem and to the market for food but also to the gigantic, increasingly energy-intensive US food industry. As such it became impossible to regulate, the demand for industrial by-products overwhelming any influence that conservation officials, much less the fishery's ecology, might have had on management of the resource (McEvoy 1986, Ueber and MacCall 1992, Scofield 1938).

Sardine harvests grew in pace with energy-intensive agriculture until by the mid-thirties the fishery, now spread as far north as Vancouver, landed more than 700,000 metric tons each season. Biologists working for the State of California grew concerned about the size of the harvest; some recommended limiting the catch, perhaps to 250,000 tons, while others recommended prohibiting the reduction of whole fish to by products so as to insulate the stock from demand pressure (Greene 1927). Neither policy made much headway, particularly as agribusiness firms effectively resisted such efforts in the state legislature. Catches began to come up short in the late 1930s, as the harvest bumped up against the fishery's capacity to produce and as the favorable marine conditions of the turn of the century gave way to a less stable, less productive regime overall (Clark 1935, Murphy 1966).

Scientists had observed irregular fluctuations in the harvest since the beginning of the fishery; California had established a State Fisheries Laboratory in Los Angeles in 1917. State scientists, whose responsibility it was to conserve the resource, pointed to overfishing as the likely cause and recommended both that the state impose limits on the catch and prohibit the reduction of whole fish to by products, so as to insulate the stock from demand pressure. Scientists working for the United States Bureau of Fisheries, who had better ties to the industry and no responsibility for conserving the fishery, traced the observed anomalies to "environmental" causes independent of fishing pressure (Radovich 1982, Clark and Marr 1955). Processors and their allies in agribusiness, meanwhile, made sure that the state biologists' increasingly urgent warnings about overfishing made no headway in the state legislature, whose responsibility it was actually to regulate commercial fishing. The result was a policy stalemate under which pressure on the stock continued unabated (McEvoy 1986).

The fishery collapsed suddenly, in a cascade, in the late 1940s. A few unfavorable seasons after 1945 wiped out several generations of new fish, while overharvesting stripped the population of the older fish that normally would buffer such shocks to the population. The stock began to decline steeply, first at its northern edges and steadily southward into its spawning area off the coast of southern California and Mexico. Boats and workers followed the stock southward until the entire fishery packed into the waters off Los Angeles; there they made short work of what remained of the harvest until by the mid-1960s sardine became statistically undetectable in California waters. Demand for fishmeal remained strong, however, and to meet it California sardine processors moved their plant and equipment to Peru, where by the early 1970s they had colonized, developed, and ultimately destroyed an even larger fishery for the biologically-similar Peruvian anchoveta. Research in the 1960s indicated that, while environmental fluctuations might have disrupted the sardine harvest temporarily, the enormous harvests of the thirties and forties so depressed the stock's natural resilience that collapse became inevitable (Murphy 1966, MacCall 1979, Radovich 1982).

Our knowledge of the complex relationships between fishing and environment continues to develop, although significant controversy persists. Some authors observe that populations of sardine-like fishes fluctuate both over wide geographical areas and far back into the geological record and discount the significance of fishing pressure (Baumgartner *et al.* 1992, Jacobson *et al.* 2001, Chavez *et al.* 2003). Others maintain that fishing pressure interacts with environmental change: some claim that exploited fish populations respond more dramatically to fluctuations in climatic conditions because harvesting alters the age composition and the geographic distribution of the target stock (Hseih 2005a, 2008, Anderson *et al.* 2008). In a similar vein, others argue that harvesting exerts a disproportionately larger impact on depleted fisheries, thus exacerbating their decline (Myers *et al.* 1995, Hutchings 2000, Shertzer and Prager 2007). These scientists urge a more precautionary approach to managing such fisheries (Hutchings 2001). Sardine stocks off the Pacific Coast of North America began to recover in the 1980s: fishing, which California had put under moratorium in 1967, began again under tight control by U.S. and Canadian agencies (Wolf 1992, Hill *et al.* 2007). Continued differences in scientific opinion notwithstanding, the sardine disaster seems to have triggered a shift in the regulatory regime, at least.

A sardine boat might not at first blush seem to belong in the same class of technology as a Space Shuttle or a deep-water oil rig. What they have in common, however, is that they all represent significant capital investments put to work in unstable, imperfectly knowable environments, subject to legal regimes that, in the last analysis, discounted environmental risk in favor of development. The sardine fishery was an integrated system made up of the ocean environment, agribusiness, and government: the system collapsed when random climatic disruption cascaded through it in ways that people foresaw only dimly but which the high intensity of the harvest, relative to the volatility of the resource, amplified to the level of disaster. Courts, legislatures, and administrative agencies charged with managing the industry not only failed to prevent the collapse but hasted its coming, even if by default, by permitting the uncontrolled expansion of the harvest in spite of the economic waste and the scientific risk that it entailed. The fishery left a significantly damaged natural system in its wake. The last, ominous lesson of the sardine fishery is that it continued its campaign of destruction, sustained by prices that reached as high as a dollar each for what few fish anyone could find, until the business withered away entirely. Meaningful control over the industry, in this case, became possible only when there was no longer any capital invested in it.

## THE SACRAMENTO VALLEY FLOODS

The same dynamics of intensive development, tight coupling to a volatile ecology, and catastrophic failure played out in the Sacramento Valley floods of the late nineteenth century. The floods, which struck the valley in the 1870s and 1880s, inundated cities, destroyed newly-developed farmland, and polluted fisheries as far away as San Francisco Bay. They triggered a significant change in California's political economy, as mining yielded its hegemony to agriculture. The immediate cause of the floods was excessive rainfall, to be sure, but what made a particular level of precipitation "excessive" in this case was the way in which the mining industry, using legal tools, had transformed the hydrology of the Central Valley in the decades after the Gold Rush of the late 1840s and early 1850s.

People who came to California to mine gold in the late 1840s and early 1850s encountered a climate that was on the whole stable and benign (U.S. National Oceanic and Atmospheric Administration [NOAA] 1988). There were a few very rainy seasons during the Gold Rush, and the geology of the Valley is such that floods are very common to the region; seasonal flooding was, indeed, the main source of the Valley's tremendous

161

agricultural productivity (Thompson 1960). The floods did little damage during the first few years of Euro-American settlement because business activity in the region consisted mostly of placer mining and its supply, none of which required much in the way of construction or other capital investment. Working only with hand tools and the natural flow of the streambeds they prospected, placer miners displaced tons of gold-bearing rock through the 1850s but without causing a great deal of damage to the system. A significant flood in January 1862 washed a decades' worth of mining debris down into the Sacramento Valley and out into San Francisco Bay, flooding the new capital at Sacramento and covering what few riparian farms there were with a concrete-like mixture of sand, mud, and gravel known as "slickens," but the region seems to have recovered without too much trouble (Gilbert 1917). Miners had depleted most of the easy placer deposits by then, so that damage to the industry itself was negligible.

The mining industry was not yet finished with the Sierra, however. Because most of the Gold Rush took place during dry years, early California law concerned itself primarily with the problem of getting scarce water to the mines in the lower foothills. This required legal engineering as well as the civil kind: in 1855 the California Supreme Court ratified the miners' informal practice of appropriating rights to use water by diverting it from its natural course; thus inventing, for the benefit of miners, the system of water rights that would come to dominate the western half of the United States. The state legislature even authorized miners to exercise the power of eminent domain, allowing them to ditch across private land as they needed to deliver water to their works. In 1859 the state made appropriation rights transferable, which made it possible for corporations to accumulate water in the amounts needed for high-intensity mining (Pisani 1992, McCurdy 1976, Kelley 1959).

Appropriation and transferability made it possible for mining to enter a new and more destructive phase. So-called "hydraulic" mining collected great quantities of water under high pressure and washed entire hillsides of mud and gravel into placer sluices in order to get at what gold there was to be had (Kelley 1959). During the mostly dry years of the 1860s, hydraulic mines loaded millions of cubic yards of debris into the watercourses of the lower Sierra. Canyons that earlier would have contained floodwater and buffered its flow now had so much of the concrete-like debris in them "that a railroad track might be laid upon their beds for 75 miles or more," as one court put it. In 1884 the bed of the Sacramento River was in some places twenty feet higher than it had been in 1860. Towns like Marysville, where the riverbed rose above street level, had to protect themselves with ever-more complicated systems of dikes and sloughs. Mining, agriculture, and town life became tightly coupled to Sierra Nevada hydrology and correspondingly vulnerable to random perturbations in the flow of water.

The rains that came to the Sacramento Valley in 1875 and 1881 were unremarkable: at 24 and 26 inches, respectively, they were just over one standard deviation from the historical mean but far less than the 36 inches that fell in 1862, for example. So degraded was the Sacramento watershed's capacity to buffer floodwater, however, that the floods of '75 and '81 did far more damage than their larger precursors. Many more farmers and town dwellers occupied the Central Valley than in the 1860s, moreover, and the precarious stopgaps that they had built up to protect them from flooding were unequal to the task (Kelley 1959). In 1882 Edwards Woodruff, who had some 1,700 acres under wheat near Marysville, sued the largest of the Yuba River mines for nuisance. The permanent injunction that came down two years later, in *Woodruff v. North Bloomfield Gravel Mining Company*, ended the mining industry's hegemony over California business and politics.[1] The case now famously stands for the proposition that nuisance law shifts entitlements between competing economic interests in response to changes in their relative contributions to net social product.

Legal agencies played a crucial role in bringing hydraulic mining to an end, just as they had from the beginning created the industry, sustained its growth, and encouraged its socially destructive habits. Prior appropriation predominated in the Sierra, not because it was peculiarly adapted to the California environment but because it made large-scale corporate mining convenient and it enabled the mines to collect the ever-increasing volumes of water they needed to draw out what remained of the Sierra's gold. Mining debris flushed out of the Sacramento River system in a gigantic, slow-moving wave over the decades following the industry's demise (Gilbert 1917). In its place, though, California farms and cities re-engineered the Sacramento-San Joaquin system to a level of intensity higher than the most ambitious mining executive could have imagined. Today, indeed, there are few more tightly coupled, high-intensity, disaster-prone resource systems in the world than the Central Valley watershed (Reisner 1993, Glennon 2009).

## LA CONCHITA

My third exemplar is a relatively small one: a landslide that took place in the coastal Southern California town of La Conchita in 2005. The La Conchita slide left few traces behind it, except on the lives of people who lost homes or loved ones and in the pastiche of scars that mark the landscape behind the tiny beach town. It did not catalyze significant social change, as did the oil blowout that took place just up the coast at Santa Barbara in 1969. Nor did La Conchita enable regulatory reform by destroying the capital investments hitherto impeding it, as did the California sardine collapse of the 1950s. Despite the nationwide press coverage that attended it, the La Conchita slides ultimately generated little more than a handful of lawsuits and—despite their significance for the parties—despite

---

[1] Woodruff v. North Bloomfield Gravel Mining Co., 18 F. 753 (C.C. Cal. 1884).

their significance for the parties—not ones important enough to make anybody rethink the structure of property entitlements in that little neighborhood. What makes the story useful here is that, as in the other two cases, what turned ordinary events into disasters was people's insistence on getting in the way and staying there, using every available legal mechanism to do so.

There are two ways in which we can usefully consider the La Conchita slide, however. One is as a species of "normal accident", in the sense that the sociologist Charles Perrow (1984) used the term: the kind of catastrophic failure that seems to be endemic to highly-engineered, intensive technologies like nuclear reactors, offshore oil rigs, or the Space Shuttle. In this case, California's more-or-less integrated schemes for managing land and water use make up just the kind of high-flux, disaster-prone system that Perrow described, with the interesting difference that in this case legal agencies rather than technicians did the engineering. We can also think of the La Conchita slide as a control case, in which we can see the law working in its everyday capacity to allocate environmental risk. As such, La Conchita is an interesting study in the ways in which the law, in its workaday mode, uses abstract principles of property and tort to do that allocation. It offers a peek at what Willard Hurst called the "working principles" of our legal order: principles "defined and expressed primarily by action"; principles of law "not so much as it may appear to philosophers, but more as it ha[s] meaning for workaday people and [is] shaped by them to their wants and vision" (Hurst 1956, p. 5).

La Conchita is a little unincorporated area of maybe 160 houses on the coast below Santa Barbara, just across the Ventura County line. Anyone who has driven north from Los Angeles on the 101 freeway has passed by it, likely without noticing it. A *Los Angeles Times* article (Saillant 2008) described La Conchita as "a place where working people could find a little slice of coastal paradise—a haven for surfers, fishermen, construction workers, retirees and assorted oddballs." R.W. Jibson of the U.S. Geological Service, on the other hand, marked La Conchita as one of the most unstable bits of real estate on the continent, packed as it is into an 800-foot wide strip between the highway and a 600-foot high, 35° bluff of porous marine sediment with an active seismic fault running across its face (Jibson 2005).

Developers first built houses on the parcel in 1924. Before then it belonged to the Southern Pacific Railroad, whose tracks run along the coast here. The SP had some buildings on the site, but after a landslide destroyed one of its trains and killed four of its workers in 1909 the railroad levelled the parcel and sold it off a few years later. What started out as a collection of weekend homes became a permanent community during the post-World War II southern California boom. The "surfers and oddballs" of La Conchita share their little slice of coastal paradise with the La Conchita Ranch Company, which in the mid-1970s began irrigating avocado and lemon trees at the top of the bluff, which had formerly been given over to lima beans and other dry-farmed crops. By the 1990s there were some 40,000 trees on the bluff (Johnson 1999, Kelley and Saillant 2005a, 2005b). The company had a permit from the California Coastal Commission to build the ranch, conditioned on its promise to implement a drainage and erosion-control plan that apparently never took form. Indeed, in the early 1980s the ranch apparently replaced its drip irrigation system with a more water-intensive one as the avocado trees planted in the 1970s reached maturity. The company restructured itself as a limited partnership in 1991, allegedly to insulate itself from liability for landslides (Polakovic 1998a, 1998b).

Rainy season along the Southern California Bight typically runs from October through May; records going back to the 1860s show a seasonal mean of a little more than 18 inches. January and February are the wettest months, averaging about four inches each per year (Santa Barbara Flood Control District 2012). In 1909, the year a slide killed four railroad workers, annual rainfall exceeded 36 inches. More than 15 inches fell in January of that year alone. The heaviest single month on record is January, 1995, which had almost 22 inches. In March of that year 600,000 tons of earth broke away from the bluff and destroyed nine houses. 2004-05 was another wet year, just under 37 inches in all; this was Santa Barbara's third-highest total on record. On January 10, after 15 days of moderate-to-heavy rain, part of the 1995 slide remobilized and slid down the bluff, in a few seconds as opposed to the several minutes that the 1995 slide had lasted. This time, the slide took 36 houses and 10 lives with it (Jibson 2005).

Rainstorms and unstable landscapes are nothing new in Southern California, although the South Coast has had more above-average rainy seasons in the last ten years than in any comparable period since World War I. The period from 1945-1975, on the other hand—the period during which Southern California experienced its most rapid development—was one of the calmest, driest climatic episodes in the region's history. Volatility is the norm here. Extreme volatility also characterizes the market for La Conchita real estate: houses whose assessed value had gone nearly to zero in the wake of the 1995 slide—as lenders and insurers refused to touch them—brought half a million dollars or more ten years later (Reed 1997, Garvey and Kelley 2005). Homeowners who might have left in the wake of 2005 slide reported that the size of their mortgages prevented them from taking advantages of federal relocation loans that were available to them.

Throughout, the law—legislatures, agencies, courts both state and federal—has worked assiduously to maintain the Southern California land market at high levels of flux, tightly coupled to ancillary systems for water supply, fire suppression, and so on. Legal agencies like the Coastal Commission and the State Department of Water Resources do their best to accommodate competing uses like housing and agriculture, favoring no one interest over another but allowing them all to generate as much wealth as possible. To keep the town operating after the 1995 slide, for example, Ventura County rebuilt the street that runs along the bottom of the bluff and put up a retaining wall to hold back debris from the slide.

The county also secured waivers against future liability from people who owned homes in the slide area (Kelley and Saillant 2005a). For good measure the county declared La Conchita a "geological hazard area", and required homeowners to post "Enter at your own risk" signs on their buildings.

The courts, also, worked to accommodate competing claims to this ephemeral property in the wake of the '95 slide, fine-tuning the allocation of risk while allowing different uses to continue unimpeded as much as possible. La Conchita residents sued the ranch in 1996, alleging that its irrigation had caused the previous winter's slide. Most of the plaintiffs settled for undisclosed sums and waivers against future liability (Reed 1997). A few went to trial, wherein the Ventura County Superior Court found for the ranch on the ground that excessive rainfall, not irrigation runoff, had caused the slide.[2] The ranch's lawyer characterized the slide as "part of a natural geologic progression that had long plagued the area and the rest of the California coast"; "a continuation of a geological progression that had been ongoing for eons." "I feel bad for the people, but then again, I don't live under a 500-foot bluff, either", the lawyer told reporters. "It's a risk you take" (Polakovic 1998a, 1998b). The slide, as the *Los Angeles Times* paraphrased defendants' argument, "was a natural disaster—unfortunate, but no one's fault" (Alvarez 1999). Much of the testimony, then, consisted of experts advocating one side or the other of the question of "whether negligent irrigation practices or natural processes caused the disaster," as the *Times* characterized it (Polakovic 1998b, 1998c). Posing the question in this way—Nature or negligence—elided the causal significance of the ranch's activity in that particular environment, thus shifting risk onto the residents. The decision did, however, allow both residential and agricultural uses to continue unabated for the time being.

A more likely explanation for the slide is that excessive rainfall and overwatering were jointly responsible for triggering the slide. It turns out that avocado trees require a great deal of water: the University of California Extension Service reports that it takes 36 acre-inches of water per acre per season to irrigate mature avocado trees; in only four years for which we have records has that much water fallen naturally onto that bluff (Takele *et al.* 2002). Irrigation, moreover, takes place during the growing season, which is normally dry. Geological Service photographs from September 2004 show clearly that the section of bluff that gave way six months later was already saturated with water, at the end of the dry season (Jibson 2005).

Victims of the 2005 slide sued again. They tried the case to a jury this time, but under a causal theory very different from the one that had lost in 1996: this time the 36 plaintiffs alleged that the ranch had negligently

---

[2] Bateman v. La Conchita Ranch Co., Civ. No. 156906 (Superior Court, Ventura County); see also Federal Home Loan Mortgage Corp. v. La Conchita Ranch Co., 68 Cal. App. 4th 856, 80 Cal. Rptr. 2d 634 (Cal. App. Dept. Super. Ct. 1998).

failed to provide adequate drainage from its property, without specifying whether it was rainwater or tailwater that had actually caused the slide. Plaintiffs won their verdict in August, 2008: under California's comparative-fault system, which allows juries to discount plaintiffs' awards to the extent that they contributed to the harm, the jury in *Alvis et al. v. La Conchita Ranch* split their verdicts more or less evenly between the ranch and individual plaintiffs. The jury held some plaintiffs who were landowners liable to their renters; at the same time the jury exonerated both the ranch manager and Ventura County.[3] Two months later, defendants settled the case by turning over $5 million in insurance proceeds and the keys to the ranch (Saillant 2008, Hernandez 2008a).

Defendants did not suffer greatly in the outcome, inasmuch as the ranch had consistently lost money and the company had been trying, unsuccessfully, to sell it for the past 15 years. Defendant's attorney "wished the plaintiffs luck in trying to sell this piece of property," he said, because the place was uninsurable: "so to the extent that [defendants] were able to give this ranch to the plaintiffs with all those problems and walk away from future problems, they [defendants] are actually very happy" (Hernandez 2008b). The plaintiffs ultimately sold the ranch "as is" to a buyer from Carpenteria, another town just up the beach from La Conchita, for $2.5 million (Hernandez 2008c). The new owner continued to operate the ranch for citrus and avocado, although the Ventura County Star reported in 2010 that he had "done a lot to divert water from the landslide area, making it much safer" (Barlow 2010).

The La Conchita story lacks the moral punch of the California sardine collapse, much less that of the *Challenger* or the *Deepwater Horizon* disasters. One thing that stands out, however, is the interesting role that private law—in this case the law of causation in tort—played in discounting the risks of land- and water- use at La Conchita. The 1995 plaintiffs lost their case because they could not successfully argue that human forces interacted with "natural" ones to generate risk; the 2005 plaintiffs, for their part, won not by registering the fact of synergy on the legal system but by finessing the issue. That causal synergy seems to be hard to argue in court suggests a persistence in our law of the nature-culture dichotomy that lots of people have written about, long after we all know better. The practical effect of this difficulty seems to be to privilege developers who would off-load the environmental risk of their activities to the public at large. Where the sardine fishery died out and left something of a vacuum for regulation to fill in its wake, however, at this writing people are still using state water to flood the cliff at La Conchita.

---

[3] Alvis *et al.* v. La Conchita Ranch Co. Superior Court for Ventura County, Case No. CIV 238700 (filed August 19, 2008).

## CONCLUSION

The La Conchita landslide, then, was as much a legal artifact as it was a natural event. As in the other disasters catalogued here—the sardine collapse, the Marysville floods—otherwise unexceptional natural perturbations led to human misery when people intensified production from natural systems to the point where disaster became more or less inevitable. In each case people used law to sustain development at as high a level as possible: through research and development if need be, by rescue and rehabilitation at times, and always by adjusting a delicate balance between competing development interests. Sustaining production and profits that their highest possible levels was the job of the legal system: indeed, the measure of its commitment to liberty and progress.

Committed as our culture remains to economic individualism, our legal system does most of its pro-development work invisibly, much as it did in the nineteenth century, by adjusting the ground rules through which people do business. Even in the environmental area, those rules work best—we think—that most resemble speed limits and least interfere with the substantive choices that people make about how actually to use their property. Public efforts to balance human affairs with the natural order are a good bit clumsier. Government research responds better to interest groups in temporary crisis than it does either to economic rationality or to the long-term good of the community. Government provides rescue and rehabilitation to the victims of crisis, but only if the particular event qualifies as a disaster through some calculus of politics, empathy, and causal attribution. Others, if they get noticed at all, are left to their fate and private insurance. In its overt activity as well as in its more hidden, systemic role, our system works mainly to balance power by means of a steadily rising economy, even when increased output intensifies pressure on resources and couples their natural fluctuations more tightly to public risk.

Indeed, in our own day much government resource allocation takes the form of shifting burdens of risk: of accident, illness, unemployment, or natural calamity. Were nuclear utilities left to the private market for insurance, for example, they would likely be unable to operate: the industry exists only because federal law since 1957 has limited the utilities' total liability for nuclear accidents to a set amount ($12.6 billion since 2005) and assigns any liability above that to the government.[4] In the 1970s and 1980s, the D.C. Circuit Court of Appeals allowed nuclear utilities to discount the risk of catastrophic accidents to zero because the utilities themselves deemed such accidents as so unlikely as to be immeasurable.[5] An

---

[4] Energy Policy Act of 2005, PL-109-58, 42 U.S.C. §§2210 *et seq.*

[5] Carolina Environmental Study Group v. United States, 510 F.2d 796 (D.C. Cir. 1975); see also San Luis Obispo Mothers for Peace v. NRC, 751 F.2d 1287 (D.C. Cir. 1984), *vacated in part,* 760 F.2d 1320 (D.C. Cir. 1985).

even more subtle form of risk allocation, which may have contributed to the *Deepwater Horizon* disaster, was the Reagan Administration Council on Environmental Quality's decision, later upheld by the Supreme Court, to repeal its requirement that environmental impact statements discuss "worst-case" impacts of projects under review.[6] On a more local level, struggles over risk allocation between public and private agencies did much to determine the pattern of land use in La Conchita, California. The political scientist Jacob Hacker (2006) has argued that the systematic, downward transfer of risks of all kinds in the United States since the 1970s has amounted to a significant redistribution of wealth and power in the society as a whole.

The word "disaster," then, is a conventional term rather than a scientific one. It is easy enough to claim that people generally do not notice that the rain comes and goes, sea bluffs collapse, wildlife populations rise and fall unless they have investments at stake. It is a little more of a stretch to claim that development intensifies natural events themselves, though there is good evidence that changes in harvesting pressure triggered the collapse of the California sardine, that hydraulic mining magnified the flood potential of rainfall in the Sierra, and that irrigation destabilized the bluff at La Conchita. Best hidden, perhaps, is the systematic role that law plays in creating these disasters at every level. The law, indeed, works hard to disguise its instrumental role, as it shifts burdens and benefits from hand to hand in the abstract generalities of individual rights and public welfare.

Natural disasters, so-called, take place when people, deliberately or no, build or invest themselves into situations in which otherwise ordinary natural events, like drought or flood, have catastrophic social consequences. All three of the catastrophes noted here—the collapse of the sardine fishery, the Sacramento Valley floods of the late nineteenth century, and the La Conchita landslide of 2005—manifested themselves as "disasters" not because of any intrinsic quality of the natural forces that set them in motion but because people intensified their use of the resources to such a degree that random fluctuations in the environment cascaded disastrously through the tightly-coupled environment-economy system. Intensive development, in turn, was only possible because people used legal devices to overcome obstacles to growth and to shift the risks of enterprise onto future generations and society at large. Disasters are thus both social and environmental phenomena: They may be less an exogenous source of instability in human affairs than they are their manifestation and measure.

---

[6] 40 CFR 1502.22(b); see Robertson v. Methow Valley Citizens Council, 490 U.S. 332 (1989).

## Bibliography

Energy Policy Act of 2005, PL-109-58, 42 U.S.C. §§2210 *et seq.*

Alvarez, F., 1999. Ranch Free of Blame in Landslide. *Los Angeles Times* [online], 16 Jan. Available from: http://articles.latimes.com/1999/jan/16/local/me-64045 [Accessed 29 March 2013].

Anderson, C. N. K., *et al.*, 2008. Why Fishing Magnifies Fluctuations in Fish Abundance. *Nature,* 452, 835-839.

Barlow, Z., 2010. La Conchita Keeps Eye on Impending Storms. *Ventura County Star* [online], 21 Dec. Available from: http://www.vcstar.com/news/2010/dec/21/la-conchita-residents-keep-watchful-eye-on/ [Accessed 29 March 2013].

Baumgartner, T.R., *et al.*, 1992. Reconstruction of the History of Pacific Sardine and Northern Anchovy Populations over the Past Two Millennia from Sediments of the Santa Barbara Basin, California. *California Cooperative Oceanic Fisheries Investigations Reports,* 33, 24-40. Available from: http://www.calcofi.org/publications/calcofireports/v33/Vol_33_Baumgartner_etal.pdf [Accessed 29 March 2013].

Chavez, F.P., *et al.,* 2003. From Anchovies to Sardines and Back: Multidecadal Change in the Pacific Ocean. *Science,* 299, 217-221.

Clark, F. N. and Marr, J.C., 1955. Population Dynamics of the Pacific Sardine. *California Cooperative Oceanic Fisheries Investigations Reports.* Available from: http://www.calcofi.org/publications/calcofireports/v04/Vol_04_Popn_Dynamics_Clark___Marr.pdf [Accessed 29 March 2013].

Clark, F. N., 1935. A Summary of the Life-History of the California Sardine. *California Fish and Game,* 21, 1-9.

Columbia Accident Investigation Board, 2003. *Report, Volume 1.* National Aeronautics and Space Administration. Washington, D. C.: Government Printing Office. Available from: http://www.nasa.gov/columbia/home/CAIB_Vol1.html [Accessed 29 March 2013].

Douglas, M., and Wildavsky, A., 1982. *Risk and Culture: An Essay on the Selection of Technological and Environmental Dangers.* Berkeley and Los Angeles: University of California Press.

Friedman, L.M., and Thompson, J., 2003. Total Disaster and Total Justice: Responses to Man-Made Tragedy. *DePaul Law Review,* 53, 251-287.

Garvey, M., and Kelley, D., 2005. Why They Are Drawn to Danger. *Los Angeles Times* [online], 14 Jan. Available from: http://articles.latimes.com/2005/jan/14/local/me-realestate14 [Accessed 29 March 2013].

Gilbert, G.K., 1917. Hydraulic Mining Debris in the Sierra Nevada. *U.S. Geological Survey Professional Paper,* 273. Washington: Government Printing Office. Available from: http://pubs.usgs.gov/pp/0105/report.pdf [Accessed 29 March 2013].

Glennon, R., 2009. *Unquenchable: America's Water Crisis and What to Do About It.* Washington, D.C.: Island Press.

Gordon, R. W., 1975. J. Willard Hurst and the Common-Law Tradition in American Legal Historiography. *Law & Society Review* 10, 9-55.

Greene, B.D.M., 1927. An Historical Review of the Legal Aspects of the Use of Food Fish for Reduction Purposes. *California Fish and Game*, 13, 1-17.

Hacker, J., 2006. *The Great Risk Shift*. New York: Oxford University Press.

Haines, F., 2009. Regulatory Failures and Regulatory Solutions: A Characteristic Analysis of the Aftermath of Disaster. *Law & Social Inquiry*, 34 (1), 31-60.

Hartog, H., 1994. Snakes in Ireland: A Conversation with Willard Hurst. *Law and History Review*, 12 (2), 370-390.

Hernandez, R., 2008a. La Conchita Plaintiffs to Get Ranch. *Ventura County Star* [online], 9 Sep. Available from: http://www.vcstar.com/news/2008/sep/09/la-conchita-plaintiffs-to-get-ranch/ [Accessed 29 March 2013].

Hernandez, R., 2008b. Judge Approves Cost of La Conchita Erosion Study. *Ventura County Star* [online], 11 Oct. Available from: http://www.vcstar.com/news/2008/oct/11/nb1fclaconchitahearing11/ [Accessed 29 March 2013].

Hernandez, R., 2008c. La Conchita Ranch is Sold For $2.5 Million. *Ventura County Star* [online], 22 Nov. Available from: http://www.vcstar.com/news/2008/nov/22/la-conchita-ranch-is-sold-for-25-million/ [Accessed 29 March 2013].

Hill, K.T., *et al.*, 2007. *Assessment of the Pacific Sardine Resource in 2007 for U.S. Management in 2008. U.S. National Marine Fisheries Service Technical Memorandum NOAA-TM-NMFS-SWFC-413* [online]. La Jolla: Southwest Fisheries Science Center. Available from: http://swfsc.noaa.gov/publications/TM/SWFSC/NOAA-TM-NMFS-SWFSC-413.PDF [Accessed 29 Mach 2013].

Hsieh, C.-H., *et al.*, 2005a. Distinguishing Random Environmental Fluctuations from Ecological Catastrophes for the North Pacific Ocean. *Nature*, 435, 336-340.

Hsieh, C.-H., *et al.*, 2005b. A Comparison of Long-Term Trends and Variability in Populations of Larvae of Exploited and Unexploited Fishes in the Southern California Region: A Community Approach. *Progress in Oceanography*, 67 (1-52), 160-185.

Hsieh, C.-H., *et al.*, 2008. Spatial Analysis Shows that Fishing Enhances the Climatic Sensitivity of Marine Fishes. *Canadian Journal of Fisheries and Aquatic Sciences*, 65 (5), 947-961.

Hurst, J.W., 1944. Treason in the United States. I. Treason down to the Constitution. *Harvard Law Review*, 58 (2), 226-272.

Hurst, J.W., 1945a. Treason in the United States. II. The Constitution. *Harvard Law Review*, 58 (3), 395-444.

Hurst, J.W., 1945b. Treason in the United States. III. Under the Constitution. *Harvard Law Review*, 58 (6), 806-857.

Hurst, J.W., 1950. *The Growth of American Law: The Law Makers*. Boston, MA: Little, Brown.

Hurst, J.W., 1956. *Law and the Conditions of Freedom in the Nineteenth-Century United States*. Madison, WI: University of Wisconsin Press.

Hurst, J.W., 1964. *Law and Economic Growth: The Legal History of the Lumber Industry in Wisconsin, 1835-1915*. Cambridge, MA: Harvard University Press.

Hutchings, J.A., 2000. Collapse and Recovery of Marine Fishes. *Nature (UK)*, 406, 882-885.

Hutchings, J.A., 2001. Conservation Biology of Marine Fishes: Perceptions and Caveats Regarding Assignment of Extinction Risk. *Canadian Journal of Fisheries and Aquatic Sciences*, 58 (1), 108-121.

Jacobson, L.D., *et al.*, 2001. Surplus Production, Variability, and Climate Change in the Great Sardine and Anchovy Fisheries. *Canadian Journal of Fisheries and Aquatic Sciences* 58 (9), 1891-1903.

Jibson, R.W., 2005. *Landslide Hazards at La Conchita, California*. U.S. Geological Survey Open-File Report (February 17, 2005) [online]. Washington: Government Printing Office. Available from: http://pubs.usgs.gov/of/2005/1067/index.htm [Accessed 29 March 2013].

Johnson, P.J., 1999. La Conchita Residents to Pursue Slide Dispute. *Los Angeles Times* [online], 19 Jan. Available from: http://articles.latimes.com/1999/jan/19/local/me-64979 [Accessed 29 March 2013].

Kelley, D.L. and Saillant, C., 2005a. Southland's Record Rainfall: Risk Goes Hand in Hand with Beauty. *Los Angeles Times* [online], 12 Jan. Available from: http://articles.latimes.com/2005/jan/12/local/me-laconchita12 [Accessed 29 March 2013].

Kelley, D.L. and Saillant, C., 2005b. Southland's Record Rainfall: Increased Monitoring Urged. *Los Angeles Times* [online], 13 Jan. Available from: http://articles.latimes.com/2005/jan/13/local/me-cause13 [Accessed 29 March 2013].

Kelley, R.L., 1959. *Gold vs. Grain: The Hydraulic Mining Controversy in California's Central Valley: A Chapter in the Decline of the Concept of Laissez-Faire*. Glendale, CA: Arthur H. Clark Co.

Landis, M.L., 1999. Fate, Responsibility, and "Natural" Disaster Relief Narrating the American Welfare State. *Law & Society Review*, 33, 257-318.

MacCall, A.D., 1979. Population Estimates for the Waning Years of the Pacific Sardine Fishery. *California Cooperative Oceanic Fisheries Investigations Reports* [online], 20, 72-82. Available from: http://www.calcofi.org/publications/calcofireports/v20/Vol_20_MacCall.pdf [Accessed 29 March 2013].

McAteer, J.D., *et al.*, 2011. *Upper Big Branch: The April 5, 2010 Explosion: A Failure of Basic Coal Mine Safety Practices*. West Virginia Governor's Independent Investigation Panel [online]. Wheeling: National Technology Transfer Center. Available from: http://www.nttc.edu/programs&projects/minesafety/disasterinvestigations/upperbigbranch/UpperBigBranchReport.pdf [Accessed 29 March 2013].

McCurdy, C.W., 1976. Stephen J. Field and Public Land Law Development in California, 1850-1866: A Case Study of Judicial Resource Allocation in Nineteenth-Century America. *Law & Society Review* 10, 235-266.

McEvoy, A.F., 1986. *The Fisherman's Problem: Ecology and Law in the California Fisheries, 1850-1980.* Cambridge University Press.

Murphy, G.I., 1966. Population Biology of the Pacific Sardine (*Sardinopscaerulea*). *Proceedings of the California Academy of Sciences* [online], Series 4, 34(1), 1-84. Available from: http://biostor.org/reference/78371 [Accessed 29 March 2013].

Myers, R.A., *et al.*, 1995. Population Dynamics of Exploited Fish Stocks at Low Population Levels. *Science,* 269, 1106-1108.

National Commission on the BP Deepwater Horizon Oil Spill and Offshore Drilling, 2011. *Deep Water: The Gulf Oil Disaster and the Future of Offshore Drilling.* Washington D.C.: Government Printing Office. Available from: http://www.gpo.gov/fdsys/pkg/GPO-OILCOMMISSION/content-detail.html [Accessed 29 March 2013].

Perrow, C., 1984. *Normal Accidents: Living With High-Risk Technologies.* New York: Basic Books.

Pisani, D.J., 1992. *To Reclaim a Divided West: Water, Law, and Public Policy, 1848-1902.* Albuquerque, NM: University of New Mexico Press.

Polakovic, G., 1998a. 2nd La Conchita Landslide Trial Set to Begin. *Los Angeles Times* [online], 19 Nov. Available from: http://articles.latimes.com/1998/nov/16/local/me-43343 [Accessed 29 March 2013].

Polakovic, G., 1998b. Judge Hears Rival Views on Slide at La Conchita. *Los Angeles Times* [online], 19 Nov. Available from: http://articles.latimes.com/1998/nov/19/local/me-44338 [Accessed 29 March 2013].

Polakovic, G., 1998c. Testimony Phase of La Conchita Landslide Suit Comes To An End. *Los Angeles Times* [online], 18 Dec. Available from: http://articles.latimes.com/1998/dec/18/local/me-55183 [Accessed 29 March 2013].

Radovich, J.C., 1982. The Collapse of the California Sardine Fishery: What Have We Learned? *California Cooperative Oceanic Fisheries Investigations Reports* [online], 23, 56-78. Available from: http://calcofi.ucsd.edu/newhome/publications/CalCOFI_Reports/v23/pdfs/Vol_23_Radovich.pdf [Accessed 29 March 2013].

Reed, M., 1997. La Conchita Landowners Settle Lawsuit Over '95 Slide. *Los Angeles Times* [online], 12 Jun. Available from: http://articles.latimes.com/1997-06-12/local/me-2563_1_la-conchita [Accessed 29 March 2013].

Reisner, M., 1993. *Cadillac Desert: The American West and Its Disappearing Water.* New York: Viking Press.

Saillant, C., 2008. Firm to Settle Suit over Slide. *Los Angeles Times* [online], 9 Sep. Available from: http://articles.latimes.com/2008/sep/09/local/me-laconchita9 [Accessed 29 March 2013].

Santa Barbara County Flood Control District, 2012. *Official Monthly and Yearly Rainfall Record.* Available from: http://countyofsb.org/pwd/water/downloads/hydro/234mdd.pdf [Accessed 29 March 2013].

Scheffer, M., *et al.*, 2009. Early-Warning Signs for Critical Transitions. *Nature,* 461, 53-59.

Scofield, W.L., 1921. Fertilizer, Stockfood, and Oil from Sardine Offal. *California Fish and Game,* 7, 7-8.

Scofield, W.L., 1938. Sardine Oil in Our Troubled Waters. *California Fish and Game,* 24, 210-233.

Shertzer, K.W. and Prager, M.H., 2007. Delay in Fishery Management: Diminished Yield, Longer Rebuilding, and Increased Probability of Stock Collapse. *ICES Journal of Marine Science* [online], 64 (1), 149-159. Available from: http://icesjms.oxfordjournals.org/content/64/1/149.full.pdf [Accessed 29 March 2013].

Short, J.F. Jr., 1984. The Social Fabric at Risk: Toward the Social Transformation of Risk Analysis. *American Sociological Review,* 49, 711-725.

Smith, P.E., 1978. Biological Effects of Ocean Variability: Time and Space Scales of Biological Response. *Rapports et Proces-Verbaux des Reunions, Conseil Internationale pour l'Exploration de la Mer,* 173, 117-127.

Soutar, A., and Isaacs, J.D., 1969. History of Fish Populations Inferred from Fish Scales in Anaerobic Sediments off California. *California Cooperative Oceanic Fisheries Investigations Reports* [online], 13, 63-70. Available from: http://www.calcofi.org/publications/calcofireports/v13/Vol_13_Soutar___Isaacs.pdf [Accessed 29 March 2013].

Takele, E., *et al.*, 2002. *Avocado Sample and Establishment Costs and Profitability Analysis for San Diego and Riverside Counties* [online]. Davis, CA: University of California Cooperative Extension. Available from: http://coststudies.ucdavis.edu/files/avosdiego2001.pdf [Accessed 29 March 2013].

Thompson, K., 1960. Historic Flooding in the Sacramento Valley. *Pacific Historical Review,* 29 (4), 349-360.

Thompson, W.F., 1919. The Scientific Investigation of Marine Fisheries, as Related to the Work of the Fish and Game Commission in Southern California. *California Fish and Game Commission Fish Bulletin* [online], 2. Available from: http://www.escholarship.org/uc/item/5d50q7vf#page-3 [Accessed 29 March 2013].

Turrentine, J.W., 1915. Utilization of Fish Waste of the Pacific Coast in the Manufacture of Fertilizer. *USDA Bulletin,* 150.

U.S. Department of Agriculture, Bureau of Chemistry. Food Research Laboratory, 1922. Rations for Feeding Poultry in the Packing House. *USDA Bulletin,* 1052.

U.S. National Oceanic and Atmospheric Administration, National Weather Service, 1988. Climate of Sacramento, California. *NOAA Technical Memorandum NWS WR-65.*

Ueber, E. and MacCall, A., 1992. The Rise and Fall of the California Sardine Empire. *In:* M. H. Glantz, ed. *Climate Variability, Climate Change, and Fisheries.* Cambridge University Press.

Vaughan, D., 1997. *The Challenger Launch Decision: Risky Technology, Culture, and Deviance at NASA.* University of Chicago Press.

Vaughan, D., 1999. The Dark Side of Organizations: Mistake Misconduct, and Disaster. *Annual Review of Sociology,* 25, 271-305.

Weber, F.C., 1916. Fish Meal: Its Use as a Stock and Poultry Feed. *USDA Bulletin,* 378.

Wolf, P., 1992. Recovery of the Pacific Sardine and the California Sardine Industry. *California Cooperative Oceanic Fisheries Investigations Reports* [online], 33, 76-86. Available from: http://calcofi.ucsd.edu/newhome/publications/ CalCOFI_Reports/v33/pdfs/Vol_33_Wolf.pdf [Accessed 29 March 2013].

Worster, D., 1979, *Dust Bowl: The Southern Plains in the 1930s.* New York: Oxford University Press.

Worster, D., 1992. *Rivers of Empire: Water, Aridity, and the American West.* New York: Oxford University Press.

**Cases cited**

Alvis *et al.* v. La Conchita Ranch Co., Superior Court for Ventura County, Case No. CIV 238700 (filed August 19, 2008).

Bateman v. La Conchita Ranch Co., Civ. No. 156906 (Superior Court, Ventura County).

Carolina Environmental StudyGroup v. United States, 510 F.2d 796 (D.C. Cir. 1975).

Federal Home Loan Mortgage Corp. v. La Conchita Ranch Co., 68 Cal. App. 4th 856, 80 Cal. Rptr. 2d 634 (Cal. App. Dept. Super. Ct. 1998).

Robertson v. Methow Valley Citizens Council, 490 U.S. 332 (1989).

San Luis Obispo Mothers for Peace v. NRC, 751 F.2d 1287 (D.C. Cir. 1984), *vacated in part,* 760 F.2d 1320 (D.C. Cir. 1985).

Woodruff v. North Bloomfield Gravel Mining Co., 18 F. 753 (C.C. Cal. 1884).

# 8

## MULTI-LEVEL GOVERNANCE IN ENVIRONMENTAL RISK MANAGEMENT

### Petra Hiller

**ABSTRACT**

The chapter examines regulatory strategies in the field of ecological disaster management with reference to the sociology of risk. The risk perspective draws attention to the fact that political strategies of regulation are to be understood as processes of risk transformation. The behavior of regulatory agencies is related to their perception of risks and opportunities. From this point of view, efforts in the field of disaster management appear as processes that turn perceived environmental threats into risks and opportunities for the agencies involved. The study shows the course of such a governance process which transforms environmental disasters into organizational risks and opportunities. This leads to the following research question: Which types of organizations favor strategies of risk avoidance and which organizations rather allow active pursuit of opportunities? The empirical part of this study is based on data obtained by field research in a multi-level negotiation system set up for managing hazardous wastes. Empirical findings support the assumption that organizational stability is a central condition for active pursuit of opportunities whereas organizational instability supports an orientation towards the avoidance of organizational risk.

El artículo examina las estrategias reguladoras en el ámbito de la gestión de los desastres ecológicos, haciendo referencia a la sociología del riesgo. La perspectiva de riesgo pone su atención sobre el hecho de que las estrategias políticas de regulación se deben entender como procesos de transformación de riesgos. El comportamiento de las agencias reguladoras se relaciona con su percepción de los riesgos y oportunidades. Desde este punto de vista, los esfuerzos en el campo de la gestión de catástrofes se convierten en procesos que transforman las amenazas medioambientales (percibidas) en riesgos y oportunidades para las agencias involucradas. El artículo muestra el desarrollo de este tipo de gobierno que convierte los desastres medioambientales en riesgos y oportunidades organizativas. Esto lleva a la siguiente pregunta de investigación: ¿Qué tipo de organizaciones favorecen las estrategias de prevención de riesgos y qué organizaciones permiten la búsqueda activa de oportunidades? La parte empírica de este estudio se basa en datos obtenidos en estudios de campo en un sistema de negociación multi-nivel, creado para gestionar residuos peligrosos. Los resultados empíricos apoyan la hipótesis de que la estabilidad de las organizaciones es una condición básica para la búsqueda activa de oportunidades mientras que la inestabilidad organizacional favorece una orientación hacia la prevención de riesgos en las organizaciones.

## INTRODUCTION

Topics of risk management have been studied intensively by social scientists over the last decades. Michael Power (2007) states an "explosion" of publications in the field since the mid-1990s. While the designation switches between *risk management, risk regulation,* and *governance of risk* (Hood, Rothstein and Baldwin 2001), Power demonstrates how the risk management discourse penetrates various areas of social life. This shift in the risk discourse indicates the generalisation of the risk management semantics. Power (2004) alludes to this as the "Risk Management of Everything."

How government *organizations* in particular deal with issues of risk and risk management, however, is still a question that requires more exploration (Hutter and Power 2005). I will connect at this point. This study will show how organizational perceptions of risks and opportunities are shaped and constrained by institutional contexts and organizational settings.[1] On the basis of an empirical case study,[2] it will examine the following research question: *Which forms of organization and which constellations of organized actors favour strategies of risk avoidance and which allow rather an active pursuit of opportunities?*

The chapter will refer to a case of environmental risk management in the cleaning up of contaminated land, considering the specific political setting after German re-unification. Special emphasis will be put on the institutionalization of a multi-level governance network between federal and state governments in the new federal states of Germany.

In order to investigate the research question of what the conditions and possibilities of active avoidance of risks or pursuit of opportunities on the part of the participating organizations would be, the chapter will sketch the empirical background and theoretical framework of this study (Section 2). It will then describe the regulatory program and its institutionalization as a multi-level governance regime for regulating contaminated land (Section 3). Section 4 elaborates on the risk and opportunity orientations of the organizations participating in the multi-level govern-

---

[1] Institutional contexts include legal, cultural, political and professional conditions (Scott 1995). Organizational settings are characterized by, amongst others, the type of organization as private or public, the formal structure, the organizational domain and the position of a focal organization within a network of organizations (Pfeffer and Salancik 1978).

[2] The empirical basis of this case study are the data I obtained through participant observation and analysis of documents in a process of decision making concerning the redevelopment of areas with contaminated land in the federal state of Saxony in 1994 and 1995. I would like to thank all members of the Operating Committee "Large-Scale Ecological Project SAXONIA" for their support and for consenting to my attendance of their meetings. In order to guarantee the anonymity of individual persons, I will express the following statements in a generalized manner and refer to governing bodies and organizations, respectively.

ance network. In Section 5 the question is asked as to how organizational structure affects the transformation of environmental hazards into organizational risks or opportunities. The closing section (Section 6) summarizes the results of this study.

EMPIRICAL BACKGROUND AND THEORETICAL FRAMEWORK

Prior to German unification in the year 1990, the political regulation of the cleaning up of contaminated land was not counted among the most politically salient environmental issues in the Federal Republic of Germany. Public attention was limited to individual cases which were at the center of a scandal in the early 1980s and receded again thereafter. With the German unification, this has changed fundamentally. The ecological dangers of industrially produced contaminated land quickly moved to the center of political debate on the environment in the new federal states of Germany.[3]

The origins of the present type of regulation of the cleaning up of contaminated land in the new federal states of Germany were of an economic nature, which can be traced back to the final phases of the GDR.[4] The last GDR government, which was in power from December 1989 to March 1990, realized that contaminated land would constitute an obstacle to privatization and investment. It was feared that investors would refrain from taking on the risks which would be passed on to them with the acquisition of contaminated premises and estates. Therefore, the GDR legislators, after coming to an agreement with the then Federal Government of the Federal Republic of Germany, decided that the legal and financial responsibility for cleaning up contaminated land in the area of the former GDR should be taken over by the new federal states.

The taking on of economic risks through State policy followed the political notion that the process of restoring Germany's unity could be forced particularly effectively by restructuring the economy in the new federal states. This required that state government provide for measures to support the economy. The most important policy instrument used was the so-called "exemption from responsibility for contaminated land" (*Altlastenfreistellung*), which was stipulated in the "Obstacle Removal Law."[5] This provision of exemption meant that whoever purchased stretches of

---

[3] The federal structure was abolished by the East German government in 1952. After reunification in 1990 the five so called "new" federal states were re-constituted by the Federal Republic of Germany.

[4] The name of the former socialist East German part was German Democratic Republic of Germany (GDR).

[5] "Law for the removal of obstacles in the privatization of companies and for the support of investment" of March 22nd, 1991 (Gesetz zur Beseitigung von Hemmnissen bei der Privatisierung von Unternehmen und zur Förderung von Investitionen vom 22. März 1991, BGBl. I, p. 766).

land or property that were polluted by hazardous wastes would be "exempt" from any responsibility and liability for damages incurred before July 1st, 1990 for a period of ten years. Instead, the respective federal state was to take on the responsibility, especially in financial and legal terms, for this ecological contamination.

This decision concerning regulation, made at the federal government level, failed to be implemented due to the resistance of the new federal states. The federal states were soon not willing to take on the financial load that this involved. The sheer flood of applications for *exemption from responsibility* for contaminated land presented by potential investors made it clear that taking over those costs would break the federal state budgets of the new federal states. The five new German federal states practically refused to implement this part of the "Obstacle Removal Law" by not processing a considerable amount of these applications for exemption. The economic-political instrument of exemption from responsibility for contaminated land threatened to fail. But none of the actors representing government wanted this to happen, since the improvement of the economic conditions in the new federal states was considered among the most important signs of political success for both the federal and the federal state governments in the process of unification. The East German federal state governments therefore demanded a noticeable financial commitment on the part of the Federal Government in the cleaning up of contaminated land. In drawn-out negotiations with the Federal Government they succeeded in reaching an agreement on the joint-financing of the cleaning up of contaminated land as far as the enterprises owned by the *Treuhandanstalt* (THA) were concerned.[6] The ensuing regulation policy and its implementation will be described in further detail below in regard to its function of distributing risk and opportunity orientations among the organizations involved.

The extent of contaminated land in the new federal states—virtually gigantic according to West German standards—required a regulatory program in the field of environmental policy which had had no precedent prior to 1990 in the Federal Republic of Germany. Despite this, a new type of regulation, suited to the demands at hand, was *not* developed. In order to deal with contaminated land, politicians thus fell back on a governance structure firmly established in the political system of the Federal Republic of Germany: the *joint decision making between federal and federal state governments* (Scharpf 1978). The mode of joint decision making is distinguished by the fact that concerned actors, by way of negotiation, look for potential decisions or problem solutions, respectively, that all the partners will consent to. The principle of consensual decision making, often shown to be counter-productive in political-administrative measures of regula-

---

[6] The Treuhandanstalt (THA) is a government trust body that deals with the privatization of former state properties. In the following I will consistently use the term "THA", even though the THA was later transformed into the Bundesanstalt für vereinigungsbedingte Sonderaufgaben (BvS) (Federal Institute for Unification-related Tasks).

tion, serves this purpose.[7] This mode of decision making is of more general interest as well. It not only represents a particular mode of problem-solving between federal and federal state governments in the Federal Republic of Germany. Decision making between member states of the European Union, for example, operates on the same basis. This makes it seem plausible that findings in this study provide insights into processes of inter-organizational risk management and multi-level governance beyond specific issues of the empirical case of contaminated land in Germany.

Unlike the familiar cases of joint political decision making in the Federal Republic, there are two aspects peculiar to this case which we have to take into consideration: firstly, in the management of the hazards of contaminated land within the area of the former (socialist) German Democratic Republic (GDR), federal state-level was represented solely by the five new federal state governments, which had little experience of the joint decision making institutionalized in the system of the Federal Republic of Germany, and from whose developing administrative system neither the required structures of implementation nor the professional patterns of orientation found in West German administrations could have been expected. Secondly, a third prominent actor entered the scene with the THA, which played a decisive role in shaping the relationship between the Federal Government and the new federal states. An essential factor of great consequence in this respect was that it was not the Federal Government and the federal states which met on the operative level of negotiations in regulation policy development. The details and the implementation of the regulation policy were accomplished by the THA and the new federal states.

In contrast to the negotiation theory of joint decision making, which describes multi-level governance as an arena characterized by conflict in which particular interests are put into effect, I will start from the assumption that organizations are not primarily related to the pursuit of interests but much rather the perceptions of risks and/or opportunities.[8] The distinction between pursuit of interests and perception of risks is a crucial line of reasoning in this chapter.

With the *risk perspective*, attention is drawn to regulatory measures in terms of processes of risk transformation (Luhmann 1993, Hiller 1993). Thus a standard assumption of negotiation theory is abandoned, according to which problem-solving oriented organizations participate in systems of negotiation established for the purpose of solving identifiable problems of regulation. "Efficiency" or "capacity for problem-solving" of

---

[7] Scharpf (1993) has investigated this mode of decision making in a number of studies and thereby gained valuable insight into a theory of multi-level governance. With respect to the European Union see Scharpf (1988).

[8] A similar approach is taken by Hutter (2005) in her article *"Ways of seeing": understandings of risks in organizational settings.*

negotiation systems, central to a control theoretical perspective is not of primary concern from a risk perspective. Instead, processes of regulation are described as processes of organizational risk management which deal with risks and opportunities that pertain to the respective organization as such. These processes of managing political risks typically take place within and through inter-organizational networks of negotiation in a multi-level governance framework. Hence, this study analyzes institution-alized modes of (risk-) regulation in policy-making with respect to their specific capacity for distributing risks and opportunities perceived by participating actors as being attached to certain policy decisions. It will show how such processes of risk transformation come about and what conditions they are subjected to. Such an analysis requires taking a closer look at the orientations towards risks and opportunities, respectively, which chiefly influence the way that organized actors operate.

## THE REGULATORY PROGRAM AND ITS IMPLEMENTATION

But what did the risk regulation between Federal Government, THA and the new federal states look like in detail? The mode of *financing* the *redevelopment of areas of contaminated land* in the new federal states which the Federal Government and federal state governments agreed on was specified in an administrative agreement.[9] In the following I will only deal with one part of redevelopment regulated in this administrative agreement: the large-scale ecological projects in the five new federal states. Large-scale ecological projects are areas of enterprise or former state-owned co-operatives (large state-owned enterprises) of regional importance which have particularly extensive problems with contaminat-ed land. The measures provided for by the "administrative agreement on financing environmental contamination" relate to two dimensions of regulation: the mode of financing and the mode of decision making. As far as the mode of financing is concerned, the administrative agreement decreed that the THA and the federal states must share the costs of rede-velopment in the area of large-scale ecological projects at a ratio of 75 (THA share) to 25 (federal states share). It turned out that the resulting unequal distribution of financial liability (mainly held by the THA) versus administrative responsibility (mainly held by the federal states) would prove to be a major obstacle to the implementation process. The structural line of conflict of such arrangements was further exasperated by the mode of decision making set up for large-scale ecological projects since the Federal Government and the new federal states agreed that all decisions

---

[9] Administrative agreement on the regulation of financing the cleaning up of contami-nated land of December 1st, 1992 (Verwaltungsabkommen über die Regelung der Finanzierung der ökologischen Altlasten, VA-Altlastenfinanzierung, Bundesanzeiger of March 10th, 1993, p. 2842). The "administrative agreement on financing environmen-tal contamination" became effective on October 15th, 1992.

on measures of redevelopment with large-scale ecological projects had to be reached *consensually*. This meant that, at the same time, each party had the power to veto any decision. The legal framework solely regulated the modes of financing and of decision making which delimited the parameters which all decisions had to be fitted into. These parameters constituted the basis for decision making and, as such, were not negotiable on the subsequent levels.

For the administrative implementation in the area of large-scale ecological projects, a multi-level negotiation system was created involving the Federal Government, THA and the five new federal states of Germany. This governance structure was designed to keep a formal division between the *decision-making* and *operative levels*. At both levels there are solely administrative bodies participating and no public participation of any kind. In this organization network Federal Government, THA and federal state administrations met according to the rules of joint political decision making, as had been typical of the Federal Republic of Germany.

The *level of decision making* consisted of the "Joint Operating Committee with representatives of the Federal Government, the THA and governmental organizations of the five new federal states" and the "joint operating committees with representatives of the Federal Government, the THA and the (respective) federal state." The activities of the Joint Operating Committee whose members represent the Federal Government, the THA and all five new federal states were restricted to dealing with basic questions and specifying a framework for the subsequent policy decision making units, i.e. the federal state-specific joint operating committees. These were in charge of approving the skeleton redevelopment plan that had to be produced for each large-scale ecological project at the operative level. The federal state-specific joint operating committee was the body that decisions could be relegated to if conflicts could not be resolved at the operative level. The joint operating committee was composed of representatives from the Federal Government, the THA and the five new federal states as well as the respective federal state joint operating committees in which, in addition to the THA, the Federal Government and federal state Departments of Finance, Economics, Employment and Environmental Affairs were represented. This particular constellation of organizations shows in which way the implementation of the "administrative agreement on the financing of environmental contamination" was not just about regulating ecological hazards but fundamentally about the transformation of political risks involving employment and the economy as well.

The *operative level* has a preparatory function with regard to decision making. It consists of federal state-specific "coordination committees" and "operating committees" specifically related to each large-scale project. In some cases the *coordination committee* is omitted, since its tasks can be taken over by the operating committee. The task of the *operating committees* is to turn contaminated land into something that can be managed in a financially viable way. If we look at a concrete case this means: to work out a skeleton redevelopment plan for the respective large-scale ecological project and submit it for approval at the decision-making level. If the skeleton redevelopment plan is approved, it is the committee at the operative level's task to specify and carry out the individual measures it contains.[10] At the operative level, thus, the fundamental decisions are made, following a pattern of "bottom-up policy making". It is here that actual plans are worked out. At this level the recommendations that are submitted to the "joint operating committee with representatives of the Federal Government, the THA and the specific federal state" are produced. The content of these recommendations is hardly ever altered any more at the decision-making level. Amongst other reasons, this is due to the fact that, for one thing, all measures presented here have to be decided upon in a consensual vote by the federal state and the THA in the operating committee. Moreover, the level of preparing recommendations to be decided upon and the level where final pertinent decisions are made are intricately interwoven through the negotiating parties' participation at more than one level.

## RISK AND OPPORTUNITY ORIENTATIONS WITHIN THE MULTI-LEVEL GOVERNANCE NETWORK

How do the processes of administrative decision making then develop in a large-scale project? Despite the large number of participants, we can reduce what is going on within the operating committee "Large-scale Ecological Project SAXONIA"[11] to the two main organizations leading the

---

[10] This is why the enterprises that regulatory measures are directed at are represented in the operating committees, beside the THA and the federal state's environmental administration authorities. The operating committee "Large-scale Ecological Project SAXONIA" consisted of the following members who were formally entitled to make decisions: State Department for Environmental Conservation and Land Development, Hazardous Wastes Division (Chair); Government Headquarters, Division Waste, Hazardous Wastes and Ground Conservation; State Environment Office, Hazardous Wastes Division; District Magistrate's Office, Environment Office; THA, Directorate Environmental Conservation/Hazardous Wastes. The following were members in an advisory function: Engineering firm hired for this project; Land Office for Environment and Geology, Hazardous Wastes Division; Land Office for Environment and Geology, Geology Division; Federal Environment Office, Hazardous Wastes Division; responsible company granted exemption, SAXONIA AG i. L.

[11] The land mass of today's SAXONIA AG i. L. had a history of exploitation reaching back to the 12th century. The decision-making process took place within the "Large-Scale Ecological Project SAXONIA," concerning a former *state-owned co-operative* of iron and steel works whose real estate property is highly contaminated to a great extent due to centuries of mining and smelting. The estate's area as a whole comprised about 53 hectares. The premises of the SAXONIA AG i. L. were classed as an area polluted by hazardous wastes of the most harmful kind; parts of the estate are impossible to redevelop. The area contained a considerable potential of hazardous wastes, such as arsenic, cadmium, lead, zinc and copper (heavy metals). At the time when the skeleton redevelopment plan was worked out, the "Large-scale Ecological Project SAXONIA"

negotiations: the THA and the Saxon Department of Environmental Affairs, which, as opponents in carrying out the project, shape the course of negotiations. With regard to the orientations of these actors in the operating committee we might hypothesize the following:

*Normatively* one would have expected the THA and the federal state's environmental administration to have been interested in finding a joint solution to the problem and to have cooperated in removing any obstacles to investment created by contaminated land in order to make subsequent economic use of industrially unused land possible. Finding a joint solution to the problem should have seemed a rational goal, since the outcome would, in any case, have been a positive one for both sides. If the cleaning up of contaminated land were carried out, then privatization of the property by the THA would be possible. Expedient privatization would serve both partners in the negotiations, the federal state as well as the THA. It would save jobs in the region and address environmental policy concerns. Lastly, conflicts should not have been expected since financial means made available through the administrative agreement (at least a hundred million German marks per large-scale project) had been estimated to be "sufficient."

*Empirically* one would have expected the federal state's environmental administration to have an interest in gaining some political profile within their policy domain and therefore to aim for a "large-scale solution" in regard to cleaning up contaminated land. The structure of the mode of financing (75% THA, 25% federal state) would have created the incentive for both organizations to try to spend as much money as possible within the boundaries of the redevelopment program, because all measures that it would not be possible carry out within this framework would have become the federal state's responsibility in the long run. With respect to the THA, it should most probably have wanted to, for one, to as quickly as possible privatize the businesses that had been included in the large-scale ecological projects program and been granted exemption. Secondly, for this reason as well as due to expenses, the THA would have pushed for a "small-scale solution" in redevelopment. Furthermore, in doing so, it would assumedly have been guided by investors' interests and the market. This means that the THA would have had to deal with protests from the public and the press and a dispute between experts about requirements of redevelopment, health hazards and redevelopment alternatives.

What did *actually* happen? In actual fact, the Saxon environmental administration acted as a supporter of the economy rather than as an organization concerned with environmental preservation. The THA, on the other side, appeared to be a money-saving inspector hindering investment rather than an active agency of privatization.

---

consisted of fifty-one individual projects and over seventy expert assessments and reports.

How is it that the environmental administration and the THA seemed to have exchanged roles with regard to the cleaning up of contaminated land? In the following I will show that this finding as well as the dynamics of the negotiating process in addition to the conditions for cooperation (which were lacking in the case of the "Large-scale Ecological Project SAXONIA") can be very well described if we recognize the organizations' ways of risk transformation as the factors which largely influence the actions taken.

In the case at hand, the Saxon Department of Environmental Affairs saw the possibility to take advantage of political opportunities in dealing with the contaminated land issue. The Department of Environmental Affairs transformed the regulation problem "dangers resulting from contaminated land" into political preferences of the agency. With the THA, the transformation proceeded in the opposite direction: the THA perceived the ecological dangers being addressed as risks for the organization itself. Accordingly, the efforts made by the THA were directed at developing strategies of risk avoidance. The Saxon Department of Environmental Affairs, however, was concerned about "making some progress in the federal state." Anything that seemed to serve this vague concern was understood as an opportunity and pursued more or less actively. It is important to note that what is meant by the pursuit of opportunities here is not about gaining specific advantages. The Department of Environmental Affairs pursued multiple opportunities which could be related to expectations of economic, ecological, financial, administrative, political and other kinds of benefits. The capability to identify potential opportunities in a policy decision-making arena characterizes an actor who would also make sure to seize opportunities in such a context. And the implementation of the "Large-scale Ecological Project SAXONIA" is an example of a situation of policy development in which potential opportunities abounded. The effects of the measures to be taken which the Saxon Department of Environmental Affairs aimed for were not necessarily tied to actually realizing the large-scale project. This project merely offered a *potential* opportunity structure and potential outcomes were thus basically contingent.

What form did the Department of Environmental Affairs' orientation towards opportunities take within the operating committee "SAXONIA"? A most significant factor, which shaped the way large-scale ecological projects were implemented in Saxony, was the Department's decision to pursue a "firm line" in carrying out the project. In comparison to the practices of carrying out large-scale ecological projects in the other new federal states, the greatest degree of centralization with respect to the steering of decision-making processes took place in Saxony. The federal state saw a chance for gaining a profile in labour market and economic policies and increased to the extent possible the political weight of the large-scale ecological projects. Besides the chance of gaining *political* profile, the federal state's environmental administration also saw opportunities of gaining *administrative profile*, which it could seize in implementing the "administrative agreement on financing environmental contamination." We can thus observe that the Saxon Department of Environmental Affairs succeeded in keeping the regulation costs low by acting as the "first mover" and defining the implementation process, thereby imposing its practices of implementation upon the THA as well as the other new federal states. The operating committee "Large-scale Ecological Project SAXONIA" had submitted the first financing framework to be approved and thereby established a model framework for the other large-scale projects in the new federal states of Germany. Another indicator of the achievement of administrative profile is that Saxony was early on the first federal state to receive funding to a considerable extent authorized by the administrative agreement. The Saxon environmental administration thus became a forerunner in "regulative competition." By succeeding in defining the way the projects were carried out, it would be able to influence multiple policy contents—in this case, labour market and economic policies in addition to environmental policy.

To sum up, if we interpret large-scale ecological projects as having offered participants in a decision-making process a chance to pursue opportunities, the strong commitment of the Saxon Department of Environmental Affairs in the implementation of the "administrative agreement on financing environmental contamination" becomes understandable. This means that the environmental agency was not concerned about improving the situation with regard to the contaminated land for its own sake. The problem of regulation became relevant only in a transformed shape. These transformations were constructions of the organized actors which led them to be able to interpret decision-making situations with orientations towards risks or opportunities.[12]

The THA's view of the situation was completely different from that of the Saxon Department of Environmental Affairs. Its behaviour in decision making was not characterized by the perception of opportunities but by that of risks. The THA transformed the problem of regulation (contaminated land) into risks that pertained to the organization itself. Its selective attention to the regulation process was directed at discovering the risks which, for the THA, were associated with the implementation of large-scale ecological projects. For the THA, anything which interfered with their criterion of success, "saving money," counted as a risk. It is this mono-referential risk perception that the decision-making behaviour of the THA triggered.

Since the new federal states had long been disputing the THA's competence in the domain of redevelopment of contaminated land, it was under pressure to justify its role. The THA is associated with the Federal Department of Finance and this association defined its position in the negotiating process. In this process it served as a controlling authority, without making any substantial contributions to problem-solving. The THA was therefore seen as the "extended arm" of the Minister of Finance

---

[12] How cognition and organization are related is shown in Hiller (2005).

by the other actors in the operating committee. To the Department of Finance the THA could present itself as successful and as necessary by controlling the expenditure in a restrictive way with regard to large-scale projects. Its formal structure was directed towards fulfilling this function.

## ORGANIZATIONAL STRUCTURE AND RISK TRANSFORMATION

Organizations specify the roles of their members by setting three parts of formal structure: decision programs, hierarchical structure and personnel structure (Luhmann 1976, 2000). The decision program of the THA followed its criterion of success, "saving money", through a rigid course of minimalist policies of redevelopment, restricting itself solely to measures directed at averting dangers. Decision-making was reduced to a simple conditional policy following Police and Regulation Law: according to this, there has to be an *immediate danger to people* in order to trigger measures to avert this danger.[13] In the view of the five new federal states of Germany the THA thus created its "own" environmental legislation which remained far behind the regulative standards of federal state-legislation. Seen against this background it was most apparent that the THA's use of the legal definition of danger clearly serves the goal of saving money: one cannot do less in the redevelopment of contaminated land than restrict oneself to such measures that prevent an immediate hazard to people.[14] Very early on the THA had already committed itself to this very simple conditional policy (Bonnenberg *et al.* 1994, p. 82). This policy is "simple" particularly because it was directed at only *one* level of contamination, i.e. immediate hazards to people. The former head of the THA explicitly refused to include other aspects in the process of considering factors relevant for redevelopment: "We operate on an economic level and are business-oriented, the political system operates on an econo-political level and is region-oriented" (Rohwedder 1991, p. 61).

Concerning hierarchical and personnel structure of the THA, restructurings took place in 1993, involving an increase in the importance of contract management, particularly in the area of controlling (Küpper and Mayr 1993, p. 332 ff.). The task of controlling privatization is to analyze sales contracts with regard to potential risks for the THA and to rectify mistakes that have been made in previous contractual agreements. Even in the area of contaminated land it was not engineers and lawyers of the division of hazardous waste but the controllers who had the final say as far as the realization of redevelopment projects was concerned. Controlling

---

[13] For a critical discussion of the causal concept of danger in Police and Regulation Law, compare Hiller (1993, pp. 116 ff.).

[14] In legal publications it is questioned whether the Police and Regulation Law can be applied to the complex subject matter of the hazardous wastes issue, in particular with regard to ground conservation (Kühl 1994 and the publications mentioned there in footnote 4, p. 54, Ladeur 1995).

became the critical authority in the decision-making process related to regulation within the THA and this facilitated its imposing restrictive practices on third parties. By increasing the importance of controlling, the THA institutionalized the risk orientation within the organization. It searched its field of operation for risks, trying to avoid those. Doing so, it destroyed potential opportunities at the same time: by staking everything on the business management rationale of controlling at the expense of engineering and administrative expertise, it could not assume a constructive and creative role in the negotiating process concerning the cleaning up of contaminated land. For the environmental agency of the federal state of Saxony, the THA was not a professionally competent partner in negotiations, with whom solutions could be worked out constructively. The THA transformed the regulation policy of the "administrative agreement on financing environmental contamination" into a question of monetary expenses, and conflicts were only dealt with as issues of expenses at the operative level of the negotiating process of the operating committee "Large-scale Ecological Project SAXONIA." By reducing the perspective of its representatives in negotiations to controlling financing, the THA caused itself and thereby the whole operating committee to be unable to negotiate. The THA had in this way indirectly resigned from its role as a partner in negotiations.

This leads to the hypothesis that the forms of risk and opportunity orientation described above regarding the Saxon Department of Environmental Affairs and the THA are related to differences in their qualities as organizations. The THA was mono-referential in defining its risks and thus acted as a *single self*, the Department of Environmental Affairs applied a complex framework for defining its opportunities and thus acted as a *multiple self*. "Single selves" pursue one objective, "multiple selves" operate in relation to various objectives at the same time (Wiesenthal 1990).[15]

Multiple selves have the more complex pattern of orientation, are more flexible and have more options to deal with insecurity, since they (for the purpose of distributing risks, for example) can point to varying levels of reference. Since they simultaneously follow different orientations (temporal horizons, definitions of benefits), multiple selves have no clear, single criterion of success. In this sense, the Saxon Department of Environmental Affairs must have made the rather vague statement of "some progress to be made in the federal state," which could have referred to economic, labour market political or ecological aims. In any case, the environmental administration did not act solely as a representative of the

---

[15] In a similar way Morgan (1986, p. 112) distinguishes "effective" from "less effective" managers according to their abilities of interpreting situations of decision making. Morgan sees these abilities as innate or acquired competences of the individual agents. What matters in this article is to show that the possibility of making use of this ability critically depends on the organizational setting that the agents (in the case at hand the negotiators) are tied up in.

"environment" and thereby increased its strategic flexibility in the policy-making process. In implementing large-scale ecological projects the Department of Environmental Affairs was in this way capable of cooperating with, for example, the Department of Economic Affairs, which was represented on a super-ordinate level of decision making in the joint operating committees. It would have been much more difficult to proceed if the Saxon Department of Environmental Affairs had understood itself as a single self, solely in terms of being responsible for the "environment". In that case, too, one would have hardly expected any support from the federal state's government, which would have been first and foremost interested in economic success. The most crucial factor, however, was that the environmental agency had a stable organizational structure, which is what makes operating with multiple reference points possible in the first place.

Unlike the environmental administration of the federal state of Saxony, the THA was from the outset supposed to be a temporary organization. Its task was to render itself redundant. It was not only exposed to an unstable environment, but also had to struggle with internal organizational problems, which resulted in a weakening of the organization. Internal power struggles and restructuring efforts were among the internal problems of the organization. A centralization of authority, a splitting of decision-making processes and frequent changes of often temporarily employed staff resulted. Personnel could hardly be expected to show outstanding commitment within the THA, since frequent staff fluctuation and the limited existence of the THA did not provide for reliable career prospects there. The staff's commitment and their identification with their task were thus considerably lower at the THA than they were in the Saxon environmental administration.

Such structural instabilities as within the THA also emerged in the operating committee "Large-scale Ecological Project SAXONIA." Responsibilities and authorities kept shifting during negotiations at that level. New representatives did not know or recognize arrangements and agreements that had been arduously worked out within the operating committee. Many things that seemed to have been decided upon were repeatedly questioned anew. The environmental administrations interpreted this as deliberate strategies on the part of the THA to cause delays.

Organizations such as this with turbulent external and internal environments are only steerable by simple conditional policies. Instead of following a "problem-centred orientation" which presupposes long-term strategic planning and complex, non-linear behavioural patterns, the THA, due to its problematic organizational structure, was guided by a rigid norm-centred orientation in accepting the Police Law's definition of danger. Given this state of affairs, the THA could not develop a complex pattern of orientation, including multiple temporal perspectives and varying preferences. It could only act as a single self in this decision-making context. In relation to the large-scale ecological projects, this took the form of an orientation towards risks related to the organization's stability: a risk was considered the lack of control over financial means. From a legal and financial point of view this was supposed to be the least risky course of action—at least if one thinks in the short term.

## CONCLUSION

It has been shown that the problem of regulation, "dangers resulting from contaminated land," became relevant in the multi-level negotiating processes of the "Large-scale Ecological Project SAXONIA" only in a transformed state, namely in the form of risks or opportunities perceived by the organizations in the process of decision making. "Problem-solving" and "cooperation" in the process of the development of the regulatory program thus appear to be chance products of convergent definitions of risks and opportunities of the negotiating partners. Therefore an analysis of negotiating processes (following the mode of joint decision making) must inquire which circumstances lead organizations in the negotiating process to tend to avoid risks, and which circumstances lead them to make the perception of opportunities the guiding principle of their actions. The case of the regulatory program of the cleaning up of contaminated land in the new federal states of Germany supports the hypothesis that different forms of risk transformation depend on an organization's quality as a single self or a multiple self in the decision-making process. Organizational *stability* constituted the basis for relating to the environment in multiple ways and was a precondition for an active pursuit of opportunities. Inversely, organizational *instability* promoted mono-referential orientation towards risks.

## Bibliography

Bonnenberg, H., *et al.*, 1994. Zur Behandlung der Altlastenproblematik im Arbeitsablauf der Treuhandanstalt. *Zeitschrift für angewandte Umweltforschung*, 5, 81-95.

Hiller, P., 1993. *Der Zeitkonflikt in der Risikogesellschaft. Risiko und Zeitorientierung in rechtsförmigen Verwaltungsentscheidungen.* Berlin: Duncker und Humblot.

Hiller, P., 2005. *Organisationswissen. Eine wissenssoziologische Neubeschreibung der Organisation.* Wiesbaden: VS.

Hood, C., Rothstein, H. and Baldwin, R., 2001. *The Government of Risk. Understanding Risk Regulation Regimes.* Oxford University Press.

Hutter, B.M., 2005. 'Ways of seeing': understandings of risk in organizational settings. *In:* B. Hutter and M. Power, eds. *Organizational Encounters with Risk.* Cambridge University Press, 67-92.

Hutter, B.M. and Power, M., eds., 2005. *Organizational Encounters with Risk.* Cambridge University Press.

Kühl, C., 1994. Altlastensanierung in Deutschland—ein föderales Finanzierungsmodell. *Zeitschrift für angewandte Umweltforschung*, 5, 51-62.

Küpper, H.-U. and Mayr, R., 1993. Vertragsgestaltung und Vertragsmanagement der Treuhandanstalt. *In:* W. Fischer, H. Hax and H.K. Schneider, eds. *Treuhandanstalt. Das Unmögliche wagen.* Berlin: Akademie-Verlag, 315-353.

Ladeur, K.-H., 1995. Öffentlich-rechtliche Haftung für Altlasten—retrospektive Zurechnung unerkannter Risiken? *Umwelt und Planungsrecht,* 15 (1), 1-8.

Luhmann, N., 1976. A General Theory of Organized Social Systems. In: G. Hofstede and M.S. Kassem, eds. *European contributions to Organization Theory.* Assen: Van Grocum, 96-113.

Luhmann, N., 1993. *Risk. A Sociological Theory.* Berlin: de Gruyter.

Luhmann, N., 2000. *Organisation und Entscheidung.* 4. Aufl. Wiesbaden: VS.

Morgan, G., 1986. *Images of Organization.* Beverly Hills: Sage.

Pfeffer, J. and Salancik, R.G., 1978. *The External Control of Organizations: A Resource Dependence Perspective.* New York, NY: Harper & Row.

Power, M., 2004. *The Risk Management of Everything.* London: Demos.

Power, M., 2007. *Organized Uncertainty. Designing a World of Risk Management.* Oxford University Press.

Rohwedder, D., 1991. Alles muß hoppla-hopp gehen. Spiegel-Gespräch. *Der Spiegel,* 45 (5), 55-61.

Scharpf, F.W., 1978. Die Theorie der Politikverflechtung: ein kurzgefaßter Leitfaden. *In:* J.J. Hesse, ed. *Politikverflechtung im föderativen Staat.* Baden-Baden: Nomos, 21-31.

Scharpf, F.W., 1988. The Joint-Decision Trap: Lessons from German Federalism and European Integration. *Public Administration Review,* 66 (3), 239-279.

Scharpf, F.W., 1993. Coordination in Hierarchies and Networks. *In:* F.W. Scharpf, ed. *Games in Hierarchies and Networks. Analytical and Empirical Approaches to the Study of Governance Institutions.* Frankfurt, *et al.*: Campus, 125-165.

Scott, R.W., 1995. *Institutions and Organizations.* Thousand Oaks, *et al.*: Sage.

Wiesenthal, H., 1990. *Unsicherheit und Multiple-Self-Identität: eine Spekulation über die Voraussetzungen strategischen Handelns* [online]. Max-Planck-Institut für Gesellschaftsforschung. MPIFG Discussion Paper 90/2. Köln. Available from: http://edoc.vifapol.de/opus/volltexte/2011/2756/pdf/dp90_2.pdf [Accessed 13 March 2013].

# 9

# INTERNAL ENVIRONMENTAL DISPLACEMENT: A GROWING CHALLENGE TO THE UNITED STATES WELFARE STATE

## Michelle A. Meyer

**ABSTRACT**

While the greatest potential for environmental displacement occurs in poorer nations, internal displacement has resulted from environmental change and disasters in the United States; and climate change will likely amplify this movement. I describe how environmental displacement is a policy drift that reduces the effectiveness of current welfare state policies to protect U.S. populations from the risk of impoverishment. Evidence from previous disasters indicates environmental displacees have particular assistance needs. I identify the four main assistance needs in my Environmental Displacement and Resilience Model then use this model to evaluate whether current policies address housing, finances, health, and discrimination needs of those displaced. My analysis highlights a gap between the country's response to disasters and the current welfare state social safety nets. Without disaster and welfare policy changes environmental displacement will continue to be a policy drift that leave displacees vulnerable to social and economic marginalization.

Mientras que el mayor potencial de desplazamientos por causas medioambientales se da en los países más pobres, en los Estados Unidos se ha producido un desplazamiento interno como resultado de cambios ambientales y desastres; y es probable que el cambio climático aumente estos movimientos. Se describe cómo los desplazamientos por causas ambientales suponen un fallo político que reduce la eficacia de las actuales políticas del estado de bienestar que se deben desarrollar para proteger a la población de Estados Unidos contra el riesgo de empobrecimiento. Evidencias de desastres anteriores indican que los desplazados por causas medioambientales tienen necesidades de asistencia especiales. Se identifican las cuatro necesidades de asistencia principales que recoge Modelo de Desplazamiento Medioambiental y Resiliciencia de la autora, para después usar este modelo para evaluar si las políticas actuales cubren las necesidades de vivienda, finanzas, salud y discriminación de los desplazados. Este análisis demuestra que hay una brecha entre la respuesta del país ante los desastres y las actuales redes de protección del estado de bienestar. Si no hay cambios en las políticas de desastres y bienestar, los desplazamientos por causas medioambientales seguirá siendo una deriva política que deja a los desplazados en una posición vulnerable frente a la marginalización social y económica.

## Introduction

The "welfare state" describes the rise of government assistance programs in industrialized nations following World War II. These programs were designed to protect citizens from a variety of risks to their social and economic livelihoods including unemployment, disability, and disasters. While not often viewed as welfare recipients, disaster victims are deemed worthy of direct governmental assistance because disasters are seen as beyond individual control. Disasters, particularly the Dust Bowl Drought of the 1930s, were even used as rhetorical tools to promote the establishment of United States (U.S.) welfare programs, and since then the effects of disaster have been continually defined as a risk to individual livelihoods that should be collectively shared (Dauber 2009).

Thus in the United States, understanding the relationship between general welfare programs and disaster assistance is important as climate change increases the intensity and frequency of environmental hazards. Moreover, in disaster after disaster, research has shown that those who face the greatest impacts and have the least ability to recover from disaster in the U.S. are those who were already in precarious social and economic positions—those who are in need or are on the verge of needing governmental assistance in daily life (Phillips *et al.* 2010). Hurricane Katrina further highlighted the need for an integrated discussion of disaster assistance and general governmental welfare assistance to ensure that the welfare state fulfills its mission of spreading certain risks collectively and prevent 21st century disaster impacts from becoming what Hacker (2004) refers to as "policy drift."

In this chapter, I focus on one specific outcome of disasters and environmental change—permanent environmental displacement—and I begin by describing how it is creating a growing chasm between policy and social conditions of risk (Hacker 2004). Using research from past events and drawing on Cernea's (1997) model of development-induced impoverishment risks, I identify four specific needs (housing, economic recovery, health, and anti-discrimination and marginalization) in the Environmental Displacement and Resilience Model to establish foci for research and welfare policy discussions on limiting the risk of impoverishment from environmental displacement. I then evaluate the ability of current disaster, general welfare, and discrimination policies to meet these needs by reviewing over 30 documents from federal agencies, Congressional records, and external research think tanks. This review raises three issues, discussed below, with the U.S. welfare state that identify environmental displacement as creating policy drift.

## Policy Drift as Welfare State Retrenchment

Hacker (2004) argued that understanding the U.S. welfare state today is less about debating the potential for major policy changes (which have been few) and more about noticing the small and often undetected changes *in society* that limit the effectiveness of welfare programs. One such change is "drift" in which social changes create new or increased risks to the financial stability of many Americans. Once the underlying forces of society have changed, the welfare state will be unable to meet its stated goals of protecting citizens from impoverishment without changes in policy. Examples of drift include changes in the economy—globalization, de-industrialization, service sector growth—or population changes—household structure change, ageing populations, growing inequality—that have put households at greater risk of falling into poverty (Piersen 2001). Without new policies or expansion of current policies, drift creates welfare state retrenchment. Thus, it mimics the effect of a major welfare policy change, namely, undermining the stated purpose of social welfare (sharing certain risks collectively) and increasing the amount of "risk privatization" in which "stable social policies have come to cover a declining portion of the risks faced by citizens" especially for already disadvantaged populations (Hacker 2004, p. 243).

The current examples of policy drift in the academic literature focus solely on societal changes. By including environmental changes, more risks can be identified. In particular, population displacement from mounting environmental change is a risk that is currently ignored by the U.S. welfare state, and much of the U.S. policy system. Environmental displacement occurs when people are forced to leave their homes due to either gradual or sudden changes in the environment (Biermann and Boas 2010). Impoverishment from environmental displacement is often perceived as a problem for low-income countries, yet a small but significant number of people in the U.S. will continue to be forced to permanently move as they have in the past (Pais and Elliott 2008). Hurricane Katrina (2005) and the Dust Bowl Drought (1930s) are examples of environmental displacement in U.S. history, along with the 1927 Louisiana flood, the 1948 Oregon flood, 1992's Hurricane Andrew, the 1993 Mississippi River Floods, and 1999's Hurricane Floyd (Levine, Esnard and Sapat 2007, Rivera and Miller 2007).

Climate change will amplify this displacement by increasing both the scale and frequency of gradual-onset events (chronic drought or sea level rise that make areas uninhabitable or unable to support certain economic sectors) and sudden-onset disasters (floods, wildfires, and tropical storms) that destroy infrastructure and homes (Field *et al.* 2007). Coupled with demographic forces such as population growth, development in hazardous areas, and increasing economic inequality, disaster and environmental changes will further increase the likelihood more people will be driven from their homes in years to come (Gutmann and Field 2010, Raleigh, Jordan and Salehyan 2008). Unfortunately, we know little about the resilience of permanently displaced populations in the U.S. since there has been little academic focus on displacement and long-term recovery; we even lack an estimate of the quantity of internal environmental displacees (Finch, Emrich and Cutter 2010). The limited evidence on U.S. environmental displacement suggests that forced environmental displacement usually leads to further insecurity and constrained resilience for U.S. populations as it does for populations elsewhere in the world (Cernea 1997, Kliot 2004).

## IMPOVERISHMENT RISKS OF U.S. ENVIRONMENTAL DISPLACEMENT

To understand how environmental displacement represents a policy drift, I adapt Cernea's (1997) model of the impoverishment risks from development projects to the U.S. situation using academic literature on U.S. disasters and displacement. Cernea identified eight impoverishment risks: landlessness, joblessness, homelessness, marginalization, increased morbidity and mortality, food insecurity, loss of access to common property, and social disarticulation. I condense these risks into four main areas of concern in the Environmental Displacement and Resilience Model (Figure 1)—housing, economic recovery, health, and anti-discrimination and marginalization—that without attention will create a secondary and often more detrimental disaster of further impoverishment and marginalization for U.S. displacees. I briefly describe how the risks that displacees face differ from those faced by populations who either voluntarily move or disaster-affected populations who are able to rebuild in place. This discussion provides foci for evaluating the welfare state's ability to attend to this issue.

Figure 1: Environmental Displacement and Resilience Model

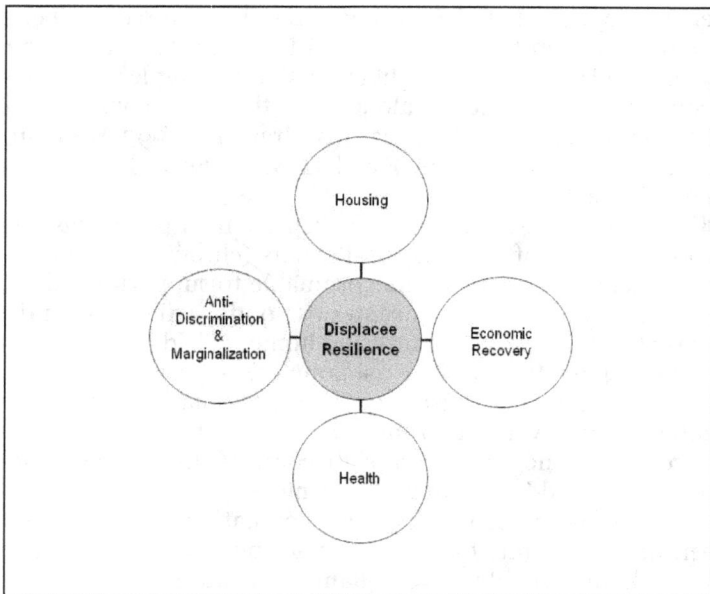

## HOUSING

Gradual environmental change negatively affects ecosystem-dependent livelihoods and sudden disasters destroy homes and businesses. Thus, the loss of lose economic and social resources for environmentally-displaced populations makes housing is a central concern for displaced populations (Cernea 1997). Specifically, environmental displacement in the U.S. results in dramatic drops in homeownership and increased public housing rates among displacees.

Many low- and middle-income households are unable to maintain homeownership through the displacement. Homeownership is foundational to Americans' economic security and homes represent the majority of households' wealth that may not be fully recouped after displacement. The loss of homes is particularly detrimental for minority and low-income households whose homes represent a larger portion of their household wealth compared to others (Finch, Emrich and Cutter 2010, Li *et al.* 2010). Not only do homeownership rates decline among environmental displacees, but there is an increase in public housing rates among those displaced compared to populations who can remain in their original location and those who voluntarily relocate. No matter their housing situation pre-event, those displaced from environmental events are at greater risk than those not displaced of relying on public housing, homeless shelters, or transitory living arrangements with friends and family for shelter, and obviously, those with the fewest resources pre-event will be at the greatest risk of becoming homeless following displacement (Hori and Schafer 2010). Low-income populations who were surviving pre-event without governmental housing assistance often meet income eligibility requirements for government housing programs following displacement (Abramson *et al.* 2010, Morrow-Jones and Morrow-Jones 1991).

The inability to get appropriate and affordable housing forces many socially vulnerable populations to relocate numerous times after the initial displacement. Morrow-Jones and Morrow-Jones (1991) found that 60% of disaster displacees changed residences within three years and Weber and Peek (2012) report that many disadvantaged Hurricane Katrina displacees relocated anywhere from 2 to more than 12 times, with African American females relocating more than other demographic groups. Without stable housing, displacees' recovery is prolonged and their financial, emotional, and educational resilience is reduced (LaRock 2005, Peek and Fothergill 2008, Picou and Marshall 2007).

## ECONOMIC RECOVERY

While housing itself is an economic concern, displacees face other economic barriers to recovery which include securing employment, beginning or restarting government welfare benefits, and the disruption of informal social networks that provide economic resources and services. This issue incorporates the many economic aspects of Cernea's model

(1997) including joblessness, food insecurity, economic marginalization, loss of social network resources, and loss of access to common pool resources (especially for Native American and ecosystem-dependent populations).

Reestablishing employment is necessary for displaced populations to begin recovery, but the loss of human, cultural, and social capital reserves following displacement makes finding new employment opportunities and surviving difficult. For example, displacees from Hurricane Katrina had greater declines in income than those not displaced, and African American displacees had the lowest likelihood of employment recovery (Hori, Schafer and Bowman 2009). Loss of ecosystem-based economic sectors will affect resource-dependent laborers who may need to retrain to find employment in another sector; and Native Americans are already the most economically disadvantaged group in the U.S., making displacement for those that pursue traditional livelihoods particularly dire. Finally, for populations already living in or near poverty, any financial setback dramatically alters their life chances. Even those who were receiving governmental welfare benefits pre-event may find that displacement, especially across jurisdictional lines, can interrupt and possibly reduce this economic support (Lein *et al.* 2012).

Because of their lack of economic resources pre-displacement, many disadvantaged populations are dependent on social networks (family, friends, and neighbors) for financial assistance, childcare, food, and shelter. Environmental displacement highlights some weaknesses of social network resource dependence (Litt 2008). First, poor and minority populations are less likely than others to move from where they are born and less likely to have geographically diverse network connections. Thus environmental displacements can disrupt entire support networks (Li *et al.* 2010). If the resources that these social networks provided are not available in a new community, resilience is limited (Tobin-Gurley, Peek and Loomis 2010).

## HEALTH

Forced displacement increases mental and physical trauma compared to voluntary migration, resulting in increased morbidity and mortality of displacees (Cernea 1997). While the risk of death from disaster and environmental change is much lower in the U.S. than in other nations, U.S. environmental displacement still affects the health of displacees, including negative mental health outcomes and lost or limited access to physical health resources.

Forced relocation following Hurricane Katrina resulted in the separation of families, resettlement in unfamiliar cities, and lack of access to recovery information, which amplified the emotional toll of the storm (Whaley 2009). Moreover, displacees may have negative perceptions of the new community, which further constricts their emotional and mental resources during recovery (Erikson 1976, Kuntz 1973, Yabiku *et al.* 2009).

Tobin-Gurley, Peek and Loomis (2010) found that successful mental health recovery (complicated by pre-existing issues for many disadvantaged individuals) was the most important factor in overall recovery for Katrina displacees.

Physical health needs of displacees extend beyond the immediate crisis period and often conflate with pre-existing problems. For populations with few resources before displacement, they are more likely to lack health insurance pre-event, lose employment-based health benefits if they lost employment during displacement, or face disruption in government-provided healthcare as they reapply for coverage in a new location. Other physical health impacts of displacement include the loss of primary care physicians, loss of medical records, and disruptions in prescription coverage (Abramson and Garfield 2006).

ANTI-DISCRIMINATION AND MARGINALIZATION

A final concern affecting U.S. environmental displacees is discrimination and social marginalization, including the loss of social standing and cultural practices (Cernea 1997). Discrimination and marginalization are included in the Environmental Displacement and Resilience Model because ethnic and racial minorities are more likely to live in environmentally risky areas and are disproportionately poor. This makes them more likely to be represented among the environmentally displaced *and* displacement exacerbates pre-existing societal tensions based on race, ethnicity, religion, and class (Lueck 2011). While discrimination is common in the U.S. during non-disaster times, trauma from the initial environmental impact and unknown surroundings after displacement amplify the effect of direct and indirect discrimination and marginalization.

Displacement transports affected populations to other communities with their own pattern of racism and population segregation. This was evident in Hurricane Katrina after which displacees recounted racial slurs, accusations of being undocumented immigrants and criminals, employment discrimination, racial discrimination from private citizens offering assistance, and refusal of leasing agents to accept federally-funded assistance (Fussell, Sastry and Vanlandingham 2010, Weber and Peek 2012). Undocumented immigrants are specifically vulnerable as they face possible deportation as well as racial discrimination because immigration regulations are enforced during disaster recovery (Wing 2006). Discrimination in housing, labor markets, and social assistance organizations can reinforce the funneling of displacees into economically- and ethnically-segregated communities, slowing their recovery and fostering continued marginalization (Foulkes and Newbold 2000, Portes and Rumbaut 1996). Conflict in neighborhoods undergoing immigration may be amplified in areas taking in environmental displacees.

Even without direct racial or ethnic discrimination, environmental displacement increases the demand for services, infrastructure, and resources in the host community, which leads to resentment and hostility against displaced populations (Moore and Smith 1995, O'Lear 1997). Because the public perceives disasters as temporary phenomena, displacees have short timeframes to return to "normal" and the host community expects displacees to integrate or move back home quickly. Many Hurricane Katrina displacees were unable to return home or become self-sufficient quickly, which caused compassion for them from the host communities to dissipate within a few months (Peek 2012). Displacees' social status, which was weakened during displacement, quickly transformed from "victim" and worthy of assistance to "competitors" for jobs, social services, and other amenities or "outsiders" changing the racial, cultural, and economic composition of the receiving community.

Direct and indirect discrimination reinforces marginalization, social isolation, and loss of community experienced by displacees. Forced resettlement without regard to kinship relations, housing type or location, neighborhood configurations, or cultural norms disrupts relationships and cultural sources of strength (Erikson 1976). Displacement can also create cleavages within populations, increasing internal conflict over scarce resources during recovery (Gill and Picou 1998). Forced displacement, the intensification of internal cleavages, and damage to agricultural and fishery practices may also cause the loss of distinct cultural traditions. For example, traditional lifestyles of Native American Cajun communities, whose fishing livelihoods have lasted centuries in the coastal wetlands of Louisiana, may disintegrate as sea level rise and erosion bring the Gulf of Mexico closer to their homes each year. The loss that will be experienced in these communities is irreplaceable, thus attention to the increasing marginalization of entire cultures is an important and understudied topic in the United States.

## ENVIRONMENTAL DISPLACEMENT AS DRIFT: THREE ISSUES

From the Environmental Displacement and Resilience model, we see that needs of displaced populations are often extenuations of the everyday needs of the poor and marginalized in the U.S. These needs include timely access to affordable housing, including rental options, public housing, and affordable loans to regain home-ownership; employment and cash assistance for food, childcare, and transportation; long-term physical and mental health assistance; and policies that address discrimination and segregation in relocation communities, help maintain community ties, and are sensitive to relocation options including land type, traditional livelihoods, housing structures, food assistance, and community cohesion. Increasing resilience in these four areas becomes a multifaceted project that includes both immediate and long-term needs of affected populations.

These issues raise questions about the ability of the current welfare state to address the risk of impoverishment for environmental displacees. Effective assistance programs help ensure displacees have pre-event resources to mitigate and prepare for and adapt to environmental change and have access to post-event recovery resources and programs to be resilient in a new location (Gajewski *et al.* 2011). While these needs could theoretically be addressed through a variety of measures, including a mix of private and public resources, there is currently *no* discussion of environmental displacement as a risk to livelihoods in the U.S. in these realms. In fact of the policy documents evaluated, only *one*, a Brookings Institution (2010) policy critique, even mentions permanent environmental displacement, and they focus solely on Native Alaskan populations facing sea level rise. Because of this issue and because the U.S. welfare state involves a complicated mix of centralized and state-based assistance programs, my goal in this section is to discuss the implications of environmental displacement on the ideals of the welfare state. Thus, I limit my following discussion to an overview of general concerns presented by environmental displacement and future research will be needed to determine the effectiveness of a variety of policy and legal options (e.g. insurance, mitigation, direct assistance, etc.).

As Hacker (2004, p. 246) discussed, policy drift implicates policymakers in the question of, "whether and how to respond to the growing gap between the original aims of a policy and the new realities that shifting social conditions have fostered." If the risks highlighted above are to be addressed and the ideals of the welfare state to share risk collectively upheld, policymakers have three issues to address: inadequate assistance timeframes, ignorance of small and gradual-onset events, and targeted assistance to those most in need.

## INADEQUATE ASSISTANCE TIMEFRAME

Environmental displacees have both immediate short-term needs, especially during disasters, and also often take longer to fully recover following displacement than populations who voluntarily relocate or those able to rebuild in place—thus an apparent challenge presented by permanent environmental displacement is the timeframe for assistance. Disaster policy, which provides immediate assistance, and general welfare policy, which addresses continued need, should together cover environmental displacees' needs, but long-term and permanent displacement highlights the temporal gap in practice between these programs.

Federal disaster policy only has procedures for short-term and temporary assistance to populations affected by environmental events. The Federal Emergency Management Agency (FEMA) coordinates disaster assistance through the *National Disaster Housing Strategy* and the National Disaster Recovery Framework. In terms of housing assistance, populations displaced from a federally-declared disaster can receive rental assistance and home repairs funding for 18 months or receive a set monetary allotment (adjusted yearly for inflation). Homeowners may request assistance to get a loan for a new property. Several federal agencies from the Department of Housing and Urban Development (HUD) to the Small Business Administration run over 30 programs that administer emergency disaster housing assistance (FEMA 2009). The *National Disaster Housing Strategy* clearly emphasizes the immediacy of disaster assistance programming by identifying the need to secure stable housing *quickly* as a central goal of disaster housing assistance. Unfortunately, the document does not create new or extend current housing programs to do so (FEMA 2009). Disaster economic assistance is provided for an even shorter time period than housing assistance—26 weeks of disaster unemployment insurance and financial support. This assistance is provided through a multitude of programs, which were recently converted to a case management approach in which FEMA and nonprofit employees provide referrals to a multitude of governmental and nongovernmental assistance programs and assist individuals in selecting and applying for assistance (FEMA 20011a).

The current standard of 18 months for housing assistance and 26 weeks of financial assistance may be appropriate for those able to quickly return and rebuild but these programs may end even before other displacees determine whether they can or will return (FEMA 2011a). For example, over five years after Hurricane Katrina, hundreds of FEMA temporary housing trailers were still occupied by the most disadvantaged displacees. Even extra appropriations to social service programs during large-scale disasters are too short-lived to fulfill their mission. For example, the Department of Labor created special career counseling and construction training programs following Hurricane Katrina which lasted only six months (GAO 2009a).

In recent decades, attention to mental healthcare following disasters has increased with large-scale mobilization of professional volunteers to disaster sites (Whaley 2009). The bulk of counseling for displaced populations falls to volunteers and non-profit organizations that offer immediate assistance in extreme situations. There are no specific programs offering long-term counseling for displacees, which may be the most needed assistance to promote overall resilience following displacement (Tobin-Gurley, Peek and Loomis 2010). Disaster financial assistance can be used to cover health insurance costs among other financial needs but there is no specific program addressing the healthcare (physical or mental) of environmentally-displaced populations.

The extended recovery period of both previously disadvantaged and newly disadvantaged displacees is meant to be addressed by transitioning from disaster programs to traditional welfare programs. But as the GAO states, "a disaster can exacerbate the long-standing challenges at-risk populations have in accessing needed assistance from multiple programs" (GAO 2008, p. 42). These programs include unemployment insurance, job placement and assistance, food vouchers, breakfast and lunch programs at schools, early childhood education programs, bus transit programs, and healthcare programs (GAO 2010, Winston *et al.* 2006). For financial and medical assistance, families with dependent children or pregnant women are also eligible for the Temporary Assistance to Needy Families program, the 1996 replacement to entitlement-based welfare assistance, along with Medicaid or Medicare (GAO 2009a). But, these programs respond poorly to sudden changes in the overall level of need, which may occur after a large disaster. Furthermore, the transition from disaster assistance to general welfare programs once the timeframe for disaster aid ends requires updated or new applications, which are bureaucratically complicated and often result in individuals losing assistance during review.

Even if environmental displacees do manage to transfer to general welfare programs, their prolonged recovery needs may still be unmet. Welfare programs are critiqued in general as ineffective in addressing the long-term and chronic needs of many low-income households (GAO 2010). General welfare programs are meant to provide temporary assistance and thus most social service programs have either continuous time limits (such as two years of continual support) or lifetime limits on assistance (such as five years for the Temporary Assistance to Needy Families cash assistance program). These time limits mean populations who received assistance pre-displacement have a limited timeframe for assistance post-event and thus have less time to become self-sufficient. For example, some displacees from Hurricane Katrina still needed assistance five years after the event—long after disaster *and* general welfare programs withdraw assistance. Recent research indicates that it can take nearly a decade for full disaster recovery, much longer than any assistance programs (FEMA 2011b).

Reducing prejudicial treatment based on race, ethnicity, religion, and class from other individuals and institutions and creating culturally-sensitive recovery options is central to promoting resilience, but this may be the most complicated component of the Environmental Displacement and Resilience Model to address in a timely manner. Direct discrimination following displacement falls under general federal anti-discrimination policy such as the Civil Rights Act and the Fair Housing Act. Together these policies prohibit intentional discrimination in federally-funded programs, employment, and housing transactions and were used following Hurricane Katrina to address racism in assistance programs (Feder 2008, HUD 2010). But, the sudden surge in discrimination following displacement challenges the effectiveness of these policies because the recourse options are time consuming and cannot provide the necessary assistance in a timely manner. Recourse for discrimination under these policies requires an official complaint to the federal government or a lawsuit against a specific individual or organization perpetrating the discrimination. When needing *immediate* housing and employment, displacees have little time, energy, or money to follow through with the required discrimination complaint or lawsuit that takes months or years to adjudicate. Unfortunately, neither welfare or civil rights programs nor revisions to disaster assistance policy following Hurricane Katrina acknowledge that environmental displacement is a unique impoverishment risk that raises questions about the timeframe of assistance programs or how to address both short- and long-term needs of displacees.

## EVENT-BASED ASSISTANCE

The types of environmental events that trigger displacement also highlight the changing nature of risk. Disaster policy provides a politically feasible access point for addressing environmental displacement, and has been used to support relocation following large-scale disasters. But, outside large-scale, sudden disasters, environmental displacement will likely follow current patterns of economic migration, which is smaller in scale and potential circular (Warner 2011). Small-scale events and slow-onset events creating this pattern of displacement are unaccounted for in current disaster assistance schemes.

Local governments have primary responsible for preparing for, responding to, and recovering from disasters; the federal government intervenes when local and state capacity is overwhelmed (when a *federal* disaster is declared). Disaster-based assistance provided by FEMA requires a federal disaster declaration (Stafford Act 1988). Small and most gradual-onset events are often overlooked in this process, leaving displacees from these events without access to federal disaster-based assistance and local and state governments without access to federal assistance to supply for the needs of victims. For example, from 1953 through 2010, droughts comprised only 2.5% of federally-declared disasters and there is no standard for sea level rise to induce a federal declaration without storm impacts (FEMA 2010). Thus, FEMA lacks a mandate to assist Native Alaskan and Cajun populations who are *already* experiencing displacement induced by climate change. During large-scale catastrophic events, Congress can relax eligibility requirements or provide additional funding to assist lower levels of government. This is a special outcome, seen most recently in Hurricane Katrina, and the general lack of federal attention results in the invisibility of displacees from certain environmental hazards. While FEMA is working to improve housing, economic, and health assistance to disaster victims, increasing environmental displacement from types of events not traditionally covered by disaster policy contributes to the "growing gulf between social risks and benefits" (Hacker 2004).

The potential for displacees to be excluded from disaster-based assistance means that other assistance programs will face increased need. Even in small-scale displacements, the level of need for general welfare programs will rise as economic losses make more individuals eligible for assistance. The ability of current assistance programs to meet the needs of more disadvantaged populations is an ongoing concern.

## ASSISTANCE TO THOSE MOST IN NEED

From research following previous disasters, we know that disasters are social phenomenon in which the risk of impact and ability to recover are mediated by social structures. "Social vulnerability" is used to describe these "social, economic, and political processes that influence how hazards affect people in varying ways and with differing intensities" (Wisner *et al.* 2004, p. 7). Economic structures—e.g. homeownership, financial assets, future income potential, insurance coverage—and social status—e.g. political power, marginalization, minority status, education, gender, age—influence individuals' and households' ability to prepare for, mitigate, respond to, and recover from disaster impacts (Cutter, Boruff and Shirley 2003, Phillips *et al.* 2010). The social vulnerability perspective also highlights the role of social structures in determining risk of climate change impacts and also the risk of displacement from environmental events (Adger 2006). Populations range from being "environmentally motivated" to "environmentally forced" depending on the intensity of environmental impact and *the feasibility of their in-place recovery or adaptation* (Warner 2010). The feasibility of in-place recovery or adaptation is contingent upon social, economic, and political resources available. As Fussell and Elliot (2009, p. 389) stated, environmental displacement will mimic disaster impacts as socially-structured phenomena with environmental and climate impacts filtering through the U.S. social structure to result in "multiple and highly unequal processes of resettlement."

While all displaced populations will face the potential of impoverishment, previous vulnerabilities are exacerbated during and following displacement leaving socially vulnerable groups to face more and larger obstacles to recovery from the initial environmental impacts *and* the displacement process (Fothergill and Peek 2004, Hunter 2005, Weber and Peek 2012). For example, in a seminal study on this issue, Morrow-Jones and Morrow-Jones (1991) found that those displaced by disasters in the U.S. were more likely to be female-headed households, minority group members, and from lower income and education brackets than those who relocated for other reasons. As noted in policy drift in general, individuals living at or near the bottom of economic and social hierarchies are the most affected by increasing risk privatization.

Figure 2 depicts the process of environmental displacement in the U.S. and highlights the likelihood of displacement for socially vulnerable populations as the cumulative outcome from a series of risks triggered by an initial environmental change (see Lueck 2011 for detailed discussion). This figure emphasizes that the most vulnerable populations will be over-represented among those *forced* to *permanently* relocate. Thus populations most in need of general welfare assistance in daily life will have the increased burden of displacement and the impoverishment that follows because "the way in which migration occurs and the resources migrants are able to access before, during, and after moving will necessarily shape social outcomes for environmental migrants" (Marino 2012).

Figure 2: Multi-phase model of U.S. environmental displacement

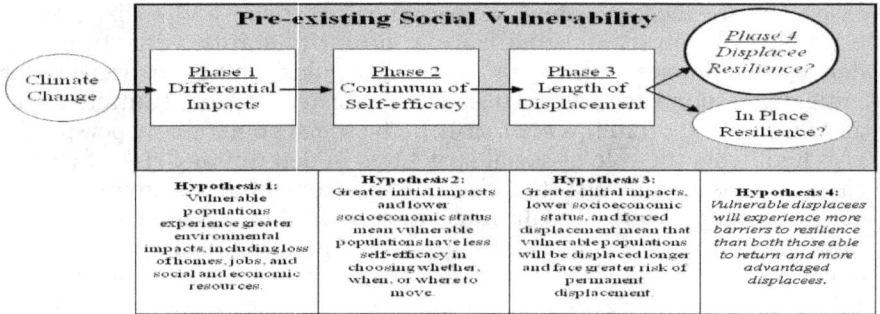

Note: Adapted from Lueck (2011)

Welfare state policies are meant to provide social safety nets for impoverishment. If populations already disadvantaged, either living in or near poverty, are most at risk of environmental displacement and face the most difficulty recovering, they are those most likely in need of the social safety net discussed here. Targeted legal planning, for the four resilience concerns presented here *and* the populations most vulnerable, is superior to more general approaches (Berke *et al.* 2010). Current policies take an "all-population" approach and, in addressing discrimination, a purportedly "color-blind" one. For example, disaster policy distributes funds based on geographic proximity to the impact and amount of lost assets, not pre-existing need, which obviously benefits those already advantaged in U.S. society. The *National Disaster Housing Strategy* is meant to streamline public, private, and non-profit collaboration related to disaster housing assistance, and it calls for specific attention to low-income and special needs populations (those with disabilities, children, and the elderly). But the document includes only vague statements about achieving this goal (FEMA 2009, GAO 2009b). More specifically, none of the six fully-funded disaster housing programs target socially vulnerable populations (FEMA 2011a).

The need for affordable housing and public housing options highlight the complex issues surrounding assistance to disadvantaged populations in the U.S. During disasters, loss of housing supply causes inflation in housing costs, especially rentals, and during gradual-onset events more people are trying to get low-income housing in communities that are often already at full capacity (Fischer and Sard 2005). The lack of affordable housing in the U.S. is a chronic problem that will affect environmental displacees. The *National Disaster Housing Strategy* acknowledges this problem but proposes only tax-credits for developers to rebuild low-income and public housing in place and geographically transferable HUD housing subsidies for eligible individuals. HUD runs the general housing programs supporting low-income populations by providing housing vouchers and assistance programs. HUD assistance is meant to be transferable from one location to another. But getting assistance in a new location again depends on the amount of affordable and subsidized housing available in the new community and, if displacees cross a state line, the amount of assistance that that state provides (which may be less than what displacees were receiving previously). Also, HUD's programs require individuals to find their own housing, which is difficult when displaced to unfamiliar communities or without access to transportation to locate adequate housing (Paradee 2012). The risk of losing housing and rising housing costs facing displacees cannot be addressed without reconsidering the role of the state in housing markets and generating more affordable housing options in *all* communities—a perfect example of drift that leaves the current welfare state incapable of maintaining a social safety net for the most needy populations.

General welfare policy assists poor and low-income individuals and households through means-tested income measures without providing specific attention to marginalized or disadvantaged groups or other differentiation beyond income. Specific groups face increased challenges, for example single mothers, which are complex and often require these groups to seek multiple governmental and nonprofit programs to cover all their needs (Tobin-Gurley, Peek and Loomis 2010). Disaster policy revisions following Hurricane Katrina drew attention broadly to socially vulnerable groups, identifying the socio-economically disadvantaged, minorities, educationally disenfranchised, women and children, individuals with disabilities, and the elderly as deserving special attention. But there is little specific guidance from FEMA on assisting these groups or on addressing discrimination, segregation, or marginalization—the greatest challenge to policy directed at displacee resilience (Cernea 1997, Farber *et al.* 2010). The Government Accountability Office (GAO 2008) acknowledged that current disaster programs were unable to assist disabled, unemployed, and homeless displacees following Hurricane Katrina. Overall case management programs had discontinuous funding streams, lack of support or clear assignments, high employee turnover, and ineffective or incomplete outreach to the most vulnerable populations which limited and complicated the ability for populations to get continuous economic assistance (GAO 2009a).

Finally, the consequences of environmental displacement on racial and cultural minorities are a growing risk that "color-blind" approaches insufficiently address. The pervasive and historical legacy of discrimination and marginalization in the U.S. that is amplified during environmental displacement requires culturally sensitive and targeted aid programs, not just complaint–based recourse (Henkel, Dovidio and Gaertner 2006). Current discrimination policies overlook unintentional discrimination, e.g. language barriers in the application processes and private citizens offering assistance to certain races, genders, and family types (Crowley 2006, HUD 2010). Furthermore, the impact on cultural heritage, specifically for Native American populations, is the invisible impact of environmental change (Collins 2008). Current discrimination policy is incapable of addressing cultural loss or entire community disarticulation, unintentional or institutional discrimination, and passive forms of racial and cultural indifference. While Native Alaskan populations are the only group acknowledged as potential U.S. environmental displacees, the discussion of relocation options and goals remains superficial and ignores the question of cultural heritage maintenance. Increased participation of these groups may draw attention to discrimination and eliminate the need for disaster-specific "Citizens' Bill of Rights" as was implemented after Hurricane Katrina (Sanyika 2009), but policy-makers have yet to fully engage a discussion of these issues for environmental displacement. This final area of displacee resilience raises the most direct policy and legal questions in the space between disaster, welfare, and civil rights policy (Sterett 2009).

## CONCLUSION

While lawsuits following Hurricane Katrina challenged federal disaster assistance programs highlighting these three issues, no policies or programs were changed in the practice of FEMA *beyond* Hurricane Katrina survivors. Hurricane Katrina was a large-scale example of what environmental displacees in the U.S. will likely encounter in the future: inadequate assistance and risk of impoverishment because changed environmental and societal circumstances leave current policies ineffective in addressing their needs.

> Some residents who were just 'getting by' in New Orleans and others who were already impoverished were thrown into deeper poverty during prolonged displacement—a problem that could not be adequately addressed by either disaster assistance programs or local social assistance programs alone. (Fussell and Elliott 2009, p. 386)

There is no simple or quick solution, and because of the current political climate, it is unlikely that welfare assistance programs will be expanded. This does not negate the fact that the need for welfare assistance in the U.S. continues to increase. For example, the poverty rate grew from 11% to over 14%, with racial and ethnic minorities experiencing almost twice those numbers, and individuals receiving food assistance more than doubled to 39 million from 2000 through 2010 (GAO 2010). With more frequent and severe disaster impacts becoming "the new normal" for the U.S. under climate change (Kolmannskog 2009) and social inequality increasing, the number of potential displacees will increase and in turn creates even more inequality as more people risk falling into poverty due to displacement. While the recent housing crisis resulted in more homes lost and increased the risk of displacement for many U.S. populations (JCHS 2008), the growing risk of environmental displacement only adds to these increasing risks of displacement under current economic and political conditions.

In this chapter, I outlined a framework for understanding how environmental changes also affect the social landscape in which the U.S. welfare state operates, and thus changes in the environment along with social changes result in increasing privatization of the risk of impoverishment from environmental displacement. "Displacement is a caused disruption, not a natural disaster, and its perverse effects must and can be counterbalanced" (Cernea 1997, p. 1570), and thus I identified both the needs of environmental displacees and the issues with which policymakers will likely grapple. The needs of displacees are intertwined and interdependent, so it is difficult to support full recovery through programs that address only one issue—emphasizing the need to integrate the welfare state and displaced populations into the discussion about disaster and climate change response and recovery. Whether new policy is developed or current policies are adapted, the U.S. must acknowledge that environmental displacement is not an unfortunate and unlikely event resulting only from extremely catastrophic disasters, but a normal part of life in the U.S. (Bullock, Haddow and Haddow 2009, Lauten and Lietz 2008). Focusing on socially vulnerable displacees will move the disaster resilience discussion from immediate humanitarian assistance and rebuilding in place towards encouraging environmental justice and fostering resilience to our changing climate (Berke *et al.* 2010, Meertens 2010, O'Brien *et al.* 2006).

## Bibliography

Abramson, D., and Garfield, R., 2006. *On the edge: Children and families displaced by Hurricanes Katrina and Rita face a looming medical and mental health crisis*. New York: National Center for Disaster Preparedness and Operation Assist.

Abramson, D., *et al.*, 2010. Measuring individual disaster recovery: A socioecological framework. *Disaster medicine and public health preparedness*, 4 (Supplement 1), S46-S54.

Adger, W.N., 2006. Vulnerability. *Global environmental change*, 16 (3), 268-281.

Berke, P., *et al.*, 2010. Disaster plans: Challenges and choices to build the resiliency of vulnerable populations. *International journal of mass emergencies and disasters*, 28 (3), 368-394.

Biermann, F., and Boas, I., 2010. Preparing for a warmer world: Towards a global governance system to protect climate refugees. *Global environmental politics*, 10 (1), 60-88.

Brookings Institution, 2010. *Comments on FEMA's National Disaster Recovery Framework* [online]. Washington, DC: Brookings Institution. Available from: http://www.brookings.edu/opinions/2010/0226_natural_disasters.aspx?p+1 [Accessed 3 April 2013].

Bullock, J., Haddow, G., and Haddow, K., 2009. *Global warming, natural hazards, and emergency management*. Boca Raton, FL: CRC Press.

Cernea, M., 1997. The risks and reconstruction model for resettling displaced populations. *World development,* 25 (10), 1569-1587.

Collins, R., 2008. Missed by the mass media: The Houma, Pointe-au-Chien, and Hurricanes Katrina and Rita. *American indian culture and research journal,* 32 (2), 43-53.

Crowley, S., 2006. Where is home? Housing for low-income people after the 2005 hurricanes. *In:* C. Hartman, and G.D. Squires, eds. *There is no such thing as a natural disaster: Race, class, and Hurricane Katrina.* New York City: Routledge, 121-166.

Cutter, S.L., Boruff, B.J., and Shirley, W., 2003. Social vulnerability to environmental hazards. *Social science quarterly,* 84 (2), 242-261.

Dauber, M.L., 2009. The real third rail of American politics. *In:* A. Sarat, and J. Lezaun, eds. *Catastrophe: Law, politics, and the humanitarian impulse.* Amherst: University of Massachusetts Press, 60-82.

Erikson, K., 1976. *Everything in its path: Destruction of community in the Buffalo Creek Flood.* New York: Simon and Schuster.

Farber, D.A., *et al.,* 2010. *Disaster law and policy.* New York: Aspen Publishers.

Feder, J., 2008. *Federal civil rights statutes: A primer.* Washington, DC: Congressional Research Service.

FEMA, 2009. *National Disaster Housing Strategy and Annexes.* Washington, DC: Federal Emergency Management Agency.Available from: http://www.fema.gov/national-disaster-housing-strategy-document-annexes [Accessed 9 April 2013].

FEMA, 2010. *Declared disasters by year or state* [online]. Washington, DC: Federal Emergency Management Agency. Available from: http://www.fema.gov/disasters [Accessed 1 April 2010].

FEMA, 2011a. *National Disaster Recovery Framework* [online]. Washington, DC: Federal Emergency Management Agency.Available from: http://www.fema.gov/pdf/recoveryframework/ndrf.pdf [Accessed 2 April 2013].

FEMA, 2011b. *A whole community approach to emergency management: Principles, themes, and pathways for action* [online]. Washington, DC: Federal Emergency Management Agency. Available from: http://www.fema.gov/whole-community [Accessed 2 April 2013].

Field, C.B., *et al.,* 2007. North America. *In:* M.L. Parry, *et al.,* eds. *Climate change 2007: Impacts, adaption and vulnerability. Contribution of working group ii to the fourth assessment report of the Intergovernmental Panel on Climate Change.* Cambridge University Press, 617-652.

Finch, C., Emrich, C., and Cutter, S., 2010. Disaster disparities and differential recovery in New Orleans. *Population and environment,* 31 (4), 179-202.

Fischer, W., and Sard, B., 2005. *Bringing Katrina's poorest victims home: Targeted federal assistance will be needed to give neediest evacuees option to return to their hometowns.* Washington, DC: Center on Budget and Policy Priorities.

Fothergill, A., and Peek, L., 2004. Poverty and disasters in the United States: A review of recent sociological findings. *Natural hazards,* 32 (1), 89-110.

Foulkes, M., and Newbold, K.B., 2000. Migration propensities, patterns, and the role of human capital: Comparing Mexican, Cuban, and Puerto Rican interstate migration, 1985-1990. *The professional geographer,* 52 (1), 133-145.

Fussell, E., and Elliott, J.R., 2009. Introduction: Social organization of demographic responses to disaster: Studying population—environment interactions in the case of Hurricane Katrina. *Organization and environment,* 22 (4), 379-394.

Fussell, E., Sastry, N., and Vanlandingham, M., 2010. Race, socioeconomic status, and return migration to New Orleans after Hurricane Katrina. *Population and environment,* 31 (1), 20-42.

Gajewski, S., *et al.,* 2011. Complexity and instability: The response of nongovernmental organizations to the recovery of Hurricane Katrina survivors in a host community. *Nonprofit and voluntary sector quarterly,* 40 (2), 389-403.

GAO, 2008. *Disaster assistance: Federal efforts to assist group site residents with employment, services for families and children, and transportation* (GAO-09-81) [online]. Washington, DC: US Government Accountability Office. Available from: http://www.gao.gov/products/GAO-09-81 [Accessed 3 April 2013].

GAO, 2009a. *Disaster assistance: Greater coordination and an evaluation of programs' outcomes could improve disaster case management (GAO-09-561)* [online]. Washington, DC: US Government Accountability Office. Available from: http://www.gao.gov/products/GAO-09-561 [Accessed 3 April 2013].

GAO, 2009b. *Disaster housing: FEMA needs more detailed guidance and performance measures to help ensure effective assistance after major disasters (GAO-09-796)* [online]. Washington, DC: US Government Accountability Office. Available from: http://www.gao.gov/products/GAO-09-796 [Accessed 3 April 2013].

GAO, 2010. *Support for low-income individuals and families (GAO-10-342r)* [online]. Washington, DC: US Government Accountability Office. Available from: http://www.gao.gov/products/GAO-10-342r [Accessed 3 April 2013].

Gill, D.A., and Picou, J.S., 1998. Technological disaster and chronic community stress. *Society & natural resources,* 11 (8), 795-815.

Gutmann, M.P., and Field, V., 2010. Katrina in historical context: Environment and migration in the US. *Population and environment,* 31 (1-3), 3-19.

Hacker, J.S., 2004. Privatizing risk without privatizing the welfare state: The hidden politics of social policy retrenchment in the United States. *The American political science review,* 98 (2), 243-260.

Henkel, K.E., Dovidio, J.F., and Gaertner, S.L., 2006. Institutional discrimination, individual racism, and Hurricane Katrina. *Analyses of social issues and public policy,* 6 (1), 99-124.

Hori, M., and Schafer, M.J., 2010. Social costs of displacement in Louisiana after Hurricanes Katrina and Rita. *Population and environment,* 31 (1-3), 64-86.

Hori, M., Schafer, M.J., and Bowman, D.J., 2009. Displacement dynamics in southern Louisiana after Hurricanes Katrina and Rita. *Population research and policy review*, 28 (1), 45-65.

HUD, 2010. *Fair Housing Laws* [online]. Washington, DC: HUD. Available from: http://www.hud.gov/offices/fheo/FHLaws/index.cfm [Accessed 1 May 2010].

Hunter, L.M., 2005. Migration and environmental hazards. *Population and environment*, 26 (4), 273-302.

JCHS, 2008. *The State of the Nation's Housing 2008* [online]. Cambridge, MA: Joint Center for Housing Studies of Harvard University. Available from: http://www.jchs.harvard.edu/sites/jchs.harvard.edu/files/son2008.pdf [Accessed 3 April 2013].

Kliot, N., 2004. Environmentally induced population movements: Their complex sources and consequences. *In:* J.D. Unruh, M.S. Krol, and N. Kliot, eds. *Environmental change and its implications for population movement.* Dordrecht, The Netherlands: Kluwer Academic Publishers, 69-100.

Kolmannskog, V., 2009. *Climate changed: People displaced.* Oslo: Norwegian Refugee Council.

Kunz, E.F., 1973. The refugee in flight: Kinetic models and forms of displacement. *International migration review*, 7 (2), 125-146.

LaRock, J.D., 2005. Katrina and Rita: What can the United States learn from international experiences with education in displacement? *Harvard educational review* [online], 75 (4), 357-363.Available from: http://hepg.org/her/abstract/1 [Accessed 3 April 2013].

Lauten, A.W., and Lietz, K., 2008. A look at the standards gap: Comparing child protection responses in the aftermath of Hurricane Katrina and the Indian Ocean Tsunami. *Children, youth and environments*, 18 (1), 158-201.

Lein, L., *et al.*, 2012. The basement of extreme poverty: Katrina survivors and poverty programs. *In:* L. Weber, and L. Peek, eds. *Displaced: Life in the Katrina Diaspora.* Austin, TX: University of Texas Press, 47-62.

Levine, J.N., Esnard, A.-M., and Sapat, A., 2007. Population displacement and housing dilemmas due to catastrophic disasters. *Journal of planning literature*, 22 (1), 3-15.

Li, W., *et al.*, 2010. Katrina and migration: Evacuation and return by African Americans and Vietnamese Americans in an eastern New Orleans suburb. *The professional geographer* [online], 62 (1), 103-118. Available from: http://www.tandfonline.com/doi/full/10.1080/00330120903404934 [Accessed 3 April 2013].

Litt, J., 2008. Getting out or staying put: An African American women's network in evacuation from Katrina. *NWSA journal,* 20 (3), 32-48.

Lueck, M.M., 2011. United States environmental migration: Vulnerability, resilience, and policy options for internally displaced persons. *In:* M. Leighton, X. Shen, and K. Warner, eds. *Climate change and migration: Rethinking policies for adaptation and disaster risk reduction.* Bonn, Germany: United Nations University Institute for Environment and Human Security, 48-62.

Marino, E., 2012. The long history of environmental migration: Assessing vulnerability construction and obstacles to successful relocation in Shishmaref, Alaska. *Global environmental change,* 22 (2), 374-381.

Meertens, D., 2010. Forced displacement and women's security in Columbia. *Disasters,* 34 (S2), S147-164.

Moore, E.J., and Smith, J.W., 1995. Climatic change and migration from Oceania— implications for Australia, New Zealand and the United States of America. *Population and environment,* 17 (2), 105-122.

Morrow-Jones, H.A., and Morrow-Jones, C.R., 1991. Mobility due to natural disaster: Theoretical considerations and preliminary analyses. *Disasters,* 15 (2), 126-132.

O'Brien, G., *et al.,* 2006. Climate change and disaster management. *Disasters,* 30 (1), 64-80.

O'Lear, S., 1997. Migration and the environment: A review of recent literature. *Social science quarterly,* 78 (2), 606-618.

Pais, J., and Elliott, J., 2008. Places as recovery machines: Vulnerability and neighborhood change after major hurricanes. *Social forces,* 86 (4), 1415-1452.

Paradee, J., 2012. Living through displacement: Housing insecurity among low-income evacuees. *In:* L. Weber, and L. Peek, eds. *Displaced: Life in the Katrina Diaspora.* Austin, TX: University of Texas Press, 63-78.

Peek, L., 2012. They call it "Katrina fatigue": Displaced families and discrimination in Colorado. *In:* L. Weber, and L. Peek, eds. *Displaced: Life in the Katrina Diaspora.* Austin, TX: University of Texas Press, 31-46.

Peek, L., and Fothergill, A., 2008. Displacement, gender, and the challenges of parenting after Hurricane Katrina. *NWSA journal,* 20 (3), 69-105.

Phillips, B.D., *et al.,* eds., 2010. *Social vulnerability to disasters.* Boca Raton, FL: CRC Press.

Picou, J.S., and Marshall, B.K., 2007. Social impacts of Hurricane Katrina on displaced K-12 students and educational institutions in coastal Alabama counties: Some preliminary observations. *Sociological spectrum,* 27 (6), 767-780.

Piersen, P., 2001. Post-industrial pressures on the mature welfare states. *In:* P. Piersen, ed. *The new politics of the welfare state.* Oxford University Press, 80-104.

Portes, A., and Rumbaut, R.G., 1996. *Immigrant America: A portrait.* Berkeley, CA: University of California Press.

Raleigh, C., Jordan, L., and Salehyan, I., 2008. Assessing the impact of climate change on migration and conflict. *Social Deminsions of Climate Change* [online]. Washington, DC: World Bank Group. Available from: http://siteresources.worldbank.org/EXTSOCIALDEVELOPMENT/Resources/SDCCWorkingPaper_MigrationandConflict.pdf [Accessed 3 April 2013].

Rivera, J.D., and Miller, D.S., 2007. Continually neglected: Situating natural disasters in the African American experience. *Journal of black studies*, 37 (4), 502-522.

Sanyika, M., 2009. Katrina and the condition of black New Orleans: The struggle for justice, equity, and democracy. *In:* R. Bullard, and B. Wright, eds. *Race, place, and environmental justice after Hurricane Katrina: Struggles to reclaim, rebuild, and revitalize New Orleans and the Gulf Coast.* Boulder, CO: Westview Press, 87-111.

Stafford Act, 1988. *Robert T. Stafford Disaster Relief and Emergency Preparedness Act. United StatesPL 100-707* [online]. Available from: http://www.fema.gov/robert-t-stafford-disaster-relief-and-emergency-assistance-act-public-law-93-288-amended [Accessed 9 April 2013].

Sterett, S.M., 2009. New Orleans everywhere: Bureaucratic accountability and housing policy after Katrina. *In:* A. Sarat, and J. Lezaun, eds. *Catastrophe: Law, politics, and the humanitarian impulse.* Amherst: University of Massachusetts Press, 83-115.

Tobin-Gurley, J., Peek, L., and Loomis, J., 2010. Displaced single mothers in the aftermath of Hurricane Katrina: Resource needs and resource acquisition. *International journal of mass emergencies and disasters*, 28 (2), 170-206.

Warner, K., 2010. Global environmental change and migration: Governance challenges. *Global environmental change*, 20 (3), 402-413.

Warner, K., 2011. Environmental change and migration: Methodological considerations from ground-breaking global survey. *Population and environment*, 33 (1), 3-27.

Weber, L., and Peek, L., 2012. *Displaced: Life in the Katrina diaspora.* Austin, TX: University of Texas Press.

Whaley, A., 2009. Trauma among survivors of Hurricane Katrina: Considerations and recommendations for mental health care. *Journal of loss and trauma*, 14 (6), 459-476.

Wing, A.K., 2006. From wrongs to rights: Hurricane Katrina in a global perspective. *Colorlines*, 9 (3), 41-44.

Winston, P., *et al.*, 2006. *Federalism after Hurricane Katrina: How can social programs respond to a major disaster?* [online]. Washington, DC: The Urban Institute. Available from: http://www.urban.org/UploadedPDF/311344_after_katrina.pdf [Accessed 3 April 2013].

Wisner, B., *et al.*, 2004. The challenge of disasters and our approach. *In:* B. Wisner, *et al.*, eds. *At risk: Natural hazards, people's vulnerability and disasters.* 2nd ed. London: Routledge, 3-48.

Yabiku, S.T., *et al.*, 2009. Migration, health, and environment in the desert southwest. *Population and environment*, 30 (4-5), 131-158.

# 10

## LONG TERM RECOVERY IN DISASTER RESPONSE AND THE ROLE OF NON-PROFITS

### Victor B. Flatt and Jeffrey J. Stys

**ABSTRACT**

The Legal Framework of Disaster Response does not deal as well with long term recovery. In particular, the role of non-profits is unexamined. This chapter examines the role of non-profits in disaster recovery and argues for a legal framework acknowledging its important role.

El marco legal de las respuestas ante desastres no tiene en cuenta la recuperación a largo plazo. En particular, no se analiza el papel de las organizaciones sin ánimo de lucro. Este artículo estudia el papel de las organizaciones sin ánimo de lucro en la recuperación de desastres, y se muestra a favor de establecer un marco legal que reconozca la importancia de su papel.

## INTRODUCTION

In the United States, the laws of disaster preparedness and response can usually be grouped into pre-disaster activities (such as planning and preparing for disasters), emergency response to disasters, and long term response and recovery to the disaster. Short term recovery involves restoration of basic services and provision of temporary housing, whereas long term recovery is focused on the restoration (and possible enhancement) of the built environment to a prior or new stasis. Though conceptually distinct, long term recovery and short term recovery are related in that actions taken during the initial stages of disaster response will affect options in longer term recovery for better and for worse.

Long term recovery efforts usually strive to return the community to conditions that existed prior to an event, or ideally, to a condition that improves upon the social, economic, and natural environments. Long term recovery actions can include repairing or replacing homes and infrastructure, and altering zoning and building codes to lessen the probability of future harm to a location (Eadie *et al.* 2001). In this way, long term recovery is explicitly linked to planning, including planning for alterations in the status quo. Thus, improving long term disaster recovery can improve the adaptability of a location to other circumstances beyond disaster (such as population growth or sea level rise) and is critically important for both disaster issues and general planning.

Compared to short term efforts, long term recovery is considered the weaker link in the recovery picture (Smith 2011). After a location has been stabilized and headlines are over, the work of long term recovery may just be beginning and may fail to proceed in an organized or logical manner.

In the United States, the legal infrastructure of long term recovery is also very different from that of immediate disaster response. As opposed to short term disaster response, long term recovery has historically not been planned comprehensively at the federal level. Aside from the transfer of money for housing replacement, the historic federal response in long term recovery has been limited (Smith 2011). Instead, humanitarian non-profits, states, and localities have taken on the lion's share role of bringing a disaster area back to some sense of normalcy (Smith 2011).

Like it did with so many parts of disaster response, the aftermath of Hurricane Katrina shined a spotlight on deficiencies in long term recovery planning. Almost six years after the event, many displaced residents do not have permanent housing or even a settled location (Groen and Polivka 2009, Hsu 2009). Much of the critique for this response has focused on the failure to properly plan before disaster strikes (Olshansky 2006). Since response actions may need to be implemented immediately, and can impact how longer term recovery proceeds, it is particularly important to have pre-disaster planning for long term recovery (Olshansky 2006). The United States Government Accountability Office ("GAO") has emphasized the importance of pre-event planning to avoid or lessen the long term problems so obvious in the aftermath of Hurricane Katrina (GAO report 2006).

As set out in this chapter, our research indicates that non-profits often provide the necessary link between vulnerable citizens and resources that may be made available to return them to their prior lives, allowing long term recovery. Because there is no comprehensive law governing long term disaster response, the degree to which this complex network of entities is able to effectively communicate and work collaboratively can drive the effectiveness of long term recovery.

Pursuant to many of their missions, social service non-profits readily respond to the immense human need caused by natural and man-made disasters. Non-profits are often on the front lines after a disaster by providing immediate and long-term assistance to affected individuals and families. Yet there has been limited research on the non-profits sector's assets, roles, gaps and potential in providing coordinated support. Non-profits offer incredible assets but too often their efforts, although often heroic, do not measure up to the true potential based on organizational assets. Limited coordination of the sector, limited pre-planning, and unclear roles and responsibilities can severely limit the ability to assist needy individuals and families.

This chapter reviews and analyzes the experience of one of the authors, Jeffrey Stys, as the coordinator of the non-profit sector's response to Tropical Storm Allison (2001), Hurricanes Katrina and Rita (2005), and Hurricane Ike (2008). Within his capacity at the United Way of Greater Houston and as a private consultant, he organized three separate long-term recovery efforts. He oversaw efforts after Tropical Storm Allison by convening nonprofit and other voluntary agencies to provide case management and home repairs for low-income and disabled Houstonians. After Hurricanes Katrina and Rita, he organized a ten agency case management collaboration and unmet needs committee that provided over $13 million to evacuee families. During that time he also served as the main Human Services representative on Houston mayor Bill White's Disaster Response Committee.

He most recently provided consulting services to five Galveston-based philanthropic organizations on post-disaster funding priorities and assisted in the creation of a local long-term recovery organization following Hurricane Ike. From this vantage point, we can see assets and problems with the operation and role of non-profits in disaster response and make recommendations for improving that role to facilitate long term recovery.

## METHODOLOGY

This chapter's commentary and analysis concerning strengths and weaknesses of non-profits in long term recovery are based on the collected contemporaneous notes of author Jeffrey J. Stys in his capacity as non-profit coordinator for 4 different large scale gulf coast disasters (Stys

2011). Because of the nature of the problem and the immediacy of this "living laboratory," there was no pre-planning for specific methodology or human subject review (Stys 2011). While such studies are emerging with respect to planning law and disasters (Smith 2011), as well as review of emergent coordination after disasters (Drabek and McEntire 2002), the random nature of disasters and multiplicity of players makes comprehensive analysis difficult (Drabek and McEntire 2002). We believe that the observations of Mr. Stys, coupled with re-visitation and review of the occurrences at that time with the major repeat players can at least provide anecdotal data to suggest policy and/or legal options to enhance long term recovery by recognizing the roles of non-profits (Stys 2011). Thus, while not a comprehensive study with the normal checks and balances, the Stys review can provide insights and suggestions as to how law and non-profit policy may improve on long term recovery.

## THE ROLE OF NON-PROFITS IN U.S. DISASTER RELIEF

### *Defining non-profits*

The U.S. Internal Revenue Code defines more than twenty five categories of non-profit organizations that are exempt from federal income taxes. Although sector wide data is difficult to quantify, the General Accounting Office estimates that the sector's spending in recent years was eleven to twelve percent of the nation's gross domestic product, and that in 2002 it had over 9.6 million employees. The number of charitable organizations completing the IRS Form 990 for non-profit status almost tripled over the last two decades. One estimate is that the federal government funded about $317 billion to non-profit organizations in fiscal year 2004 (GAO 2007).

There are more than 1.9 million tax-exempt organizations in the United States, a number that has approximately doubled in the past thirty years. Most non-profits are small. More than seventy three percent of reporting public charities reported annual expenses less than $500,000 in 2005. Less than four percent of public charities reported expenses greater than $10 million (GAO 2007).

According to Independent Sector, a national non-profit research and advocacy group, about 1.4 million of these tax exempt organizations are registered as 501(c)(3), charitable organizations (Independent Sector 2011). There organizations fall into eight broad categories:

1. Arts, culture and humanities

2. Education and research

3. Environmental and animals

4. Health services

5. Human services

6. International and foreign affairs

7. Public and societal benefit

8. Religion

Charitable organizations are separated from other types of tax-exempt organizations by their purpose: they must benefit the broad public interest, not just the interests of their members. These organizations fall into two broad categories: public charities and private foundations. Public charities must document that they receive at least one-third of their annual income from the public, a unit of government, or an organization formed to raise money for its support. Public charities can also charge fees for their services. Private foundations derive most of their financial support from individual, family, or corporate contributions. Foundations are subject to substantially more restrictions regarding the distribution for charitable purposes. Non-profits are generally governed by a governing board model according to state law (Flatt 2003). The effectiveness of such governance structure, however, has been called in question (Flatt 2003).

The charitable organization sector shows broad diversity in terms of services provided. Some organizations deliver a very specific service such as afterschool activities while others are multiservice organizations that provide a wide range of services to individuals and families. All rely on some combination of individual, private foundation, and corporate giving. In 2008, private charitable giving totaled $307.65 billion, a 2% drop in current dollars over 2007. It is interesting to note that this represents the first decline in charitable giving since 1987 (Giving USA 2009). The GAO reports that non-profits receive significant funding from government sources, but data are limited so a thorough analysis of governmental funding trends for non-profit organizations is not readily available.

For the purposes of this report, the term "non-profit" refers to public charities under the tax code.

## *Traditional non profit organizations and disaster response*

### Non-profits involved in disaster response

There are a handful of nationally-based non-profit organizations that have clearly defined missions in disaster response. These have a strong commitment at the national level, and local chapters generally have close working relationships with local emergency management organizations. Among these are: the American Red Cross, the Salvation Army, the United Methodist Committee on Relief (UMCOR), the Lutheran Disaster Response, the Christian Reformed World Relief Committee, and the Mennonite Disaster Services (Stys 2011). As organizations formed, at least in part, to respond to disasters, these organizations have assumed various roles in disaster recovery, including immediate needs, aid, and organizational distribution (Stys 2011). These organizations may work together or with government (Stys 2011). The religious based organizations, in particular, may also work with their local affiliates in long term recovery aid (Stys 2011).

### Other non-profits in disaster response

Though such national "disaster" non-profits are important in disaster recovery, many recovery roles (particularly long term recovery roles) fall to more general and local non-profits.

As mission-based organizations, human service organizations deem it their mission to respond when disasters are imminent or occur. Although most non-profits would not consider themselves disaster responders, the vast majority will react after a manmade or natural disaster. For example, if a hurricane warning is issued, a Meals-on-Wheels organization may spring into action with activities to ensure that food recipients are provided several days' worth of non-perishable foods prior to storm landing. Homeless service organizations may make additional bed space available to provide shelter to the street homeless during the most violent parts of the storm. In times of disasters, non-profit agencies face two realities: the needs of existing clients become more acute while at the same time new clients arrive seeking service. These needs and services may be temporary or long term based on the nature and severity of the disaster. Below is a discussion of the characteristics of non-profits that make them an important partner in delivering services to vulnerable individuals and families prior to, during, and after a disaster.

Because human service non-profits provide ongoing support to clients on a whole range of human needs, the resources, personnel, facilities, and services of non-profits can be mobilized quickly in times of crisis. For example, non-profits are generally supported by community leadership and have positive relationships with local elected officials and can be called upon to support first responders. They have buildings that can be used to provide shelter and distribute goods and information. Other tangible assets include communications networks or automobiles that can be used to support vulnerable citizens. Most importantly, they have established relationships with individuals that will likely need additional support such as people with disabilities, senior citizens, and families with limited financial resources.

These existing relationships make service providers at non-profits critical liaisons with vulnerable clients right before and after a disaster, as they make recommendations for disaster preparedness for their clients and complete well-being checks after an event. In general, non-profit professionals are used to working with emergencies, albeit on much smaller scale than a natural or manmade disaster. They are used to responding to human need and finding creative solutions to often very complex situations.

Drabek and McEntire conclude from their review of the literature on multi-organizational collaboration in disasters, that new coordination may emerge from existing non-profits, other organizations and government because of the perceived need for disaster response (Drabek and McEntire 2002). They also note, however, that these emergent organizations face significant problems in coordination and response (Drabek and McEntire 2002). In particular, past literature has focused on problems of goals and communications. The gulf coast disasters demonstrate these problems and also provided a larger scale to look at them and at possible solutions (Stys 2011).

It is important to note that the varying strengths and roles that non-profits play within the community will differ based on the local situation and the specific mission and resources of the agency. Organizations may be solely focused on the clients they serve or they may be more willing to provide new or additional services based on community needs created or exacerbated by the disaster. Despite their assets, non-profits may be limited in their response to disasters.

For non-profits not primarily focused on disaster relief as their mission, there are significant barriers that may inhibit the ability of a non-profit to respond systematically to disasters. First, non-profits within the disaster zone may be unable to respond if their facilities and communication infrastructure have been damaged and if their employees are affected by the disaster.

Secondly, non-profits function on very tight budget constraints. Most non-profits have very limited, if any, emergency financial reserves and have a 'pay as you go' philosophy. Although additional funds may be available after a disaster, there is no guarantee that funds will be available through fundraising, governmental sources, or partnership.

Third, there may be conflict between non-profits and the funding agencies for long-term recovery. This is most true for smaller agencies or those with client-peer leadership, i.e. substance abuse recovery agencies. Many non-profits lack within their agencies a continuity of operations plans and may not have established relationships with local emergency responders. As a general rule, these non-profits do not have the necessary internal planning skills, nor do they take the time to engage in developing relationships with local emergency responders. This can often lead to strained relationships when each sector has unrealistic expectations of the other in its ability to respond during times of disaster.

There are significant cultural and tactical differences that can exacerbate the strife between non-profits and emergency responders. First, emergency response organizations function under clear command and control models. There is a clear leader and chain of command. As individual organizations, non-profits have clear organizational models but in most communities there is little *sector* coordination. Larger communities may have thousands of non-profits but there is no single central-organizing structure. When coordination efforts are attempted, there is a priority on consensus driven action and equal access to input into the process. Although there is clear benefit to this model, it is time consuming and not necessarily effective post-disaster when quick, decisive action may be needed. This decentralized model can be a strength when working with vulnerable individuals but can limit the efficacy and efficiency of overall response efforts.

With a few notable exceptions such as the American Red Cross and the Salvation Army, experiences with the major gulf disasters show that non-profits are rarely included in the regular disaster planning events of local jurisdictions. Although this is changing ever so slightly, there have been challenges in getting non-profits to take an active role in planning. As mentioned earlier, non-profits often do not have the necessary skills nor do they believe they have the time to be involved in planning efforts. For example, the HUD "Sequence of Delivery" has voluntary agencies as key organizations at the beginning and end of the disaster recovery process (Cahill *et al.* 2009). The role of these organizations has been determined by a government agency, but they are likely to be left out at the local level of the planning processes and resource decisions.

UNIQUE ROLE OF LOCAL NON-PROFITS
IN SHORT AND LONG TERM RECOVERY

### Local non-profits in the disaster zone

Local non-profits in disaster zones provide a variety of services to existing and new cliental before and immediately after a disaster. The scale and scope of assistance provided will be greatly influence by the resources of the organization and the existing client base. Most organizations will engage in several general activities that support those affected by the disaster. Common roles of non-profits include:

- Assisting by providing up to date information pre and post event

- Assisting with FEMA forms for those with limited literacy or English proficiency

- Distributing donations—clothing, food, other supplies

- Monitoring vulnerable clients and notifying authorities if there is a dangerous situation

The chart on the following page lists types of services provided in the days immediately after a disaster by a variety of non-profits. Some non-profits may provide more than one of the services listed below and many provide multiple areas of support. A discussion of non-profit roles in long term recovery is addressed below.

## Immediate and short term non-profit response

| Type of Service | Description |
|---|---|
| Senior Services | Well being checks, ensure that clients who do not have ability to travel to distribution points have food and supplies delivered |
| Child Care | If facilities allow, provide additional spaces for children of emergency providers and other critical personnel who are part of the response |
| After School / Youth Programs | May extend hours to accommodate children who are not able to attend school regularly due to damaged facilities |
| Food Pantries | Greatly increase distributions of food and water, may act as official distribution points for emergency food and supplies. May provide direct financial assistance for lost wages, sheltering cost etc. |
| Medical Providers | Increased patient visits due to disaster related injuries or closure of other medical facilities |
| Providers for Individuals with Disabilities | Do well-being checks on clients, make arrangements for those who need electricity for medical equipment or storage of medicines |
| Mental Health Providers | Provide on-scene mental health services and be of service to other agencies as they find individuals that need services |
| Homeless Providers | May make additional beds available prior to the event |
| Community Centers | Act as distribution points for food, water, supplies and information<br><br>Act as source of information for non English speakers or people with low literacy levels |

### Roles and issues for local non-profits in long-term recovery

After an initial disaster, non-profits react to support the needs of clients and other vulnerable citizens. However, their presumed roles and responsibilities for long term disasters often leads to confusion and sometimes hostility since no clear definition of "long term recovery" exists, with clear divergence in what Emergency Managers and Non-profits consider long term recovery. The Department of Homeland Security has "Economic and Community Recovery" as one of the thirty-seven Technical Capabilities (DHS 2007, p. 567). This capability covers many aspects of an overall recovery process but does not address specific roles for non-profits or mention the need to support vulnerable citizens.

FEMA representatives regularly state that "all disasters start and end locally." This means that FEMA expects local organizations to complete the recovery process for vulnerable citizens. FEMA representatives often tell local communities that long term recovery lasts "between three and five years." In the consultant's experience this is accurate as recovery efforts from Tropical Storm Allison (2001) had recently wrapped up when Hurricane Katrina (2005) hit the Gulf Coast. The federal government is empowered to coordinate all disaster relief efforts, including volunteer, state and local efforts. This includes providing technical assistance to local governments for the provision of essential services[1] and assisting with the distribution of supplies (42 U.S.C. § 5170(a)).

FEMA will deploy Voluntary Agency Liaisons (VAL) to declared disaster zones. These individual are generally the point of contact for non-profit agencies. They are also important in educating non-profits on their potential roles in long term recovery (Stys 2011). There may be variation in the quality of these individuals. In general, VALs with extensive experience can be true allies and supporters of long term recovery. They understand the federal resources that can be used to support the local community and see themselves as a support to the overall long-term recovery efforts (Stys 2011). Others that appear to have been trained on their role after FEMA became a part of the Department of Homeland Security have not been as effective. They may not understand federal resources or may simply not feel it is their role to communicate such information (Stys 2011). They appear to approach communities with differing agendas and do not understand their role of supporting local community organizations in their efforts. For instance, VALs may wait to be asked for resources when, in reality, local communities do not know what to ask for. Much of this confusion may be because neither the government, nor localities understand what their roles in long term recovery are (Stys 2011).

For instance, the work of non-profits in long term recovery may be seen in opposition to the government role, i.e the government provides financial aid with restrictions, and the non-profits assist the vulnerable public with understanding and managing the restrictions. With respect to

---

[1] 42 U.S.C. § 5170(a)(3).

long term recovery, non-profit agencies focus on helping low income and other special populations with case management services and home repair (Stys 2011). This includes assistance directly to clients and managing volunteers that want to assist. For many citizens, dealing with the paperwork of insurance claims and FEMA forms is overwhelming. Quality case management involves an initial assessment, client created goals, and assistance in finding resources to meet goals. In the example of Hurricane Katrina evacuees, case management played a key role in helping people establish themselves in Houston by assisting them to find appropriate housing and employment, and in getting children enrolled in school or assisting the family to move back to the New Orleans area (Stys 2011). In other disasters, case management has focused mainly on home repair. Most home repair utilizing volunteer labor is focused on owner-occupied units of low-income disaster victims. There is an effort to assist the family to use personal resources wisely and identify other available financial assistance. There are national groups that can send teams of skilled volunteer labor for extended periods of time for home repair activities. These volunteer teams need varying levels of financial support. Some groups bring not only labor but financial support for needy families while other groups may need local support for housing and meals.

No matter what level of financial support they bring, the volunteer teams need clearly identified clients that have been locally "approved" for volunteer building support. The "pre-work" of home repair process that is handled through case management is an analysis of the family's income, scope of damages, and third party payments for damages. As each family and volunteer group is different, each home must be matched to the appropriate volunteer group. This non-profit function of volunteer management is labor intensive but was a significant factor in stretching financial and human resources after Hurricanes Katrina and Rita (Stys 2011)

Non-profit agencies involved in long term recovery need those resources clearly defined where case managers can bring a client's "unmet needs." These are needs that remain after all family resources and other support in the community have been exhausted.

One unique model from the gulf coast disasters that provided a cornerstone of effective long term recovery was the creation of a "common pool" of funds administered by one agency participating in the long term recovery (Stys 2011). All agencies that are performing case management are able to approach the fund for their specific clients. For example, after Hurricane Katrina, the United Way of Greater Houston raised money and Neighbor Centers Inc. provided financial controls. An Unmet Needs Committee made up of various experienced case management supervisors oversaw the committee's day to day operations. The fund allocated almost $2 million in local funds and $10 million in funding from the American Red Cross. Ten agencies that were working within the collaborative were able to approach the fund (Stys 2011). For many families, it meant an additional sum of money to complete the home repair process. For other families it meant funds for replacing necessary work tools that were destroyed in the disaster. For this function to occur, a centralized agency must have a dedicated source of funding and a clearly defined process that can be used for these needs.

The process can be further complicated by how the federal response agencies have set up the processing of claims. For instance, with Hurricane Ike, FEMA sought to hire victims of the Hurricane (many from minority and low income communities) who, while having connections with the locality, were not well trained in how to take in and process the information for disbursement of funds. While FEMA was meeting one need of recovery (providing employment), it was failing in another (providing efficient services to those in need).

This type of long-term recovery is at least a three to five year commitment. Identifying needy clients, available financial resources, and volunteer labor is often a slow and arduous process (Stys 2011). It is best handled within a well-defined recovery system. The challenge for most communities is that the system needs to be created within the chaos of the post-disaster world. Even without the challenges of the disaster, creating a recovery organization is a challenge in most communities. In Houston after the massive urban flooding of Tropical Storm Allison, it took community organizations more than six months to work out a suitable recovery structure. Up to that point, many organizations were working at cross-purposes and duplicating efforts. Recovery systems must be a collaboration of many different organizations as no one organization has all the resources needed to be successful.

As noted above, the experiences of the gulf coast provide contrasting lessons concerning the effectiveness of local non-profits in recovery depending on organizational planning. Thus, systems and organization present the most pressing issues to address as non-profits coordinate with other long term recovery groups, organize, launch operations, and work to ensure that vulnerable citizens are able to recover from disasters (Stys 2011).

## CREATING SYSTEMS COLLABORATIONS WITH NON-PROFITS

The Gulf Coast disasters demonstrate that post–disaster communities that have an existing coordination mechanism for non-profit organizations are generally better equipped to design and implement a long term recovery response (Stys 2011). Large local and out of state philanthropic organizations are more likely to make large scale financial investments in established collaboratives or consortium of non-profit organizations. These groups can effectively communicate the needs of their organizations and clients and devise innovative solutions often better than single organizations. Communities that have a centralized convener of the non-profit sector can offer a location to begin discussing the needs, assets, and a structure for long term recovery.

## Coverage by voluntary organizations active in disaster (VOAD)

In recent years, there have been active attempts to organize organizations that have disaster response as part of their mission. These groups often form Voluntary Organizations Active in Disaster (VOAD) groups. Local VOAD groups often have representatives of the American Red Cross and theSalvation Army and local representatives of national faith-based groups. Each local VOAD is structured differently, some are formal 501(c)(3) organizations and others are not. Each VOAD has the mission of improving pre- and post-disaster communication, cooperation, collaboration, and coordination. It is important to note that in most situations the VOAD does not respond to events, individual members respond based on the organization's mission and resources.

Local VOADs often play a role in providing a forum for the development of an appropriate long term recovery response. In the consultant's experience they are not well equipped to handle the organizing and operational needs of a long term recovery.[2]

## Common issues in long-term recovery

After a disaster, participating local and national non-profit organizations may create a Long Term Recovery Organization (LTRO). The LTRO is charged with carrying out the specific functions involved in long term recovery efforts. There are several serious challenges with forming a LTRO. First and foremost, putting together a mission-based organization of various organizations in a time of chaos is likely to be a new experience for most organizations involved. Basically, a critical organization has to be created "out of nothing" quickly in the midst of chaos. As an "organization of organizations" the LTRO needs to create a very intentional balance between collaboration and a focus on accountability. This is an unusual non-profit organizational model, and in most communities there may be little experience or expertise in working through the complex issues of developing a functioning organization.

The Long Term Recovery Organization is dedicated to performing certain tasks. Figure 1 shows an organizational structure that was based on experience with Texas-based disasters. This organizational chart represents a way to structure a recovery or other community problem solving effort. This model attempts to increase the effectiveness of the *overall recovery system*. The system supports the overall recovery and those organizations and individuals working within the recovery. In the consultant's past disaster experience, it is the system efforts that often do not receive adequate support and hamper overall recovery efforts. It's

---

[2] Often times, federal authorities will use the term VOAD as a term of art for non-profit agencies active in disaster response. This can be confusing as many non-VOAD members will also activate after a disaster.

important to note that these sections do not need to be specific employees paid by the leadership group. They could be leadership committee members or subcommittees, community volunteers, or strong non-profit organizations. The central point is that someone (or some organization) must assume leadership responsibility and create and support clear lines of communication with all components of the recovery process leadership team.

In addition to the specific LTRO functions, it is important to create a forum for all non-profit organizations to learn about disaster related needs and resources. After a disaster, programs are created, funding becomes available or disappears, and new needs emerge. The forum is a centralized place where all of this information can be shared with the non-profit community. This may take the form of a weekly or monthly meeting or a regularly updated website. Although this may seem obvious, it is one of the most overlooked yet effective tools in getting information to those who work with vulnerable clients.

### *LTRO organizational model*

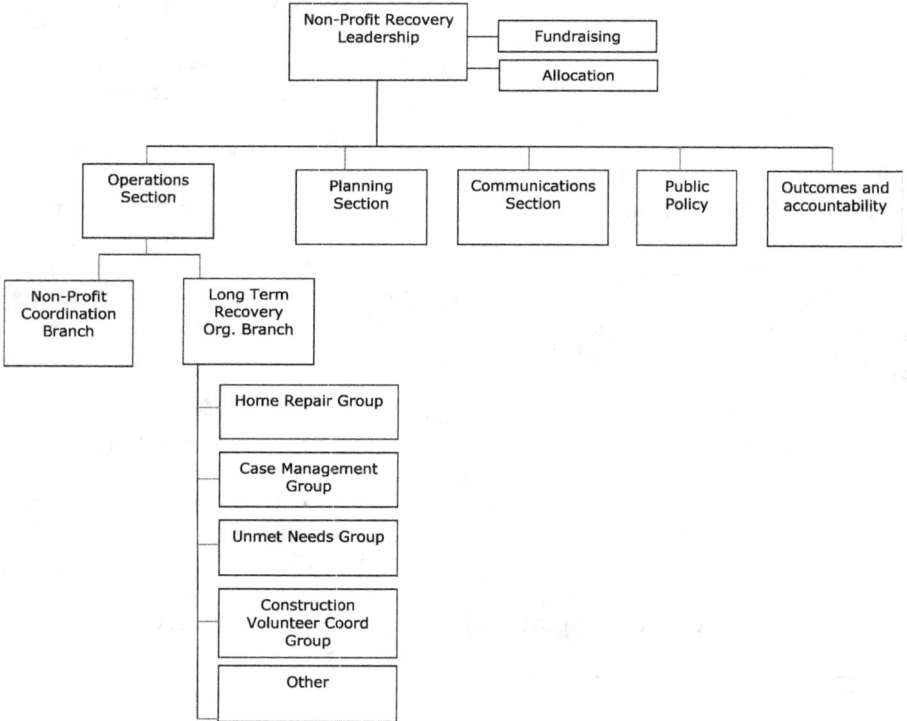

Figure 1

### *Developing an effective long term recovery organization*

Essentially, most long term recovery organizations are "virtual" organizations made up of non-profit service organizations. They usually do not establish physical offices and have few, if any, staff. Foundational documents such as mission statements and by-laws must be developed. Yet more importantly there needs to be effective leadership who can convene the key partners, help members identify key principles, and establish cultural norms of work. These "softer" skills are especially important in working with varying personal styles and organizational cultures that inevitably make up a long term recovery. Effective communication skills are critical in motivating members and dealing with inevitable conflicts. Leaders should be able to communicate effectively as well as implement structures such as regular meetings, communications networks, and organizational charts to ensure each partner can easily see how the entire recovery effort fits together and relates to outside organizations.

Key LTRO functions include:

**Fundraising and Allocation Decisions**

Financial resources are a critical component of long term recovery success. Individual organizations will bring financial resources but the LTRO will need to identify funding and ensure that funds and results are accounted for. In the consultant's experience, it is best to develop a leadership group that has the responsibility for raising money and making resource allocation decisions. This has been a successful model as long as there is clear and consistent communications with the operational aspects of recovery.

**Accountability of All Partners**

As an organization of organizations, it is critical to set up accountability between and among functions of the LTRO. This is challenging within a non-hierarchical organization. Once again, it is important to have formal reporting structures in place, but it is also important to build a culture of accountability.

**Research and Data**

For long term success, it is important to have the research and data to clearly identify the scope of the existing need. This can be used to communicate with outside stakeholders to attract financial resources. Data is also needed to identify potential clients that need assistance. It is also important to quantify and communicate the scope of work that has been accomplished. Individual organizations are used to doing this but there should be a quantitative report of work accomplished by all of the members of the LTRO. Data reports that can be effectively communicated will likely attract additional outside resources

**Communication/Publicity**

The LTRO needs to be able to communicate with the public and government agencies effectively. This may seem obvious but it can be difficult since the LTRO is collaboration of many organizations. There can be confusion and conflict over who the organization's spokesperson is and how member organizations may or may not be highlighted. Yet, without this function, the recovery can be hampered as the general public or other stakeholders may believe the efforts are completed or severely inadequate.

**Public Policy and Government Relations**

Government organizations must be considered partners in the recovery efforts. Outside of FEMA, there are substantial funding sources that should closely align with LTRO activities. In past disasters, Social Service Block Grant funding has been an important source of funding for recovery efforts. The recovery team will be required to build relationships with government entities to inform them of current efforts and needs but also to have an impact on allocation decisions. Additionally, it is important that government efforts facilitate and enhance the abilities of the LTRO and not block or interfere with them.

## RECOMMENDATIONS

### Additional disaster planning for non-profits

*Continuity of Operations:* These plans help organizations plan for the continuation of critical services after a disaster. Every organization should have a plan of how to protect human and physical assets. It is especially important for non-profits to consider developing continuity of operations plans as demands for their services will increase after a disaster.

*Community Planning for Recovery Operations:* Every community should identify the key organizations that will be needed to implement an effective recovery. These groups should discuss likely roles and responsibilities and can begin to identify key leadership and functional gaps.

### Additional connection to emergency response organizations

Non-profit organizations should communicate with local emergency planners and responders. For communities that have had disasters, non-profits should engage in after-action reporting and share these results with emergency responders. In this way, they can be invited into the planning process. The non-profits may also engage in a conversation about how to better handle appropriate 'hand-off' of potential clients. Emergency responders will often find people needing more help than they are authorized to provide. There should be a formalized way to ensure individuals do not fall through the cracks. Approaching this before a disaster may help minimize some of the problems of organizing during the emergency.

### *Official communication networks*

*Among non-profits:* Communications networks are critical during a disaster. It is best practice to develop these networks prior to a disaster. This network will look different in different communities. It may be a physical place everyone agrees to meet at a specific time period after an event, a list of current names, address and phone numbers or website that can be activated on short notice. It is important to develop this mechanism prior to an event. Of course, these can be used on a regular basis outside of a disaster event.

*Between non-profits and emergency responders:* Emergency responders have the latest information from federal, state, and local authorities. It is important that all shared information comes from authenticated sources. The relationship should be based on two-way communications. The non-profit sector is important in providing information to emergency responders that can be used in rumor control and in providing information to individuals who are in life-threatening situations. Again, communications networks should be set up a head of time.

*Between non-profits and federal and state disaster action and funding agencies:* Generally, federal and state governments administer many of the grants and funds that can be used for long term recovery. Non-profits usually have the most information about the needs of the community.

### Long-Term recovery organizational structures that ensure efficacy and accountability

Long term recovery is a commitment of time and resources. Many organizations want to be of assistance but cannot commit to the process. The resources of many organizations are needed, but the involvement of so many groups can lead to confusion and frustration. It's important to have a clear leadership structure, clearly defined roles and responsibilities, and a structure for horizontal and vertical communications.

### *Funding*

Private dollars should be used to develop effective delivery models, meet initial needs, and lay groundwork for public funding. Private contributions generally come into a disaster stricken community quickly after a disaster. Government funding may not hit the ground until many months after the disaster. Long Term Recovery efforts should focus on putting up effective response systems quickly and on communicating with government officials. LTRO and non-profits can create the platform for effective programs to meet community needs. Generally, government funding is greater than privately donated dollars and the non-profit sector can greatly multiply their impact by making sure government funding meets the needs of local citizens with effective programs.

Pre-event governmental planning funding for non-profit coordination should be considered and implemented.

## *Recognition of non-profit roles in law and regulation*

Because of the importance of non-profits in providing unmet services and enhancing the effectiveness of government disaster response (both short and long term), federal and state disaster planning and response laws and regulations should provide a legal and regulatory mechanism for effective coordination of roles, responsibilities, and funding, as well as pre-disaster planning.

For instance, disaster recovery regulation could recognize the role of non-profits in assisting citizens with securing government aid, and then provide training and pre-event certification for certain of these non-profits to do this more effectively. This could curb the current adversarial nature between government entities that are to provide aid to citizens and the non-profits that seek to assist them in receiving the aid, and create more efficient and effective use of limited funds.

### CONCLUSION

The mix of law and regulation governing disaster preparedness and response, particularly long term response, is broad and in flux. In addition to government responders, in the United States much of the needs of a community in recovery are met by non-profits. These non-profits have the information on the most vulnerable citizens in a community and know how best to effectively coordinate and disburse aid. However, the recent disasters in the Gulf Coast show that there is much confusion about roles and coordination among non-profits, and between non-profits and other organizations. Steps taken over time between an early disaster and a later disaster provide a way to analyze how non-profits operate, and what can be improved. Our research sets out what we believe is the problem, and how it can be improved.

In many ways, the research is specific to the United States in that the U.S. utilizes non-profits more than other developed countries to provide services to vulnerable populations. Nevertheless, international humanitarian aid often comes through non-profits as well, and the need for coordination and planning between these organizations and governments seems apparent from many recent international disasters.

We hope that the study of non-profits continues—and that these recommendations may assist in disaster response, and in particular long term recovery.

### *Bibliography*

*United States Code* Annotated (USCA), Title 42, § 5170(a).

Cahill, A.W., *et al.*, 2009. *Directory of Disaster Response and Recovery Resources* [online]. Canavan Associates, prepared for the United States Department of Housing and Urban Development, Office of Community Planning and Development, Office of Special Needs Assistance Programs. Available from:

http://www.hudhre.info/documents/DisasterRecoveryDirectory_June2009.pdf [Accessed 15 June 2011].

DHS—United States Department of Homeland Security, 2007. *Target List Capabilities: A Companion to the National Preparedness Guidelines* [online]. Washington D.C.: U.S. Department of Homeland Security. Available from: http://www.fema.gov/pdf/government/training/tcl.pdf [Accessed 15 June 2011].

Drabek, T.E. and McEntire, D.A., 2002. Emergent Phenomena and Multiorganizational Coordination in Disasters: Lessons from the Research Literature. *International Journal of Emergencies and Disasters* [online], 20 (2), 197-224. Available from: http://ijmed.org/articles/574/download/ [Accessed 29 October 2012].

Eadie, C., *et al.*, 2001. *Holistic Disaster Recovery: Ideas for Building Local Sustainability After a Natural Disaster*. Fairfax, Virginia: Public Entity Risk Institute.

Flatt, V.B., 2003. Notice and Comment for Nonprofit organizations. *Rutgers University Law Review*, 55 (1) 65-85.

FEMA, 2012. *Long-Term Community Recovery Cadre Information* [online]. Washington: Federal Emergency Management Agency. Available from: http://www.fema.gov/long-term-community-recovery-cadre-information [Accessed 1 November 2012].

GAO—United States Government Accountability Office (GAO), 2006. *Testimony before the Senate Homeland Security and Government Affairs Committee, Hurricane Katrina: GAO's Preliminary Observations Regarding Preparedness, Response, and Recovery* [online], March 8, 2006, GAO-06-442T. Available from: http://www.gao.gov/new.items/d06442t.pdf [Accessed 14 June 2011].

GAO—United States Government Accountability Office (GAO), 2007. *Testimony before the Subcommittee on Oversight, Nonprofit Sector: Increasing Numbers and Key Role in Delivering Federal Services*, GAO-07-1084T.

Giving USA, 2009. *Press Release, U.S. Charitable Giving Estimated to be $307.65 Billion in 2008* [online]. Chicago, IL: Giving USA Foundation,. Available from: http://www.philanthropy.iupui.edu/News/2009/docs/ GivingReaches300billion_06102009.pdf [Accessed 14 June 2011].

Groen, J.A. and Polivka, A.E., 2009. *Going Home after Hurricane Katrina: Determinants of Return Migration and Changes in Affected Areas* [online]. Washington: Bureau of Labor Statistics. Working Paper No. 428. Available from: http://www.bls.gov/osmr/pdf/ec090060.pdf [Accessed 14 June 2011].

Hsu, S.S., 2009. Permanence Eludes Some Katrina Victims. *Washington Post* [online], 13 June. Available from: http://www.washingtonpost.com/ wpdyn/content/article/2009/06/12/AR2009061203958.html [Accessed 15 June 2011].

Independent Sector, 2011. *Scope of the Nonprofit Sector* [online]. Washington, D.C.: Independent Sector. Available from: http://independentsector.org/ scope_of_the_sector [Accessed 15 June 2011].

Olshansky, R.B., 2006. Planning After Hurricane Katrina. *Journal of the American Planning Association*, 72 (2), 147-53.

Smith, G., 2011. Addressing the Challenges of the Disaster Recovery Assistance Framework: Creating the Disaster Recovery Act, at 33. *In: Planning for Post Disaster recovery: A Review of the United States Disaster Assistance Framework*. Fairfax, Virginia: Public Entity Risk Institute, 321-376.

Stys, J.J., 2011. *Nonprofit Involvement in Disaster Response and Recovery* [online]. Prepared for the Center for Law, Environment, Adaptation and Resources (CLEAR) at the University of North Carolina School of Law, January 17, 2011. Available from: http://www.law.unc.edu/documents/clear/nonprofit.pdf [Accessed 14 June 2011].

United Methodist Committee on Relief (UMCOR), 2008. *Annual Report 2008* [online]. New York: United Methodist Committee on Relief (UMCOR). Available from: http://new.gbgm-umc.org/umcor/about/annual-report/annual-report-2008/ [Accessed 15 June 2011].

# 11

## DISASTERS, FOCUSING EVENTS, AND SOCIOLEGAL STUDIES

### Thomas A. Birkland

**ABSTRACT**

This final chapter discusses natural disaster research from agenda setting and public policy perspectives. I note the lack of such a large contribution of sociolegal research to the broader social science of disaster, and argue that there can be fruitful connections between sociolegal studies and the interdisciplinary and rapidly evolving field of disaster research. Legal scholars have a great deal to contribute to our understanding of social responses and behaviours in the face of these often-frightening events.

Este artículo analiza la investigación sobre desastres naturales desde la perspectiva de establecer un calendario y de política pública. Se menciona la falta de una investigación sociojurídica tan completa en el campo más amplio de las ciencias sociales de desastres, y se defiende que pueden darse conexiones fructíferas entre los estudios sociojurídicos y el campo interdisciplinario y en rápida evolución de la investigación de desastres. Los profesores de derecho pueden hacer una gran contribución a nuestra comprensión de las respuestas y comportamientos sociales frente a estos acontecimientos, a menudo aterradores.

## INTRODUCTION

Natural disasters, industrial accidents, and terrorism have become major concerns among governments and peoples around the world, as their frequency and socioeconomic costs increase (Keen and Pakkot 2011, Roberts 2009). These costs—and the social disruptions they represent—continue to grow even as the low probability of these events striking in any one place has inhibited careful understanding of the possibility of "worst cases" (Clarke 2005). Events like the Japan tsunami and Fukushima nuclear plant disaster, Hurricane Katrina, the Deepwater Horizon oil spill, and the September 11 attacks have increased thinking about "catastrophic" disasters that render local and sometimes national governments unable to effectively respond to the disaster (Birkland 2009a, Quarantelli 2005). Other events, such as Hurricane Sandy, raise alert communities to the possibility of even worse outcomes from stronger disasters in the future.

Disasters are important because they disrupt the normal, expected workings of society. But, paradoxically, their effects do not often alter existing organizational or stakeholder relationships based on economic or political power. Indeed, in many cases, the differential impact of disasters on the wealthy and the poor simply reflects existing distributions of power and resources, as was seen most starkly in the United States in the immediate aftermath of Hurricane Katrina (Cutter 1996, Laska and Morrow 2006, Norris 2002). Such events can open opportunities to address inequity, but do not often do so.

Disasters and catastrophes can reveal policy failures in two fundamental ways. First, disasters reveal existing distributional inequities that are the result of policy failures, such as a failure to enforce building codes (Mittler 1991, Burby, French, and Nelson 1998, Burby *et al.* 2000). Second, since disasters cause significant losses of life and property, citizens, political leaders, and interest groups (Birkland 1997, 1998) may look for policy failures and ask whether policies to prepare for, mitigate, respond to, and recover from disasters should be improved. They can also lead to questions about the appropriate distribution of responsibility between the central government and the local governments, or, in federal systems, between the national government and the state or provincial and local governments (Birkland and DeYoung 2011). Similar questions arise with respect the different goals of national governments and supragovernmental systems, such as NGOs involved in disaster relief. Disasters are therefore *focusing events* that rapidly expand (and, often, fade) on the news media and on governmental agendas. In the policy literature, focusing events provide a rather short "window of opportunity" (Kingdon 2003) for policy change; we can also think of this window as opening for social and cultural change, and as an opportunity to change the contours of the scholarly community that studies hazards. Any resultant policy or social change can be conceived as attempts to "learn the lessons of" an event, in a process sociologists call "sense-making." However, these claims of lesson learning are not always substantiated even as they are often contested in political debate (Birkland 2006).

Social scientists often state "there is no such thing as a *natural* disaster" (Hartman and Squires 2006) (my emphasis). A meteorological or geophysical event that happens in a sparsely populated area will not be categorized or defined as a disaster, because there are few people and little human society to disrupt. More narrowly, political scientists say that "all disasters are political" (Selves n.d.) because, both before and after disasters, the classic Lasswellian definition of "politics"—who gets what, when and how—is certainly evident (Lasswell 1958). In democratic societies, we have passionate public debate over how to rebuild parts of cities. By contrast, after a devastating 1972 earthquake, Nicaragua, an authoritarian kleptocracy, failed to rebuild Managua, in particular, because the Somoza regime encouraged corruption and theft of funds from international donors (Cueto 2010). The politics of post-earthquake Nicaragua therefore reflected and reproduced pre-existing conditions of corruption and ineffectiveness. Similarly, rebuilding structures in Haiti after the 2010 earthquake has been slow, arguably due to chronic political unrest, corruption, and poor infrastructure systems (Bilham 2010). Whether in democracies and in autocracies, it is the rare event that changes underlying politics, and, even in well-functioning systems, the debates over how to rebuild communities and, in some cases, redefine them in the wake of the disaster, are political because power and resources are at stake. These political debates are not solely pursued in what we might narrowly call "political institutions," but take place across societies, and engage questions of power, legitimacy, and law and legal institutions.

## DISASTERS AS AGENDA SETTING EVENTS

The political science literature on agenda setting suggests that societies and political system cannot devote constant attention to all the possible issues before them, so that problems—and their solutions—must compete for attention at the societal and institutional levels (Cobb and Elder 1983, Hilgartner and Bosk 1988). Focusing events can lead interest groups, government leaders, policy entrepreneurs, the news media, or members of the public to identify new problems, or to pay greater attention to existing but problems that were previously perceived to be dormant, potentially leading to a search for solutions in the wake of apparent policy failure (Birkland 1998). At the heart of this activity is the constant search by interest groups for opportunities to advocate policy change based as much on advocacy opportunities as on technically superior analysis (Kingdon 2003, Majone 1989). Claims of policy failure are therefore made by pro-change groups in an attempt to expand an issue to a broader audience.

With event-induced attention to the problem, pro-change groups may mobilize in several ways, including membership drives and appeals for donations. These tactics are much more common in industrial disasters, such as oil spills. Many groups will move to lobby legislators to press for policy change, and their group leaders will be invited to testify before congressional hearings or parliamentary commissions. Group mobilization is quite uncommon after natural disasters, although some groups have filed negligence suits against the authorities that built and maintain the levee system in and around that city.

If an event threatens to reduce the power of advantaged groups to control the agenda, these groups are likely to respond defensively to focusing events (Birkland and Nath 2000). They may argue that an event is not as important as claimed by opposing groups, that existing policy is able to deal with any problems, or that, if new policy is needed, the policy proposed by the contending groups would be ineffective or counterproductive. Groups that are more powerful will work to downplay an event's significance by providing officials and the public with alternative explanations of the meaning and significance of the event (Birkland 1997, ch. 5).

Public policy theorists continue to wrestle with the policy making implications of focusing events, including the usual debate over definitions of an "event," drivers of social and policy change as a result of this event, and whether such events really make much of a difference in the long-run trajectory of public policy. But we do know that, in the past fifteen or twenty years, large disasters have become important focusing events for the scientific and social scientific community. Disasters of various types, ranging from the *Exxon Valdez* oil spill, through various earthquakes in California and Washington State (in 1989 and 1984, and 2001, respectively), and the hugely damaging hurricanes Andrew (1992), Katrina (2005), and Sandy (2012), drew huge attention to the vulnerability of communities in the United States. The damage and disruption of these events was often equalled or exceeded by huge disasters, such as the 2004 Sumatra earthquake and tsunami, the 2011 earthquake and consequent nuclear disaster at Fukushima, Japan, and earthquakes in Sichuan, China in 2008 and Haiti in 2010.

Clearly, these events focused policy makers' attention. But they also opened the field of disaster research to a much broader group of scholars than had previously engaged in this work. While the roots of this field run to the early and mid 20th century, in sociology and in geography, the field has been propelled forward by scholarly attention to major events. Perhaps the two most important such events for disaster scholars in the United States were Hurricane Katrina and the September 11 terrorist attacks; in other countries, similar terrorist attacks, in London and Madrid, and similar natural disasters, have increased interest to the point where we can say that a global epistemic community—or set of connected epistemic communities—exists and is taking natural and technological hazards very seriously. In simplest terms, focusing events focus the attention of scholars, as well as of policy makers and citizens.

The sociolegal studies community is one such epistemic community that has been mobilized to study disasters. As I show in the remainder of this chapter, sociolegal scholars are making considerable contributions to our understandings of disasters in terms of human rights, power relations, legal mobilization, and the how law and legal institutions shape the sorts of things that communities can do to reduce their vulnerability. Law and legal institutions also shape how people respond to and recover from disasters.

A sociolegal approach to disasters and agenda setting is important because, as Sarat and Lezaun note:

> Legal, political and humanitarian responses are premised on the deep-rooted assumption that we can at least decipher the meanings of disaster, at beast correct its causes and prevent future consequences. Whatever explanatory theory one holds..., catastrophic events test our legal, political, and humanitarian resolve and resourcefulness.

> This testing is particularly salient with respect to the law. That is the case not only because the breakdown of legal order is one of the clearest signs of catastrophic disruption, but, more importantly, because the law plays a crucial role in drawing lessons from disaster, in providing relief and redress to victims, and in correcting the vulnerabilities that caused or compounded the destruction (Sarat and Lezaun 2009, p. 1).

Table 1: Representative Articles on Law in Disaster Research Journals

| *Themes* | *International J. of Mass Emergencies and Disasters* | *Natural Hazards Review* | *Disasters* | *Journal of Contingencies and Crisis Management* |
|---|---|---|---|---|
| Compensation regimes, liability, and fixing of blame or responsibility | (Huffman 1983) | | (Bruggeman, Faure, and Haritz 2011) | (Elliott and McGuinness 2002) |
| Crisis management | | | | (Jang and Chen 2009) |
| Disability | | | (Parr 1987) | |
| Governance and Management | | | (Chan 1997) | |
| Human rights | | | (Dufour *et al.* 2004, Young *et al.* 2004) | |
| Land Tenure | | | (Reale and Handmer 2011) | |
| Law as social institution | (Huffman 1989) | | | |
| Mitigation and preparedness | (Lindell 1997) | (Burby 2005) | (Luna 2001) | |

Sarat and Lezaun's statement touches on many major themes in sociopolitical studies of disaster: sense making, resilience and resourcefulness, the breakdown of legal order, and learning lessons from disaster. These questions are addressed, individually and collectively by all social scientists that study disasters. Sarat and Lezaun laid down this challenge because these questions have not been taken up in the mainstream journals either in disaster studies or in sociolegal studies. In Table 1, I show representative articles that invoke "law" or legal processes as an important subject for study in four important journals devoted to disaster social science. The few articles that were published focus on the liability, human rights, and compensation and "blame fixing." Very few of these articles make direct reference to important sociolegal questions, including how legal practices and institutions shape societal responses to problems, or how legal institutions can help or hinder effective action in times of rapid change and urgency. A few articles address issues of particular interest to law and society, such as Reale and Handmer's (2011) article on land tenure and vulnerability, and Meyer's (1984) article on "relief workers and violations of humanitarian law," which engages important transnational questions in a field that sometimes focuses on one state at a time. Unsurprisingly in disaster journals, the one theme that three journals had in common is discussions of the legal aspects of disaster preparedness and mitigation.

Clearly, there is plenty of room for sociolegal scholars to share more of their knowledge with the disaster research community. Indeed, this community, being consciously interdisciplinary, would welcome such participation. Indeed, much greater interest—but not discernibly increased interest in publishing in disaster journals—was apparent after Hurricane Katrina. This event opened the window of opportunity for change, sense making, and reconceptualization of disaster that had never occurred before.

Of course, it is unsurprising that sociolegal scholars would want to publish their results in their most important disciplinary or interdisciplinary journals. Still, law and society scholars have not integrated much of the "disaster science" and "agenda setting" literature into their published work, and their work has not penetrated the disaster research field. This is, of course, true in the opposite direction. Very few disaster scholars have sought to publish in standard sociolegal journals. Indeed, a search on the term "disaster" in the full title and abstract of articles indexed in "law and society" journals in JSTOR reveals only 13 articles on the topic.[1] These articles are listed in Table 2.

---

[1] These journals are the *Journal of Law and Economics* 1958-2012; *Journal of Law and Society* 1982-2007; *The Journal of Legal Studies* 1972-2012; *The Justice System Journal* 1974-2009; *Law and Contemporary Problems* 1933-2007; *Law and History Review* 1983-2009; *Law and Human Behavior* 1977-2009; *Law & Social Inquiry* 1988-2007; *Law & Society Review* 1966-2009; *Oxford Journal of Legal Studies* 1981-1998; *Yale Law & Policy Review* 1982-2009.

From this small collection of work on disasters, we can see that, in the North American literature, the greatest intellectual effort has been given to four very useful articles on the origins of disaster relief schemes during the New Deal period (Dauber 2005a, 2005b, Gillman 2005, Landis 1999). These studies are very valuable in that they explain how we have come to have the policy and legal regime that has created disaster relief as an expectation of the U.S. national government, a concept that, even in the early 1950s, was still quite novel. This power to provide aid is strongly grounded in New Deal constitutional jurisprudence.

Two articles note how the administration of justice after disasters, like all social activities, be can be severely disrupted by disasters (Wasby 1998). The administration of justice during a disaster is a remarkably challenging task, because court managers must manage many different people—jurors, prosecutors, defendants and their attorneys, witnesses, and any other people who have any business in the court. They must so while protecting important legal rights, such as representation by counsel, pretrial discovery, speedy trial, and the right to confront one's witnesses (Ellard 2007). A notable example is the 1989 Loma Prieta (San Francisco) earthquake, which required the U.S. Ninth Circuit court of appeals to move to temporary office space in San Francisco while its badly damaged courthouse was being built. A perhaps more startling example was the need for the New York State courts in lower Manhattan to manage the emergency that befell their operations on September 11 (Birkland and Schneider 2007). The impact of these disasters extends outside the court-room. The WTC towers housed over 1400 lawyers and their firms, many of which lost important records that the New York State courts helped to reconstruct from their files. Similar disruption followed Hurricane Katrina, which even more profoundly shook the regional legal community.

Three articles—and four, if we consider liability regimes in the same category—are about regulatory regimes intended to prevent disaster or to regulate dangerous processes (Gunningham and Sinclair 2009, Haines 2009, Horlick-Jones 1995, Kamin and Rachlinski 1995). Other articles focus on the corrupting influence of disaster relief (Leeson and Sobel 2008), on police and official accountability in a crowd-crush disaster at a soccer match (Scraton 1999), and on insurance regimes (Kunreuther 1968), the latter of which might be considered a regulatory matter as well.

Table 2: Articles in Sociolegal Studies about Disaster

| *Article* | *Topic* |
| --- | --- |
| Scraton, Phil, 1999. Policing with Contempt: The Degrading of Truth and Denial of Justice in the Aftermath of the Hillsborough Disaster. *Journal of Law and Society*, 26 (3), 273-297. | Accountability of the police and officials in a "human" disaster (crowd crush at a soccer game). |

| | |
|---|---|
| Leeson, Peter T. and Sobel, Russell S., 2008. Weathering Corruption. *Journal of Law and Economics,* 51 (4), 667-681. | Disaster relief is associated with state corruption |
| Birkland, Thomas A., and Schneider, Carrie A., 2007. Emergency Management in the Courts: Trends After September 11 and Hurricane Katrina. *The Justice System Journal*, 28 (1), 20-35. | Disasters and the administration of justice |
| Wasby, Stephen L., 1997. Delay and a Docketing Disaster. *The Justice System Journal*, 19 (2), 240-242. | Disasters and the administration of justice |
| Kunreuther, Howard, 1968. The Case for Comprehensive Disaster Insurance. *Journal of Law and Economics*, 11 (1), 133-163. | Insurance |
| Kamin, Kim A., and Rachlinski, Jeffrey J., 1995. Ex Post ≠ Ex Ante: Determining Liability in Hindsight. *Law and Human Behavior*, 19 (1), 89-104. | Liability regimes |
| Gunningham, Neil, and Sinclair, Darren, 2009. Regulation and the Role of Trust: Reflections from the Mining Industry. *Journal of Law and Society*, 36 (2), 167-194. | Regulation in the presence of risks and disasters |
| Haines, Fiona, 2009. Regulatory Failures and Regulatory Solutions: A Characteristic Analysis of the Aftermath of Disaster. *Law & Social Inquiry*, 34 (1), 31-60. | Regulation in the presence of risks and disasters |
| Horlick-Jones, Tom, 1995. Review: Learning from Disaster: Risk Management after Bhopal, edited by Sheila Jasanoff. *Journal of Law and Society*, 22 (3), 416-419. | Regulation in the presence of risks and disasters |
| Dauber, Michele Landis, 2005. Judicial Review and the Power of the Purse. *Law and History Review*, 23 (2), 451-458. | The influence of New Deal relief spending and legal doctrines on the idea and growth of disaster relief |
| Dauber, Michele Landis, 2005. The Sympathetic State. *Law and History Review*, 23 (2), 387-442. | The influence of New Deal relief spending and legal doctrines on the idea and growth of disaster relief |
| Gillman, Howard, 2005. Disaster Relief, "Do Anything" Spending Powers, and the New Deal. *Law and History Review*, 23 (2), 443-450. | The influence of New Deal relief spending and legal doctrines on the idea and growth of disaster relief |

| | |
|---|---|
| Landis, Michele L., 1999. Fate, Responsibility, and "Natural" Disaster Relief: Narrating the American Welfare State. *Law & Society Review*, 33 (2), 257-318. | The influence of New Deal relief spending and legal doctrines on the idea and growth of disaster relief |

This set of examples is necessarily restrictive, but it does suggest that disaster research has not been a major concern in the law and society community. Nevertheless, there are signs that this is changing as sociolegal scholars begin to understand the importance of the field as risks become more costly and more important in daily life.

Some promising points of departure are found in Austin Sarat and Javier Lezaun's edited volume (Sarat and Lezaun 2009), which contains sound essays on law, bureaucratic accountability and housing policy. And while Sarat and Lezaun make and expansive claims for the role of law and legal scholarship in learning from sudden events like disasters, and putting those lessons into force, the actual literature on policy learning after disasters is not generally promising, the many claims to "lessons learned" notwithstanding (Birkland 2006, 2009b, Donahue and O'Keefe 2007, Gerber 2007). Sarat and Lezaun's call for greater attention to legal reasoning and norms within a broader social context is taken up by Sterett (2012), whose work has sought to understand how displaced people in the United States are treated by a system of disaster relief that constitutes part of the American social welfare system. She argues that the recipients of this relief made their claim to this relief by virtue of their being American citizens, not as "refugees" in the sense of people leaving their country for another, safer one. She ties citizenship to ideas of human rights, a term that is often avoided in domestic discourse about the rights of Americans within the nation's boundaries. This article innovatively ties together the fact of an event, its manifest consequences, and concepts of citizenship and rights, and is published in a journal that receives broad attention in the disaster research field.

Works like these make a significant contribution to our understanding of disasters. The legal practice and sociolegal studies communities have made substantial contributions to understanding the substance of the law as it relates to such disparate matters as bankruptcy (American Bankruptcy Institute Law Review 2007), liability and insurance regimes, questions of property rights, the legal regimes for disaster relief and assistance in disasters, and, in particular, the administration of law and order or what some mistakenly believe to be "martial law" (Davies 2000, Cook 2006). These articles have not found their way into the "mainstream" law and society journals. But have such themes found their way into the standard law reviews? A search of law review articles in the Lexis-Nexis database for articles published beginning in 2000, with the word "disaster" in their title, yielded 530 articles. I performed a very simple content analysis of terms that appeared often in these titles, and that are of concern to disaster researchers and the results are shown in Table 3.

Articles can fall into more than one topic if they address two or more topics, such as *liability* and the *Deepwater Horizon* oil spill. Clearly, natural disasters were of great concern to law review authors, with particular interest in disaster relief, although the *Deepwater Horizon* gained considerable attention—as much as Hurricane Katrina. Most of the discussion around the oil spill focused on liability and damages, as well as the law of torts. Overall, though, while we can say that lawyers are interested in disasters, these articles did not deeply engage the broader social, political, and economic questions that social scientists address. Rather, these articles focused more on the language of the law and its interpretation, and what that means in terms of government duties and powers, corporate responsibility, and the liability that arises when organizations or institutions fail in their duties. And, as noted above, the legal community is very concerned, like all organizations, with the implications of disasters on their own legal practices, which the September 11 attacks and Hurricane Katrina showed are as vulnerable as any other enterprise. Given the importance of courts and legal procedure, the effects of disaster on the practice of law are nontrivial. There is, of course, considerable value to such literature to the legal community, which, after all, must advocate for its clients and participate in shaping legal doctrine. But this is not, mostly, social science research.

Table 3: Topical Coverage of Law Review Articles on Disaster

| Topic | Count |
| --- | --- |
| natural disaster | 47 |
| hurricane | 34 |
| disaster relief | 33 |
| Deepwater Horizon | 28 |
| Hurricane Katrina | 25 |
| liability and damages | 20 |
| law practice (recovery from damage done to one's own practice) | 17 |
| risk | 13 |
| tort | 13 |
| insurance | 11 |
| catastrophe | 8 |

| disaster preparedness | 8 |
|-----------------------|---|
| disaster recovery     | 8 |
| terrorism             | 8 |
| women in disasters    | 8 |
| damages (legal)       | 6 |
| Exxon Valdez          | 6 |

This overview of the law review literature on disasters is necessarily limited by the use of the term "disaster," in the title. But we can discern from these data some trends in the study of disasters. These trends and foci of interest appear quite similar to those of the "established" disaster research community, which also tend to focus on individual disasters and on disaster relief. But this literature also contributes to understandings of disaster in terms of risks and liability, including explicitly the notion of torts in the disaster context.

Daniel Farber is a legal scholar whose work has touched on many of these themes, and his work crosses the very permeable boundary between legal studies and policy analysis. For example, he has done significant work on systems of compensation for victims of climate change, which is a very important topic in disaster research because of the increased vulnerability of communities to what were considered "minor" disasters when sea level was lower. (Farber 2011, 2008a, 2008b, 2007a, 2007b). His 2011 article is particularly important as it overtly connects environmental law and disaster law, the connections to which are not clear or often considered even by practitioners in the field.

In Japan, Leflar and his colleagues studied the relationship between survivors, their legal representatives, and the sociolegal system in the aftermath of the Fukushima earthquake and nuclear disaster. They asked, "After an earthquake, tsunami, and nuclear power plant accident of historic proportions, how can lawyers help sort out the mess?" (Leflar *et al.* 2012). Their fieldwork is an excellent example of after-event research that has supported the theory and knowledge base in disaster research. It is also an outstanding ethnographic study that helps us understand not only the lives of the survivors of this disaster, but also the lives of the lawyers that represent these people in a context and culture that often resisted demands for rapid and equitable compensation. These themes transcend time and place in disaster studies, and again point out how the law and legal institutions shape social relations before and after disasters.

In summary, disaster scholars know that the field can grow and contribute to disciplinary and societal concerns only to the extent that the field is truly interdisciplinary (National Research Council Committee on

Disaster Research in the Social Sciences 2006). This is known to legal scholars as well. This conference in Oñati spurred the development of a Collaborative Research Network under the auspices of the Law and Society Association (http://jurisprudenceofdisasters.org). According to the group's website:

> If jurisprudence is understood to be the study of the (historical, philosophi-
> cal, cultural, social, and political) roots of law and legal institutions, our
> common research focus is on two related questions:
>
> 1. How these roots can combine to create laws actually making disasters
> more likely to occur; and
>
> 2. How they can likewise create laws to correct the imbalances that can
> result in disastrous events.

As this brief review suggests, progress is well under way to address these questions, although there is yet much more to be done. We know that the sociological scholarship of disaster, could address, among other questions, how the law and legal institutions work to mitigate, or, possibly more likely, work to reproduce the unequal distribution of resources and power that make some people more vulnerable to disaster in the first place. These insights would be powerful and useful in a field that has few legal scholars, beyond law professors and practicing attorneys. I am confident that the research community, which is remarkably open to new ideas and improved analytical concepts and tools, would greatly welcome greater participation of sociolegal scholars, with their impressive record of analytic rigor and ability to tackle vexing social problems. In the end, such collaboration and scholarly attention would not only yield improved social theory, but would also help lead the way to protect people and their communities by reducing their vulnerability, increasing community resilience, and promoting equity as a fundamental principle of disaster policy.

## Bibliography

American Bankruptcy Institute Law Review, 2007. The Category 5 Crisis: How Hurricanes Katrina and Rita Exposed Deficiences in the Bankruptcy Abuse Prevention and Consumer Protection Act of 2005. *American Bankruptcy Institute Law Review*, 15, 321-359.

Bilham, R., 2010. Lessons from the Haiti Earthquake. *Nature*, 463 (7283), 878-879.

Birkland, T. A., 1997. *After Disaster: Agenda Setting, Public Policy, and Focusing Events* (American Governance and Public Policy Series). Washington, DC: Georgetown University Press.

Birkland, T. A., 1998. Focusing Events, Mobilization, and Agenda Setting. *Journal of Public Policy*, 18 (1), 53-74.

Birkland, T. A., 2006. *Lessons of Disaster: Policy Change after Catastrophic Events* (American Governance and Public Policy Series). Washington, D.C.: Georgetown University Press.

Birkland, T. A., 2009a. Disasters, Catastrophes, and Policy Failure in the Homeland Security Era. *Review of Policy Research*, 26 (4), 423-438.

Birkland, T. A., 2009b. Disasters, Lessons Learned, and Fantasy Documents. *Journal of Contingencies and Crisis Management*, 17 (3), 146-156. doi: 10.1111/j.1468-5973.2009.00575.x.

Birkland, T. A., and DeYoung, S.E., 2011. Emergency Response, Doctrinal Confusion, and Federalism in the Deepwater Horizon Oil Spill. *Publius: The Journal of Federalism*, 41 (3), 471-493. doi: 10.1093/publius/pjr011.

Birkland, T. A., and Nath, R., 2000. Business and Political Dimension in Disaster Management. *Journal of Public Policy*, 20 (3), 279-303.

Birkland, T. A., and Schneider, C.A., 2007. Emergency Management in the Courts: Trends After September 11 and Hurricane Katrina. *The Justice System Journal* [online], 28 (1), 20-35. Available from: http://www.ncsc.org/Publications/ Justice-System-Journal/~/media/Files/PDF/Publications/Justice%20System% 20Journal/emergency%20management%20in%20the%20courts.ashx [Accessed 20 March 2013].

Bruggeman, V., Faure, M., and Haritz, M., 2011. Remodelling Reparation: Changes in the Compensation of Victims of Natural Catastrophes in Belgium and the Netherlands. *Disasters*, 35 (4), 766-788. doi: 10.1111/j.1467-7717.2011.01233.x.

Burby, R.J., 2005. Have State Comprehensive Planning Mandates Reduced Insured Losses from Natural Disasters? *Natural Hazards Review*, 6 (2), 67-81. doi: 10.1061/(asce)1527-6988(2005)6:2(67).

Burby, R.J., French, S. P., and Nelson, A.C., 1998. Plans, Code Enforcement, and Damage Reduction: Evidence from the Northridge Earthquake. *Earthquake Spectra*, 14 (1), 59-74.

Burby, R.J., *et al.*, 2000. Building Code Enforcement Burdens and Central City Decline. *Journal of the American Planning Association*, 66 (2), 143-161.

Chan, N.W., 1997. Institutional Arrangements for Flood Hazards in Malaysia: An Evaluation Using the Criteria Approach. *Disasters*, 21 (3), 206-222. doi: 10.1111/1467-7717.00057.

Clarke, L., 2005. *Worst Cases: Terror and Catastrophe in the Popular Imagination*. Chicago: University of Chicago Press.

Cobb, R.W., and Elder, C.D., 1983. *Participation in American Politics: The Dynamics of Agenda-Building*. 2nd ed. Baltimore: Johns Hopkins University Press.

Cook, M., 2006. "Get Out Now Or Risk Being Taken Out By Force": Judicial Review Of State Government Emergency Power Following a Natural Disaster. *Case Western Reserve Law Review*, 57 (1), 265-300.

Cueto, M., 2010. Review of Jürgen Buchenau and Lyman L. Johnson (eds.), *Aftershocks: Earthquakes and Popular Politics in Latin America. Journal of Latin American Studies*, 42 (4), 839-840. doi: 10.1017/S0022216X10001380.

Cutter, S.L., 1996. Vulnerability to Environmental Hazards. *Progress in Human Geography*, 20 (4), 529-539. doi: 10.1177/030913259602000407.

Dauber, M.L., 2005a. Judicial Review and the Power of the Purse. *Law and History Review*, 23 (2), 451-458. doi: 10.2307/30042875.

Dauber, M.L., 2005b. The Sympathetic State. *Law and History Review*, 23 (2), 387-442. doi: 10.2307/30042873.

Davies, K.L., 2000. The Imposition of Martial Law In The United States. *Air Force Law Review* [online], 49, 67-112. Available from: http://www.afjag.af.mil/shared/media/document/AFD-081204-030.pdf [Accessed 21 March 2013].

Donahue, A.K., and O'Keefe, S., 2007. Universal Lessons from Unique Events: Perspectives from Columbia and Katrina. *Public Administration Review*, 67(s1), 77-81. doi: 10.1111/j.1540-6210.2007.00815.x.

Dufour, C., *et al.*, 2004. Rights, Standards and Quality in a Complex Humanitarian Space: Is Sphere the Right Tool? *Disasters*, 28 (2), 124-141. doi: 10.1111/j.0361-3666.2004.00248.x.

Ellard, P., 2007. Learning from Katrina: Emphasizing the Right to a Speedy Trial to Protect Constitutional Guarantees in Disasters. *American Criminal Law Review*, 44, 1207-1237.

Elliott, D., and McGuinness, M., 2002. Public Inquiry: Panacea or Placebo? *Journal of Contingencies & Crisis Management*, 10 (1), 14-25.

Farber, D.A., 2007a. Apportioning Climate Change Costs. *UCLA Journal of Environmental Law & Policy* [online], 26 (1), 21-54. Available from: http://www.thefreelibrary.com/Apportioning+climate+change+costs.-a0179133294 [Accessed 21 March 2013].

Farber, D.A., 2007b. Basic Compensation for Victims of Climate Change. *University of Pennsylvania Law Review* [online], 155 (6), 1605-1656. Available from: https://www.law.upenn.edu/journals/lawreview/articles/volume155/issue6/Farber155U.Pa.L.Rev.1605%282007%29.pdf [Accessed 21 March 2013].

Farber, D.A., 2008a. The Case for Climate Compensation: Justice for Climate Change Victims in a Complex World. *Utah Law Review* [online], 2, 377-413. Available from: http://content.lib.utah.edu/utils/getfile/collection/utlawrev/id/480/filename/14715.pdf [Accessed 21 March 2013].

Farber, D.A., 2008b. Modeling Climate Change and Its Impacts: Law, Policy, and Science. *Texas Law Review* [online], 86 (7), 1655-1699. Available from: http://scholarship.law.berkeley.edu/cgi/viewcontent.cgi?article=2639&context=facpubs [Accessed 21 March 2013].

Farber, D.A., 2011. Symposium Introduction: Navigating the Intersection of Environmental Law and Disaster Law. *Brigham Young University Law Review* [online], 6, 1783-1820. Available from: http://lawreview.byu.edu/articles/ 1342142932_farber.fin2.pdf [Accessed 21 March 2013].

Gerber, B.J., 2007. Disaster Management in the United States: Examining Key Political and Policy Challenges. *Policy Studies Journal*, 35 (2), 227-238.

Gillman, H., 2005. Disaster Relief, "Do Anything" Spending Powers, and the New Deal. *Law and History Review*, 23(2), 443-450. doi: 10.2307/30042874.

Gunningham, N., and Sinclair, D., 2009. Regulation and the Role of Trust: Reflections from the Mining Industry. *Journal of Law and Society*, 36 (2), 167-194. doi: 10.2307/40206886.

Haines, F., 2009. Regulatory Failures and Regulatory Solutions: A Characteristic Analysis of the Aftermath of Disaster. *Law & Social Inquiry*, 34 (1), 31-60. doi: 10.2307/30234214.

Hartman, C.W., and Squires, G.D., 2006. *There is No Such Thing as a Natural Disaster: Race, Class, and Hurricane Katrina*. New York: Routledge.

Hilgartner, J., and Bosk, C., 1988. The Rise and Fall of Social Problems: A Public Arenas Model. *American Journal of Sociology*, 94 (1), 53-78.

Horlick-Jones, T., 1995. Review: Learning from Disaster: Risk Managment after Bhopal, edited by Sheila Jasanoff. *Journal of Law and Society*, 22 (3), 416-419. doi: 10.2307/1410590.

Huffman, J.L., 1983. Government Liability and Natural Hazard Mitigation in Japan the Soviet Union China New Zealand and the United States. *International Journal of Mass Emergencies and Disasters* [online], 1 (3), 379-397. Available from: http://ijmed.org/articles/531/download/ [Accessed 21 March 2013].

Huffman, J.L., 1989. Law Comparative Legal Study and Disaster Taxonomy. *International Journal of Mass Emergencies and Disasters* [online], 7 (3), 329-347. Available from: http://ijmed.org/articles/237/download/ [Accessed 21 March 2013].

Jang, W.-Y., and Chen, C.-T., 2009. Defendant Firms and Response to Legal Crises: Effect on Shareholder Value. *Journal of Contingencies & Crisis Management*, 17 (2), 108-117. doi: 10.1111/j.1468-5973.2009.00570.x.

Kamin, K.A., and Rachlinski, J.J., 1995. Ex Post ≠ Ex Ante: Determining Liability in Hindsight. *Law and Human Behavior*, 19 (1), 89-104. doi: 10.2307/1394067.

Keen, B.D., and Pakkot, M.R., 2011. Monetary Policy and Natural Disasters in a DSGE Model. *Southern Economic Journal*, 77 (4), 973-990.

Kingdon, J.W., 2003. *Agendas, Alternatives, and Public Policies*. 2nd ed. New York: Longman.

Kunreuther, H., 1968. The Case for Comprehensive Disaster Insurance. *Journal of Law and Economics*, 11 (1), 133-163. doi: 10.2307/724973.

Landis, M.L., 1999. Fate, Responsibility, and "Natural" Disaster Relief: Narrating the American Welfare State. *Law & Society Review*, 33 (2), 257-318. doi: 10.2307/3115166.

Laska, S., and Morrow, B. H., 2006. Social Vulnerabilities and Hurricane Katrina: An Unnatural Disaster in New Orleans. *Marine Technology Society Journal*, 40 (4), 16-26.

Lasswell, H.D., 1958. *Politics: Who Gets What, When, How*. New York: Meridian Books.

Leeson, P.T., and Sobel, R.S., 2008. Weathering Corruption. *Journal of Law and Economics*, 51 (4), 667-681. doi: 10.1086/590129.

Leflar, R.B., *et al.*, 2012. Human Flotsam, Legal Fallout:Japan's Tsunami and Nuclear Meltdown. *Journal of Environmental Law & Litigation* [online], 27, 107-124. Available from: http://ssrn.com/abstract=2025761 [Accessed 21 March 2013].

Lindell, M., 1997. Adoption and Implementation of Hazard Adjustments. *International Journal of Mass Emergencies and Disasters* [online], 15 (3), 327-453. Available from: http://ijmed.org/articles/330/download/ [Accessed 21 March 2013].

Luna, E.M., 2001. Disaster Mitigation and Preparedness: The Case of NGOs in the Philippines. *Disasters*, 25 (3), 216-226. doi: 10.1111/1467-7717.00173.

Majone, G., 1989. *Evidence, Argument and Persuasion in the Policy Process*. New Haven: Yale University Press.

Meyer, M.A., 1984. Relief Workers and Violations of Humanitarian Law: Some Legal Considerations. *Disasters*, 8 (4), 302-306. doi: 10.1111/j.1467-7717.1984.tb00895.x.

Mittler, E., 1991. *Building Code Enforcement Following Hurricane Hugo in South Carolina, Quick Response Research Report No. 44* [online]. Boulder: Natural Hazards Research and Applications Information Center, University of Colorado. Available from: http://digital.lib.usf.edu:8080/fedora/get/usfldc:F57-00067/DOCUMENT_PDF [Accessed 21 March 2013].

National Research Council Committee on Disaster Research in the Social Sciences, 2006. *Facing Hazards and Disasters: Understanding Human Dimensions*. Washington, DC: National Academies Press.

Norris, F., 2002. Disasters in Urban Context. *Journal of Urban Health*, 79 (3), 308-314. doi: 10.1093/jurban/79.3.308.

Parr, A.R., 1987. Disasters and Disabled persons: An Examination of the Safety Needs of a Neglected Minority. *Disasters*, 11 (2), 148-159. doi: 10.1111/j.1467-7717.1987.tb00629.x.

Quarantelli, E.L., 2006. Catastrophes are Different from Disasters: Some Implications for Crisis Planning and Managing Drawn from Katrina. *Understanding Katrina: Perspectives from the Social Sciences* [online]. Available from: http://understandingkatrina.ssrc.org/Quarantelli [Accessed 21 March 2013].

Reale, A., and Handmer, J., 2011. Land tenure, Disasters and Vulnerability. *Disasters*, 35 (1), 160-182. doi: 10.1111/j.1467-7717.2010.01198.x.

Roberts, P., 2009. An Unnatural Disaster. *Administration & Society*, 41 (6), 763-769. doi: 10.1177/0095399709345628.

Sarat, A., and Lezaun, J., 2009. *Catastrophe: Law, Politics, and the Humanitarian Impulse*. Amherst, MA: University of Massachusetts Press.

Sterett, S.M., 2012. Need and Citizenship After Disaster. *Natural Hazards Review*, 13 (3), 233-245. doi: 10.1061/(ASCE)NH.1527-6996.0000072.

Scraton, P., 1999. Policing with Contempt: The Degrading of Truth and Denial of Justice in the Aftermath of the Hillsborough Disaster. *Journal of Law & Society*, 26 (3), 273-297. doi: 10.2307/1410746.

Selves, M.D., n.d. *The Politics of Disaster: Principles for Local Emergency Managers and Elected Officials* [online]. Emmitsburg, MD: Federal Emergency Management Agency. Available from: http://training.fema.gov/EMIWeb/edu/docs/hazdem/The%20Politics%20of%20Disaster.doc [Accessed 31 May 2011].

Wasby, S.L., 1998. The Effect of Disasters on Courts: An Introduction. *The Judges' Journal*, 37 (4), 4-5, 48.

Wasby, S.L., 1997. Delay and a Docketing Disaster. *The Justice System Journal*, 19 (2), 240-242.

Young, H., *et al.*, 2004. Linking Rights and Standards: The Process of Developing 'Rights-based' Minimum Standards on Food Security, Nutrition and Food Aid. *Disasters*, 28 (2), 142-159. doi: 10.1111/j.0361-3666.2004.00249.x.

**qp**

Visit us at *www.quidprobooks.com.*